THE FOOD SECTION

Rowman & Littlefield Studies in Food and Gastronomy
General Editor: Ken Albala, professor of history, University of the Pacific (kalbala@pacific.edu)

Food studies is a vibrant and thriving field encompassing not only cooking and eating habits but also issues such as health, sustainability, food safety, and animal rights. Scholars in disciplines as diverse as history, anthropology, sociology, literature, and the arts focus on food. The mission of **Rowman & Littlefield Studies in Food and Gastronomy** is to publish the best in food scholarship, harnessing the energy, ideas, and creativity of a wide array of food writers today. This broad line of food-related titles will range from food history, interdisciplinary food studies monographs, general interest series, and popular trade titles to textbooks for students and budding chefs, scholarly cookbooks, and reference works.

Titles in the Series

Appetites and Aspirations in Vietnam: Food and Drink in the Long Nineteenth Century, by Erica J. Peters

Three World Cuisines: Italian, Mexican, Chinese, by Ken Albala

Food and Social Media: You Are What You Tweet, by Signe Rousseau

Food and the Novel in Nineteenth-Century America, by Mark McWilliams

Man Bites Dog: Hot Dog Culture in America, by Bruce Kraig and Patty Carroll

New Orleans: A Food Biography, by Elizabeth M. Williams (Big City Food Biographies series)

A Year in Food and Beer: Recipes and Beer Pairings for Every Season, by Emily Baime and Darin Michaels

Breakfast: A History, by Heather Arndt Anderson (The Meals series)

Celebraciones Mexicanas: History, Traditions, and Recipes, by Andrea Lawson Gray and Adriana Almazán Lahl

Food History Almanac: Over 1,300 Years of World Culinary History, Culture, and Social Influence, by Janet Clarkson

The Food Section: Newspaper Women and the Culinary Community, by Kimberly Wilmot Voss

THE FOOD SECTION

Newspaper Women and the Culinary Community

Kimberly Wilmot Voss

ROWMAN & LITTLEFIELD
Lanham • Boulder • New York • London

Published by Rowman & Littlefield
A wholly owned subsidiary of the Rowman & Littlefield Publishing Group, Inc.
4501 Forbes Boulevard, Suite 200, Lanham, Maryland 20706
www.rowman.com

16 Carlisle Street, London W1D 3 BT, United Kingdom

British Library Cataloguing in Publication Information Available

Library of Congress Cataloging-in-Publication Data

Voss, Kimberly Wilmot, 1970–
The food section : newspaper women and the culinary community / Kimberly Wilmot Voss.
pages cm — (Rowman & Littlefield studies in food and gastronomy)
Includes bibliographical references and index.
ISBN 978-1-4422-2720-0 (cloth : alk. paper) — ISBN 978-1-4422-2721-7 (electronic)
1. Food writing—United States—History—20th century. 2. Newspapers—United States—Sections, columns, etc.—Food—History—20th century. 3. Women in journalism—United States. 4.
Food writers—United States. I. Title.
TX644.V67 2014
808'.066641—dc23
2013046690

Printed in the United States of America

CONTENTS

ACKNOWLEDGMENTS

Many years of work went into researching the material for this book. The archivists from several libraries were helpful including those at the Fales Library at New York University. The Special Collections archivists and librarians at Iowa State University were especially helpful. My thanks to Becky S. Jordan for answering questions about home economics journalism alumni.

I want to thank the children of Jane Nickerson and the daughter of Jeanne Voltz for their help. Also, the nephew of Cecily Brownstone was helpful in gathering information. Further, the oral history that Laura Shapiro conducted with Brownstone allowed for the confirmation of many facts about newspaper food journalism. Carol Haddix provided a speech she gave about her experiences as the food editor at the *Chicago Tribune*.

Women's page editor and later publisher Marjorie Paxson's creation of the National Women and Media Collection and her donation of her own papers were incredibly helpful. Paxson had the only report from the 1972 food editors conference in Houston that answered many questions. My thanks to Elizabeth E. Engel, who has helped me track down documents from the NWMC.

I also want to acknowledge the American Journalism Historians Association. My 2010 conference paper, "Food Journalism or Culinary Anthropology? Re-evaluating Soft News and the Influence of Jeanne Voltz's Food Section in the *L.A. Times*," won the Maurine Beasley Award for best research on women in journalism history and also the

William David Sloan Award for top faculty paper. The enthusiasm for
my recognition of soft news as an important part of journalism history
changed the course of my research agenda.

I want to thank my former Southern Illinois University, Edwards-
ville, colleague and current friend Laura Milsk Fowler, who alerted me
to the Foodways series with a Facebook post. I also thank the Greater
Midwest Foodways Alliance and the Culinary Historians of Chicago for
the 2013 American Midwest Foodways Scholar's Grant to study the
career of *Chicago Tribune* food editor Ruth Ellen Church.

The interlibrary loan librarians at the University of Central Florida
aided me with sometimes hard-to-find newspaper clippings. My graduate assistant Meredith Morris transcribed talks given at the Culinary
Historians of Southern California that were referred to often.

I especially want to thank my husband, Lance Speere, for his interest in the topic and support of the research, as well as his editing help. I
could not have written this book without him. Also, I appreciate my two
little boys, Curtis and Paul, who were so well behaved on the evenings
when their mother needed to write.

Lastly, thank you to my editors Ken Albala and Suzanne Staszak-
Silva for the feedback and guidance.

PREFACE

Food pages have been a part of newspapers for more than a hundred years. They were widely read by the members of the communities they served. Recipes were clipped and saved. The phone of the food editor was constantly ringing with readers' questions. Yet little research has been done on what was in these sections. This book seeks to answer the question: What content was in the food sections of newspapers during the women's page years of the 1940s to the 1970s? After all, this was the place where most Americans—especially women—got their information about food. It was a time when food was changing significantly due to developments in technology and a changing American palate. It was a time that introduced fast food, television dinners, and the need for an electric can opener. It was also a time when Americans began experimenting with French dishes and went back to baking their own bread. Newspaper recipe columns from the 1950s and 1960s prove that cookery was not just based on convenience foods, despite the stereotypes of American cooking during these decades. Food history for home cooks is more complex than has been previously described.

This book also addresses another question: Who were these women who covered the food beat at newspapers? Many false assumptions have been made about these women, that they were simple at best and unethical at worst. The truth is that most editors were trained journalists or home economists. A few others learned their craft along the way. Yet at various times these women have found themselves either marginalized or under attack. For example, in the 1950s, the Associated Press built a testing kitchen in the home of its food writer, Cecily Brownstone. This was done so that she would not be in the office of the newspaper wire service—considered an unladylike environment. Until the 1960s, food editors were still excluded from most of the press organizations based on their gender. Then, in the early 1970s, the food editors found themselves accused of wrongdoing by a senator and by some in their own industry. The accusations were unproven and led to the creation of what is called today the Association of Food Journalists. (Initially, the group was called the Newspaper Food Editors and Writers Association.) By the mid-1970s, women's pages, which had housed the food pages, had been transitioned into lifestyle sections and men had begun taking on the role of food editor.[1]

This book seeks to clarify what newspaper food journalism was by looking at the editorial content of the sections and the journalists who covered them. There have been many generalizations that the sections were fluff or pandered to advertisers. This examination challenges those views. After all, journalism historians have largely ignored soft news like food. Instead, they have more often focused on the news found on the front pages of newspapers. Culinary historians who study media coverage of food tend to lump together magazines and newspapers. Yet in practice and in ethics these two media forms are often different. There is typically a sturdy wall between the advertising and editorial sections of newspapers. Further, newspapers have a direct connection to the community that a national magazine does not. Food editors will largely write about local stores, local restaurants, and local cooks. For example, the *Akron Beacon Journal* food editor Polly Paffilas said this of her role:

> The newspaper food editor is the homemakers' best friend, mother confessor and mentor. Mrs. Jones calls us when she can't understand a recipe in a national magazine or when Graham Kerr talks about clarified butter. Mrs. Jones doesn't call the magazine or the TV station. She calls me.[2]

This book also recognizes the often rarified culinary world where food editors interacted with big names like James Beard, Poppy Cannon, and Julia Child. All three cooks became newspaper columnists—along with cookbook authors Peg Bracken and Myra Waldo. In part, those big names became big names because of positive newspaper coverage. It was an integrated community of food and journalism. The creation of this community in food-centered New York City likely began with Jane Nickerson at the *New York Times*. She was the first food editor at the newspaper, beginning in 1942. Over the years, she introduced James Beard to food editor Cecily Brownstone; the two would speak on the phone daily. They were often dinner companions, along with Nickerson and her future husband. It was Brownstone who introduced the New York food community to Irma S. Rombauer, author of the popular cookbook *Joy of Cooking*. Later, it was Beard who introduced Julia Child to the New York food community. Yet, in another example of food editor marginalization, Nickerson rarely gets the credit in historical culinary stories. Instead, she has been overshadowed by the considerable scholarship about Craig Claiborne, who followed her as food editor. In fact, she is often described as "retiring" from the New York newspaper in 1957. This is untrue; she took a few years away from her professional career to raise her children and then returned to being a newspaper food editor and cookbook author in Florida by 1973. There are a few brief references to Nickerson in a 2012 biography of Claiborne, but it does not give credit for her work. A request to the archives that house Craig Claiborne's papers found no reference to Nickerson or Brownstone.

During the course of the past decade, I have examined the women's pages of newspapers across the country. This was largely the only part of a newspaper where women could work prior to the 1970s. I took several approaches when considering which newspapers to study. First I focused on the winners and finalists of the Penney-Missouri Awards. These were the top recognition for women's sections, and awards were given in four different circulation categories. Later, I added to this list the food sections that were winners of the Vesta Awards, the only national newspaper award for food journalism until the early 1970s. More editors were added from the cookbooks produced by the newspaper food editors in 1952 and 1970. Lastly, I found food sections from several different newspapers and also the AP that had been scanned for the Google News Archive. Furthermore, I accessed dozens of articles through the paid archive of the *Omaha World-Herald*.

Additional material was drawn from archives, personal interviews, and academic studies. Only a few food editors left papers behind in archives. The previously mentioned Polly Paffilas left behind her collection of about 5,000 recipes, which are available at the Akron library,[3] and *Cleveland Plain-Dealer* food editor Janet Beighle French donated her recipes and articles to Cleveland State University.[4] Denver food editor Helen Dollaghan left her cookbook collection to the University of Denver. Brownstone left her vast collection of cookbooks and other materials to the Fales Library at New York University. Among Brownstone's papers is an oral history interview with her conducted by Laura Shapiro that provides insight to the New York food community. Clementine Paddleford, food editor at the *New York Herald Tribune*, left her papers to her alma mater, Kansas State University. Kelly Alexander and Cynthia Harris explored those papers in their book *Hometown Appetites*, which outlined her impressive career. Also, internal files from the *New York Times* about the food section were found at the New York Public Library. They were helpful in determining the role of ethics in food coverage.

Newspaper cookbooks were examined, as were cookbooks written by food editors independent of their newspapers. Many newspapers published cookbooks and cooking pamphlets over the years. Some included favorites of the food editors, and others were collections of recipes sent in by readers. Because of their stature as well-known food editors, some of the women wrote their own cookbooks. For example, Ruth Ellen Church wrote a popular blender cookbook published by the Bobbs-Merrill Company. The publisher's papers at the Lilly Library at Indiana University were helpful in understanding how cookbooks were marketed.

One of the most helpful sources in learning how food editors perceived their work was discovered in the papers of longtime women's page editor Marjorie Paxson at the National Women and Media Collection. Among her papers was a large transcription of a 1972 meeting at the University of Houston called the Food Editors Seminar. The gathering was a response to accusations made by Senator Frank Moss in a speech that was found in his papers at the University of Utah.

The Special Collections at Iowa State University included files for several food editors such as Ruth Ellen Church and Virginia Heffington, who were graduates of the home economics journalism program. These files provided information on the curriculum and the college experience of female students of that time. Several of Heffington's food sections were located at the Special Collections at University of Guelph in Ontario, Canada. This allowed for an understanding of the food page in its complete form rather than article by article, as found in online databases of some newspapers. Further, the journalism and home economics program at Arizona State University provided helpful information about Peggy Daum's undergraduate years and the home economics journalism curriculum.

Julia Child's papers at the Schlesinger Library include her columns with the *Boston Globe*. They reveal the line edits of her recipes as she updated her instructions for her recipes. Las Vegas food editor Ann Valders donated her papers to the Special Collections at the University of Nevada, Las Vegas. They provided material for the Pillsbury Bake-Off and other cooking competitions. The University of Texas at San Antonio Libraries Special Collections also had background materials about the Pillsbury Bake-Off. The papers included the names of all the food editors who attended the contest in 1968 and those who acted as judges, and provided information about what the food editors learned while at the competition. The list led me to Grace Barr, who had been the food editor at the *Orlando Sentinel*. Her son, Graham Barr, has a self-published memoir located at the Orange County Regional History Center, which provided additional information about Barr's career. Furthermore, the story of the Pillsbury Bake-Off as told by Laura Shapiro to the Culinary Historians of Southern California in 2012 was transcribed. The organization-sponsored presentation by the former food journalists from the *Los Angeles Times* in 2010 was also transcribed.

Phone interviews were conducted with *Milwaukee Journal Sentinel* food editor Nancy Stohs about Peggy Daum. I also spoke to food editor Carol DeMasters, who served as executive director/administrator at the Association of Food Journalists for many years and was the former food editor at the *Milwaukee Sentinel*. Email interviews were conducted with *Arizona Republic* food editor Dorothee Polson, the *Cleveland Plain-Dealer*'s Janet Beighle French, and Carol Haddix, who was the food editor at the *Detroit Free Press* and *Chicago Tribune*. Phone interviews with Jeanne Voltz's daughter (also named Jeanne Voltz), *Charlotte Observer* food editor Kathleen Purvis, and cookbook author Jean Anderson were conducted to learn more about Voltz. Jane Nickerson's children were helpful by email and social media in learning more about their mother. Rita Ciccone's daughter also provided details about her mother's career at the *Ft. Lauderdale News*.

Academic conference papers and theses also provide an understanding of the editors and their sections. Much of this research involved in-depth interviews and survey research of the food editors. For example, a graduate student in home economics journalism at the University of Wisconsin wrote a paper titled "Public Relations Information and Practices as Viewed by Women's Newspaper Editors" in 1973. She surveyed and interviewed the food editors at sixteen Midwest newspapers in various circulation sizes. Her research was based in five areas: general information, use of public relations materials, the use of recipes from food companies, editors' use of freebies, and what editors wanted from public relations people.[5] It was this kind of research that demonstrated that there were clear ethical guidelines and that those who accused the editors of inappropriate behavior were incorrect in their assumptions.

Lastly, some of the work of celebrity cookbook authors who also had syndicated newspaper food columnists were examined. For example, Jim Beard's newspaper columns were published in his book *Beard on Food*. Poppy Cannon, Myra Waldo, and Peg Bracken's columns are available in the newspapers found in Google News Archive. I also looked at how the food editors interacted with these food celebrities at annual meetings and visits during cookbook tours.

The cookbooks and recipe booklets from the newspaper food editors were collected through eBay and used book websites. A few specific cookbooks were particularly helpful: The 1952 *Coast to Coast* and the 1970 *Favorite Recipes of America's Food Editors* added to my food editors list and allowed for a comparison in changing trends. The two cookbooks were created by newspaper food editors and provided background about regional cooking. They also provided insights into the food editor community as they traveled the world together.

This research builds on the work of culinary historian Laura Shapiro, who examined the food sections of newspapers. In her book *Something from the Oven*, she noted that her favorite sources for food history and home cooks were the food sections. She wrote that this was because they "by virtue of their place in the community seemed likely to reflect fairly closely the needs and habits of their readers. And my favorite bits in the papers that I studied were the recipes sent in by readers themselves."[6] In one example, Shapiro examined the content of the *Boston Globe*'s cooking column, "Confidential Chat." In this book, I look at the editor of that column and of the overall food section, Dorothy Crandall.

She had a degree in home economics and served as food editor of the
Globe from 1953 to 1973. One of the stories she is best known for was a
process of cooking a roast underneath the hood of a car. The meat
cooked inside her car as she drove from Essex Junction, Vermont, to
Boston, Massachusetts.[7]

In another example mentioned previously, Shapiro gave an interesting talk about the home cooks who entered the Pillsbury Bake-Off and
what it tells us about culinary history.[8] After all, those who entered the
competition were home cooks, not professionals—the kinds of women
who read the newspaper food sections. There were numerous other
important cooking contests, from state fairs to the original national cook
competition—the Delmarva chicken cooking contest, which took place
in various cities in Delaware, Maryland, and Virginia's chicken-produc-
ing regions. This book looks at the judges of cooking contests—newspaper food editors. In the year that Shapiro described in her talk, the
judges included several newspaper food editors who are studied in this
book.

Looking at the predominantly female profession of food editor in the
1940s through the 1970s also meant addressing evolving gender roles of
the time. After all, these food editors were champions for the home
cooks in their communities, and for several editors, their own profession meant balancing work and family. This was at a time when the
question of working mothers was something to be debated publicly—as
if many women had not already been in this position for generations.[9]
Yet the editors' work in a traditional female area often made them,
along with home economics, the target of feminist leaders in the late
1960s and the early 1970s. The papers of feminist leader Robin Morgan
at Duke University were examined and revealed her role in a radical
speech given to the national home economics organization, which is
discussed in chapter 6. Gloria Steinem called for the elimination of
women's pages at newspapers as "ghettos" for women. Instead, she
wanted women to work in sections throughout the newspaper. (Steinem
did, however, reverse her views a few years later and seemed to see the
value of the sections.)

Ultimately, the women's pages were eliminated at most newspapers
by the mid-1970s. Food sections remained in newspapers but the editor
was more likely to be a man. The final chapter of this book explains
what happened to the food editors in the years after the elimination of

the women's pages. Some editors had success as they were elected into halls of fame, published more cookbooks, and developed culinary organizations. Others suffered early deaths through illness and even murder (Ruth Ellen Church) and suicide (Poppy Cannon). Other food editors lived well into old age (some into their nineties and active until the end), and a few developed retrospective cookbooks that looked back over the entirety of their careers.

The story of the newspaper food sections and the women who edited the sections is important to understanding the history of American food and home cooks. One journalism industry study, conducted in the 1940s, found that 64 percent of women discovered their new recipes in newspapers. This was obviously significant content for readers. As an American Press Institute publication noted, "It is certainly probable that they could become much more important as a source of food information by improving their performance in handling food news."[10] Newspaper food editors had to balance the traditional dishes that grounded a community and the innovations that made their reporting relevant. This is not to refute the assertion that there was some fluff in the sections; this was likely inevitable when food sections were thirty to fifty pages long, as many were.

This is also the story of new dishes, recipe testing, cookbooks, and cooking competitions. There are stories of food history, organic food, and the growth of vegetarianism. There are worries over high food prices and contaminated food. There are reviews of restaurants and questions of journalism ethics. There is an examination of cookbook reviews and the stories of the cookbooks that the editors wrote. It is about the stories of home cooks—several newspapers had weekly columns that profiled local women, often in their kitchens. These profiles were often significant in the lives of the women featured; the honor was mentioned in the obituaries of some of those women.[11] Further, the role of home economics and women's changing roles in society are addressed.

This research builds on the work of scholars who have documented the social history of food such as Shapiro, Warren Belasco, Amy Bentley, and Joanne Lamb Hayes. While these authors mentioned the food sections of newspapers, the content and who wrote it was not critically examined. For example, in his classic book about food history, *United States of Arugula*, David Kamp described the newspaper food editors as "nicey-nice lady food journalists."[12] There were certainly some editors who did fit this description. The *St. Petersburg Times*'s Ruth Gray, for example, felt so badly about writing a negative restaurant review that she would leave town for a few days after it was published. But other editors were not quite so concerned about kindness. Brownstone said about herself, "Someone told me I was bitchy. I could be bitchy occasionally."[13] *Charlotte Observer* food editor Kathleen Purvis wrote admiringly, "Voltz wasn't valued for her sweetness. Her flavor was pepper and vinegar."[14] If the food editors were perceived as an overtly nice group, it was likely true, as they needed to make a connection to their readers. Or it might be that in comparison to the battles within the New York City food establishment,[15] the other newspaper food editors seemed quite friendly. Nora Ephron quoted James Beard about a 1968 Cookbook Guild gathering in New York City: "You could barely move around at that party for fear someone would bite you in the back."[16] Yet, as explained in chapter 3, when these female food editors came under attack in 1971, they were ready to fight.

The dishes that these food journalists wrote about continue to circulate today in newspaper exchange columns and on food blogs. For example, on the website of *Oprah Magazine* is *Charlotte Observer* food editor Eudora Garrison's recipe for sherried chicken salad sandwiches.[17] *Los Angeles Times* food editor Jeanne Voltz's recipe for green corn tamales can be found on the Food Network website with a note giving credit to her acclaimed book *Barbecued Ribs, Smoked Butts and Other Great Feeds*.[18] Voltz's book was one of the first to establish barbecue as a cuisine worth valuing. Her take on barbecue was likely facilitated by the fact that she was not burdened by the food hierarchy of culinary cuisine. She simply saw an untold story. Voltz once said, "The South has the kind of climate that grows certain things the way no other place in the country does. I've worked in Los Angeles and New York, but you can't ever get away from grits and greens."[19]

This book looks at the period of 1945–1975 (and a few years before and after) for several reasons. World War II meant significant changes for women and for food. The role of home economists was extended as the government paid them to teach homemakers to stretch limited meat supplies and can the produce from their victory gardens. The technology and products that food companies developed to feed the soldiers would change what was later offered in the grocery stores and the available fast food options. It also changed women's roles in society. Spurred on by the image of Rosie the Riveter, many middle-class women entered the workforce for the first time. At newspapers, many women journalists left the women's pages and were allowed to work in every part of the newspaper. Most would return to the women's pages when peace returned.

The year 1975 was chosen as an end point because it was in the mid-1970s that the women's pages were largely eliminated from newspapers. As a result of the outcry from feminist leaders, the pages were transformed into lifestyle sections largely filled with entertainment stories. The end of the women's pages provides an interesting parallel to the end of the home economics field. It, too, was renamed with a new focus on consumer and family information. While the food pages of newspapers continued, men were now more likely to be food editors. "Food Pages No More a Woman's Domain," declared a headline on one wire story. The reasons cited were the depressed economic climate and an interest in food as a topic for investigative journalists.[20] The food sections were no longer strictly a women's domain, as they had been for decades.

I

THE ORIGINS OF FOOD JOURNALISM IN US NEWSPAPERS

THE NEW FOOD STUDIES

In recent years, there has been a renewed interest in the study of food, from its role in society to where our eating habits come from. Typically referred to as food studies, the academic field often uses the media's coverage as a top source in its research. Scholars may study food advertising (as Katherine J. Parkin did in *Food Is Love: Advertising and Gender Roles in Modern America*) or use newspaper articles from food sections to study specific types of food like baby food, white bread, or diet foods.[1] Some food studies draw on a mix of mass communication including advertising, magazine articles, and newspaper stories to look at food fads or food preparation during specific eras like World War II or the post–World War II era.[2]

Cultural studies scholars have also looked at food journalism. Jessica Weiss examined the weekly column "She Also Cooks," which ran in the *Oakland Tribune* from 1957 to 1959. She wrote that the column highlighted local women and "illustrated that they could balance both public and private life." The column, written by Kay Wahl, included an interview with the woman being featured that week, a sketch, and a recipe. While the women included were educated, middle-class, and white, it does provide insight into a certain kind of postwar employed woman. Weiss found that "Wahl's column served as evidence that women's lives were changing, and she and many of the women she interviewed emphatically endorsed these changes."[3] In other words, taking on the traditional role of home cook meant that women could seek work in a nontraditional role of paid worker in a middle-class household.

Despite how scholars have drawn on food journalism for their studies, the food journalists themselves have largely been either marginalized or mocked. For example, in Kamp's *United States of Arugula*, food writers of the women's pages are largely dismissed, relegated to only a few mentions; in one reference, he describes them as the "Jell-O abusing women's-page ladies."[4] In another example, a *Los Angeles Times* reporter in a 1984 article repeated the myth that food sections had little value and were ethically problematic, accusing the food editors of using brand names in recipes. Claims about the ethics of food columns are not new; the same accusation was initially made in the early 1970s.

Despite its long history, newspaper food journalism has long been ignored until recently. According to journalism magazines, the subject of culinary or food journalism has only become popular in the past decade or so. For example, in 2004, the industry publication *American Journalism Review* covered the increased interest in food journalism, arguing that it had gone upscale after decades of simply serving as a filler section in the paper. "Food journalism has long been an oxymoron with newspaper food pages," the author wrote. "Little more than wire service recipe dumps and magazine articles barely scraping deeper than 'what's hot and what's not.'"[5] Characterizations such as those overlooked the work found in many women's pages prior to the demise of the sections in the early 1970s, despite the evidence that it was these women's page journalists who set the foundation for food journalism. They further marginalize the work of women in journalism and culinary histories.

Newspaper food sections have long served an important purpose for home cooks and restaurant fans. Readers wrote letters and called the editors on a regular basis. These food sections were made thick with grocery store coupons and new appliance advertisements in the 1950s and 1960s. The food section of one newspaper, published the week before Thanksgiving, was as big as 90 pages.[6] Food news originated in the women's pages (typically defined as the fashion and household pages) of metropolitan dailies across the country. Few of the food sections have received much historical examination despite the important role they played in their individual communities.

Food pages—both as part of the women's pages or as stand-alone sections—have long been a staple of metropolitan newspapers. The food sections of newspapers reflected gender roles, health standards, and governmental policies about food in a community. They also reflected the developing demographic of many cities as new immigrants settled into communities and shared their dishes. This was a time, for example, when the pronunciation of the word "pizza" was clarified in the pages of the 1939 *New York Herald Tribune*, with food editor Clementine Paddleford explaining that it was "peet-za."[7] In the late 1960s, the *Los Angeles Times* food editor Jeanne Voltz introduced her readers to Chinese cooking,[8] and later she authored a cookbook devoted to California cooking, marveling, "Where else but in California will you find your Japanese neighbors barbecuing shish kebab to go with their avocado salad and the Danes up the road serving enchiladas and chiles rellenos, all washed down with California wine?"[9]

Newspaper food sections do not have a well-documented history outside of brief mentions of the women's pages. The few newspaper journalism employment options for women prior to the early 1970s were in the women's pages. These sections were known for the four Fs: family, fashion, food, and furnishings. They also included women's club coverage, society news, and wedding announcements. Food was representative of the more traditional content of the women's section—a rare area where women could claim authority prior to the women's liberation movement. These women were appealing to the average home cooks in their communities. As one academic expert said about *Denver Post* food editor Helen Dollaghan, "Her recipes were simple, she kept current, and she was so much in tune with the readers."[10]

Critics have charged that food sections were simply repositories for "just recipes." As a publication from the industry organization American Press Institute noted of newspaper food pages in newspapers, "It is certainly probable that they could become much more important as a source of food information by improving their performance in handling food news."[11] While much of this book refutes the idea that food as news was lacking in newspapers, it is unfair to dismiss recipes as somehow inferior in content. If the idea is to generate audience with relevant content, newspaper readers find recipes interesting. Exchange columns in which readers requested recipes were some of the most common, popular, and long-lasting features of the newspapers acting as a kind of early social media.

The food sections originated out of the women's pages, which ran daily and often included a bigger stand-alone section on Sundays that included content produced days in advance and made thick with department store advertising. Soon, this meant there was a daily food page that food editors had to fill along with the weekly stand-alone food section on Wednesday or Thursday and sometimes twice a week. The food editor also was expected to contribute copy and original photos to the full-color Sunday magazines being published by many metropolitan newspapers.

Most of the editors fell into two camps or a mixture of the two. Many were college-educated reporters who could not find jobs in the news sections. They made the best of their marginalization and practiced good journalism in the women's pages.[12] A second category included graduates of home economics programs who practiced their expertise as food writers.[13] A few happened into journalism because they liked to write. Regardless of their backgrounds, the food editors made a difference in the menus of their communities. They helped recognize the home cooks of their communities and examined the changing food habits of their readers.

Women's magazines and the food coverage within have been studied to some extent but the same generalizations drawn from those works cannot necessarily be applied to newspaper food sections. The two media forms usually operated quite differently. Culinary historian Laura Shapiro noted that in the 1950s, food writers may have moved back and forth between food advertising and magazines.[14] Yet, at most newspapers, there was a rather clear separation between the editorial side and the advertising side; even if the advertising side paid the bill, it did not dictate content. While there were some exceptions, most newspapers and press associations had ethics codes already in place by the 1950s.

Most metropolitan newspapers have books devoted to their histories. The women's pages or food pages are rarely mentioned, with a few exceptions. A lengthy book about the *New York Herald Tribune*, a newspaper that supported women and soft news, included some information about Paddleford.[15] A book about the history of the *Chicago Tribune* also included information about food editor Ruth Ellen

Church, known to her readers as Mary Meade.[16] Food editor Kay Savage is briefly mentioned in a history of the *Detroit Free Press*.[17] Eudora Garrison is mentioned in a book about the *Charlotte Observer*—but mostly in the role of secretary rather than as food editor.[18] In a book that chronicled the history of the *Miami Herald*, author Nixon Smiley wrote that Jeanne Voltz became the food editor because of her expertise as a gourmet cook.[19] This account is fiction, disproved by Voltz years later in a newspaper interview. According to Voltz's own account, she was a hard news journalist, not a gourmet cook, when editor Lee Hills called her into his office and told her to cover food. She did not know how to cook, she replied. Learn, he told her.[20]

THE FOOD SECTION MYTH

For years, newspaper food sections were overlooked as nothing more than a collection of casserole recipes and plugs for local grocery stores and other advertisers.[21] Some have described the food sections as the "powder puff side of journalism."[22] Yet food journalists played a significant role in the story of food. They wrote about topics such as food safety and consumer issues that would have run counter to the advertisers who funded their sections. This is how Ann Criswell described her career as a food editor at the *Houston Chronicle*:

> You may be surprised that a food editor's life isn't all champagne and caviar. There is the constant stress of deadlines; keeping up with (and explaining to readers) scientific and nutrition advancements that can change from hour to hour; learning about food safety, production and agricultural phenomena such as genetically altered foods; and having to master new computers and printing technologies (often while on deadline).[23]

Some critics viewed articles about new products as a form of advertising, but the journalists believed that new products needed to be evaluated and explained to their readers. Church wrote in 1955 that the changes in the food industry and new products during the previous decade were "revolutionary." She noted, "Fully a third of the products and foods we buy now in the supermarket were not even in existence 10 years ago: instant puddings, cake mixes, instant coffee, instant dry milk, detergents, the wide array of frozen and pre-packaged foods."[24]

Journalists also covered serious food-related issues like poverty and nutrition, but they believed in the value of recipes. Recipes were indicators of a changing American appetite following World War II and the impact of women working outside of the home. They were a way for editors to understand their communities. A 1951 journalism industry publication advised, "The food editor of a newspaper, who should be thoroughly familiar with the tastes and dominant food interests of her readers, can win and hold readers by providing the recipes sought by the housewife in her constant quest."[25] And that quest could include a mix of high-end and everyday foods. In 1952, Church indicated that readers of the *Chicago Tribune* requested the following: "Recipes for French pastry, Italian cannoli, East Indian curry; they want to know how to cook pheasant in wine and to make rich, extravagant desserts. But they also want to know how to fix the more everyday foods of such as potato salad, coleslaw, bread pudding, and corned beef hash."[26]

Food sections in metropolitan newspapers from World War II through the 1970s illustrate the intersection between gender, food, and communities. They show that the editors and journalists of these sections, far from being the "Jell-O abusing" dilettantes of David Kamp's imagination, were in fact a strong community of women who took food seriously as a beat and as a public service. They wrote for the home cooks and the restaurant goers while keeping the advertisers at bay. Newspaper editors were especially independent, in contrast to editors at magazines, where advertising and editorial often shared a friendly relationship.[27] "I thank God for that separation of the editorial and advertising departments," declared Dorothy Jurney, an editor with the Knight Newspaper chain.[28] At the Louisville newspapers, the former managing editor said that food news was treated the same way that all news was handled—with no input from the advertising department.[29]

These food editors tested recipes, reviewed restaurants, and explained new products. They wrote about war-time rations, food consumer news, and nutrition research. As technology changed how food was prepared, the food editors evaluated the ease and quality for their readers. This is how Church described her job in 1955 as she supervised a staff of five home economists, a secretary, and a kitchen assistant at the *Chicago Tribune*:

We do most of our own food photographs, conduct a daily $5 favorite recipe competition, maintain a mail and telephone service to home-makers, scout for what's new in the kitchen, test recipes and such. In addition, I write a daily and Sunday column, and supervise the publication of a number of supplements each year, notably the Thanksgiving and Christmas special sections.[30]

THE CLAIBORNE MYTH

In the book *Hometown Appetites*, the authors argue that Clementine Paddleford was a forgotten food writer. A pioneer in newspaper food journalism, Paddleford traveled the country, often piloting her own plane, to find stories. Her biographers wrote that Paddleford was over-shadowed by the combination of her early death, the popularity of *New York Times* food editor Craig Claiborne, and the end of her newspaper, the *New York Herald Tribune*. This is all true; in fact, most newspaper food journalists have been forgotten. Like their sisters in home economics, their place in the women's pages was a casualty of the 1970s fight for women's equality. Yet these sections, as well as the women who edited them, were significant in the communities where they worked and should not be overshadowed by the legacy of Claiborne or the more popular cookbook authors of the time such as James Beard or Julia Child.

Claiborne certainly had a significant impact on food journalism, especially in the area of restaurant reviewing and New York City. But his predecessor Jane Nickerson laid the foundation at the *New York Times* during her 1942 to 1957 tenure. In 2003, former *New York Times* food journalist Molly O'Neill credited Nickerson with being one of the first food journalists to apply ethics and news values to her craft. According to O'Neill, news was central to the story lines in the vast majority of the *Times'* food stories in the Nickerson years. During one period early in the 1950s, 646 out of 675 food stories possessed a news hook, as cataloged in the *New York Times* index, and the percentage remained the same throughout the 1950s.[31] According to Evan Jones's biography of James Beard, *Epicurean Delight*, Nickerson regularly went to dinner with Cicely Brownstone and Beard, as well as her future husband. "They probed New York's ethnic neighborhoods," Jones wrote, "titillating their palates and venting their curiosities about origins of recipes."[32]

When Nickerson announced her retirement in 1957, Beard was particularly saddened by what her absence could mean to food coverage in New York. Her popularity was punctuated by the number of farewell parties held in her honor, as Beard wrote in a letter to food writer Helen Evans Brown: "Going to four parties for Jane this week. She leaves next week for Florida, and how we hate to see her go. She has done more for dignified food coverage than anyone. Everyone will miss her keenly, and I more than most, for she was a good friend and a most amusing person always."[33]

Nickerson and Beard had hoped that Brown would become the second food editor at the *New York Times*. When the position went to Claiborne, they publicly supported the decision and kept their dissent private. Beard wrote to Brown that he and Nickerson had agreed Brown was the better choice, "[b]ut that is in the family and never breathe it."[34]

Claiborne's significance in New York culinary history is well documented, but it is more complex than previously understood. Claiborne's initial culinary authority was based on an article he wrote for the *New York Times* in 1959 titled "Elegance of Cuisine Is on Wane in U.S."[35] In the widely read article, he wrote, "Two time-honored symbols of the good life—great cuisine in the French tradition—are passing from the American scene." He believed this was for three reasons: costs, a lack of training facilities, and a drop in the number of master chefs from France, a result of stricter immigration laws passed in the 1930s.[36] Claiborne's memory of how he approached reporting this story differs from that of his editor. "I took it upon myself to write a devastating attack on the restaurant situation in Manhattan," he wrote in his memoir.[37] But according to his editor, Elizabeth Penrose Howkins, Claiborne did not initially want to write the article. Instead, it was her prodding that led to it being written and published. According to a memo that Howkins sent to the paper's top editor, Arthur Sulzberger,

> It is particularly gratifying to me that the story came off because, I must confess, I had an extremely difficult time getting Craig to do it. It was a touchy subject, but one that needed to be aired. In addition to feeling it was a subject that would have wide reader response, I also told Craig, very frankly, that he would never make his mark on this paper until he did a story on a big subject, such as this, with all the research and hard digging it required. Now, of course, he is

gratified as I am that I spent so much time and effort nagging him into it.[38]

Howkins's background was in women's magazines rather than newspapers—a very different form of journalism. She was an excellent judge of talent but sometimes fuzzy on newspaper norms, asking *Times* fashion reporter Nan Robertson "about how newspapers were run." Later, when Robertson became the union shop steward, Howkins asked if she could join. When Robertson responded that Howkins was in management and could not be a member, she appeared hurt.[39] While Claiborne went on to great acclaim, Robertson said Claiborne did not know how to write a lead when he was hired. Claiborne earned a journalism degree from the University of Missouri, but his focus was on advertising. "I learned absolutely nothing," he said of his college experience.[40] His big break came when Nickerson resigned (not retired) to relocate to Florida to raise her children for a few years.

Nickerson started at the *New York Times* in 1942 as the food editor—with a journalism degree from Radcliffe University and experience at a women's magazine. The *Times'* "News of Food" column had begun in 1941 and was written by Margot Murphy under the pen name of "Jane Holt." While Nickerson was at the *Times*, she said the eight major newspapers in the city were all vying for the same stories.[41] During Nickerson's tenure, recipes were tested by home economist Ruth P. Casa-Emellos, who taught at Columbia University for twenty years before Nickerson hired her in 1943 to join the food-news staff of the *Times*. Working with Nickerson, Casa-Emellos prepared the dishes that appeared in recipes and were photographed for the newspaper. She tested the recipes for accuracy in the *Times'* test kitchen and adapted them, when necessary, for home use. She also wrote occasional columns about food.

Nickerson covered the hard news of government-issued rations during World War II and the rising cost of food. She wrote about the famous chefs who headed New York City restaurants and the new food products offered in the city's department stores. She interviewed home cooks and the topics that interested homemakers. She reported from the annual food editors conferences and cooking competitions. She included stories about the history of food and the role of nutrition. Typical of many newspaper sections of the time, she included many recipes, both new and classics.

By 1957, Nickerson was ready to leave the *Times* and join her husband in Florida. That summer, Nickerson lifted a glass of Chassagne-Montrachet at the restaurant "21" and toasted her departure from the newspaper with lunch guests *Gourmet* magazine editor Eileen Gaden and *Gourmet* writer Craig Claiborne. Nickerson announced she was leaving September 1—whether her replacement had been hired or not. Reportedly, she said to Claiborne, "I honestly think the *Times* didn't believe me when I said I was leaving. People simply don't leave the *Times*. They stay there until they die or are dismissed."[42] Editors at the newspaper had interviewed many possible replacements for Nickerson, or, as she put it, "anybody who can type with one finger and who had ever scrambled an egg."[43] Initially the editors were more interested in hiring someone with a background in test kitchens rather than the "rarefied atmosphere of a publication like *Gourmet*,"[44] but ultimately Claiborne was hired. Claiborne wrote in his memoir, *A Feast Made for Laughter*, that Nickerson "was, to my mind, the most inventive and diligent food writer in Manhattan. What she did not know she researched with great gravity and concern."[45]

David Kamp, in *The United States of Arugula*, contends that Nickerson and Claiborne first met when Claiborne, back in New York after studying at a Swiss cooking school, called Nickerson and pitched a profile about himself and "Nickerson took the bait."[46] Food writer Betty Fussell wrote that Nickerson was tricked into writing about Claiborne because "as a P.R. man, he knew how to con."[47] The idea that Nickerson was somehow tricked by Claiborne seems an unnecessary twist on the interview, however. After all, Nickerson had to write regular stories and was continually looking for story ideas. Writing about a local resident who had an interesting background in cooking would have fit the news values of her position. The profile she created was informative, not puffery. "Claiborne's interest in fine cooking began when he was a child in Indianola, Miss.," Nickerson wrote. "His mother was an outstanding cook in the Southern tradition. He came from a home, where, as he put it 'elaborate food preparation was not unknown.'"[48] Nickerson did not write a gushing profile; instead, she noted critically that the fancy French techniques he had mastered while abroad "had small practicality for householders here" in the United States.[49]

Claiborne wrote about Nickerson's resignation in his memoir. He said that at the beginning of 1957, she told the *Times* that "for reasons of family" she would be resigning from the newspaper as of September 1. She had married Alexander Francis Steinberg in 1950, after meeting him while writing a *New York Times* story about becoming the first person to market yogurt commercially in the United States.[50] Within a few years, with two children at home, she was ready to move to Florida with her husband. Claiborne wrote of the decision, "I was a bit startled at the news because of my respect for Jane as a journalist and also because I knew of her devotion to the job. She was a workaholic, a lady who often went into the office seven days a week to pursue her career. She was a diligent researcher with a thoroughgoing interest in learning more about the world of cuisine."[51]

After moving to central Florida and raising her children, Nickerson returned to food journalism. She published a cookbook about Florida foods in 1973. That same year, she became the food editor at the *Ledger*, a *New York Times*–owned newspaper in Lakeland, Florida, and a syndicated columnist to ten Florida newspapers. She covered food news for what was then called the Taste section. She used a similar journalistic approach to that which she used at the *New York Times*.

THE EARLY HISTORY OF FOOD JOURNALISM IN NEWSPAPERS

Women's pages have long been a part of American newspapers. According to most official journalism histories, Joseph Pulitzer started the women's pages in 1891 for the *New York World* as a way to increase advertising for products women would buy.[52] But further study shows that other newspapers had women's pages at about the same time or even sooner.

One of the earliest food columns was in the *Milwaukee Journal*, which began covering food on November 25, 1882, with a women's page titled "Women and the Home—HER DAILY PAGE" and suggestions on how to boil corn beef and make a wine pudding sauce.[53] The *San Francisco Chronicle* began its women's page in 1895. By 1905, it had a food writer who wrote under the pen name "Jane Friendly." Later, the name was associated with food editor Jane Benet.

The *Chicago Tribune* printed a one-paragraph recipe for baked ham in 1849, just two years after it began publishing. The recipe was alongside short articles about law reform in England and Africa exploration. By 1910, the *Tribune* included recipes and household tips in a daily column called the "Tribune Cook Book," edited by Caroline S. Maddocks under the pen name "Jane Eddington" (chosen in honor of her birthplace of East Eddington, Maine). The column included instructions about home canning and the preparation of a wedding cake. According to a *Tribune* manual from the time, the intent of the food page was to "preach daily that cooking is a noble as well as an ancient duty, and an art and exacting science all in one. The department wages an unrelenting war against uninspiring, vapid and tasteless foods." Eddington retired in 1930.[54]

Other metropolitan newspapers were quick to copy these sections. The *Louisville Courier-Journal* began a daily food column in April 1924 written by Cissy Gregg, who held a degree in agriculture and home economics from the University of Kentucky. Equipped with a test kitchen and a small staff to help her, her section was the first to use color at her newspaper.[55] She traveled through Kentucky gathering news about food and lecturing to women's groups. She also had an interest in international dishes, which she shared with her readers during World War II. Her recipes still run on the newspaper's website today.

The Picayune's Creole Cook Book, initially published by the *Picayune* in New Orleans at the turn of the century, "became wildly popular by 1915."[56] The book included culinary practices passed down from "the lips of the old Creole" cooks. In 1932, the *Times-Picayune* began offering classes in its Cooking and Homemaking School, held in the Municipal Auditorium and conducted by Jessie Marie DeBoth. The classes, which ran through the 1960s, used recipes from the original *Picayune* cookbook and from DeBoth's own cookbooks.[57] Julie Duvac Bowes began her career of thirty years as the food editor of the *Times-Picayune* in 1949 under the pen name "Sue Baker." She tested on her family the recipes that she used in her twice-weekly column, published on Thursdays and in color on Sundays in the newspaper's *Dixie Roto Magazine*.

Mary Acton Hammond was hired as the *Philadelphia Bulletin*'s first food editor in 1929 and wrote under the pen name "Frances Blackwood," her grandmother's name. She worked out of her own home kitchen for fifty-three years, testing her recipes. In 1941, she traveled to England, interviewing British women about how they prepared food during the war. It led to a series of columns that First Lady Eleanor Roosevelt mentioned in her "My Day" column. The columns turned into the book *Mrs. England Goes to War.*

Grace Hartley, who had a home economics degree, was the food editor at the *Atlanta Journal* for more than four decades, from 1936 to 1970. She briefly left the newspaper during World War II when the newspaper was only a few pages due to shortages. During that time, she worked for the War Production Board. Hartley had one of the first electric ranges in Atlanta, and likely the first microwave, a massive piece of equipment that stood five feet tall, with a conventional oven underneath.[58]

THE MID-CENTURY BOOM IN FOOD SECTIONS

In the post–World War II years, newspaper food sections were made thick thanks to grocery store and kitchen product advertisements. Between the ads was increasing space for news about food, new recipes, and the results of nutrition studies. A 1948 study by the Bureau of Agriculture Economics found that 56 percent of women got their food news from newspapers and magazines.[59] Wives and girlfriends were dealing with their menfolk returning from World War II after tasting new dishes abroad and needed to turn to someone such as their local food editor for direction on how to prepare these dishes, according to Nickerson.[60] Shapiro also has pointed out that the developments in food preservation and transportation shaped the way American women prepared food.[61] As these American housewives were looking to try new dishes, it was newspaper food editors who were quick to respond.

One article in a culinary journal declared there was no such thing as a food writer prior to Craig Claiborne's hiring in 1957 at the *New York Times*.[62] Yet in 1950 the journalism industry publication *Editor & Publisher* reported that the number of newspaper food editors had grown from 240 to 561 in one year. The reporter noted, "Hundreds of newspapers, which in the past have paid scant attention to the subject, are realizing the reader interest and the advertising revenue possibilities of food and are appointing qualified editors to turn out readable food pages."[63]

The *Washington Post* created a full food section with color photos in the early 1950s. Previously, it was a single page of food coverage. Elinor Lee, who had a background in home economics and was featured on a successful radio show about homemaking, oversaw the change. She joined the newspaper in 1953.[64] She was on the editorial committee for the fundraising cookbooks for the Women's National Press Club.

In 1962, *Arizona Republic* managing editor J. Edward Murray informed food editor Dorothee Polson that she would have her own food section rather than just a page or two.[65] She was given complete control, with no advertiser influence regarding the content. "I think it helped me that there had not been a food section, because there were no rules and regulations to follow," Polson recalled in her oral history. "I could just do whatever I wanted to. And I did. I would do interviews with interesting people that had nothing to do with food and just bring in their favorite recipes, because everyone eats. Most people cook a little bit, and most people have a favorite recipe, whether it's theirs or somebody else's. No matter what I wrote about, I could bring in a food angle."[66]

The *Denver Post* began its first stand-alone weekly food section in 1974, calling it "Food and Western Outdoors."[67] However, food coverage had begun as early as 1950 at the newspaper, when Helen Messenger Cass became the women's page editor. She wrote a popular food column that ran in the newspaper's Sunday publication, *Empire Magazine*, called "Munching Through Denver with Messenger." A few years later, Helen Dollaghan was given the title of food editor and became known as an expert in high-altitude cooking.

The growth of the food sections was aided by the lively food industry scene at this time. During the 1950s and 1960s, about 125 food editors attended the annual weeklong food editors' conferences. All but a handful of the attendees each year were male. It was reported that the Associated Press had assigned a man, Jack Ryan, to cover the subject, although there is no record of his work. Rather, Cecily Brownstone was likely the food editor. Based in New York, she was at the Associated Press for thirty-nine years—from 1947 to 1986. Her widely syndicated column included five recipes and two food features each week.[68]

Food editors met annually for the weeklong industry meetings where they typically spent from breakfast through late nights together. They also traveled together regularly to try new food and products or to judge cooking competitions. This description of the *Fort Worth Star-Telegram* food editor's job was typical of the experiences of most food editors: "Mrs. Vachule's job took her around the world in the company of other food editors." This included learning about cooking pineapple in Hawaii, sampling wine and cheese in Bologna, and dining at Spago in Beverly Hills.[69] *St. Louis Post-Dispatch* food editor Barb Ostmann traveled the world, including China, Switzerland, and Cuba, and learned about international cuisine. During her travels, she ate French-fried scorpions in China, horse kidneys in Italy, and emu carpaccio in Australia.[70]

Beighle French recalled that her travel led to her learning about the food issues of bananas in Guatemala and potatoes in Peru, as well as the systemic poverty of the regions. She recalled, "The Danish government hosted us to promote its edible exports and the Spanish green olive industry promoted its product while soldiers manned every street corner."[71]

THE JOURNALISTS AND EDITORS OF THE FOOD SECTIONS

At the time, most food editors had a journalism degree or a home economics degree that involved taking journalism classes. A handful did not meet this model, such as Cecily Brownstone, who completed only one year of college. Brownstone said, "I had no food training."[72] But a majority of food editors had college degrees and followed journalistic practices that they had been taught—following traditional news values, checking facts, and using ethical guidelines. For example, *Milwaukee Journal* food editor Peggy Daum was a stickler for details, insisting that accuracy was as important in the food section as on the front page. "If someone's age is wrong, that's one thing," Daum once said in an interview. "But if the amount of flour in a recipe is wrong, then the whole recipe can be ruined."[73] Newspapers took and still take the accuracy of recipes seriously. For example, when a mistake is made in a recipe published in the *Chicago Tribune*, a correction appears in the next issue of the newspaper and the entire recipe is reprinted in the next food section. The only other time that a corrected article is reprinted in its entirety in the newspaper is an incorrect obituary.[74] Jane Nickerson was also a stickler for details, including the proper use of language. *Webster's Third New International Dictionary* used twenty-five examples of Nickerson's work as the demonstration of correct English usage of words.[75] Furthermore, she appreciated the specifics needed in a good recipe. In one story, Nickerson marveled that Cicely Brownstone's recipes were accurate down to the one-eighth of a teaspoon of salt.[76]

Clarice Rowlands covered food for the *Milwaukee Journal* in the 1950s—an interest that she said started when she was a member of the 4-H Club in high school. A 1936 graduate of the University of Wisconsin, she was often asked the question that tended to irritate many food writers: "Does she cook?" These women believed the question undermined their roles as journalists. "No," Rowlands would respond. "I am a reporter in the field and it is not more necessary for me to prepare all the food I write about than it is for the paper's crime reporter to commit the crimes about which he writes."[77] Rowlands traveled the country looking for food news and reporting on regional dishes, as did the legendary Clementine Paddleford.[78]

Paddleford was the longtime food editor at the *New York Herald Tribune* and the only female food editor to have a book devoted to her career. This was partly because of her influence and partly because she saved so many of her own papers, which were donated to her alma mater, Kansas State University, and provided a rich trove of resources on her career. She was known for traveling the country to find food stories—sometimes even flying her own plane. She connected with newspaper food editors across the country regularly, contacting them when she came to their towns looking for good restaurants or home cooks. For example, when Paddleford wanted to learn about the food of Tampa, Florida, she contacted the *Tampa Tribune* food editor, Barbara Clendinen, for advice. This led to Paddleford visiting locals such as Mrs. Eliot Fletcher and Bertha Corral for their expertise on Spanish food.

Other food editors earned degrees in home economics—a popular path for women at the time. Some programs had a specific major dedicated to home economics journalism, including Iowa State University, Kansas State University, and the University of Wisconsin. More attention has been paid to recognizing the value of home economics in recent years. As one home economics scholar wrote, "Home economics has not fared well at the hands of historians. Until recently women's historians largely dismissed home economics as little more than a conspiracy to keep women in the kitchen."[79] Another noted, "The stereotypical image of home economics belies the reality that home economics was a diverse movement whose members had ambitious goals for themselves not only as teachers, but also as reformers and professionals."[80]

Yet, for other food writers, there was a need to distance themselves from the expertise that was implied by a home economics degree. It was a way to speak as an everyday cook. Clementine Paddleford created the term "panicitis" to describe cooks who had anxiety about their skills. Paddleford described herself as an everyday cook, which, according to her biographers, "distanced herself from home economists and endeared herself to her readers."[81] Many of these women were journalists who had no compelling interest in food but developed the interest later. One columnist wrote of Denver food editor Helen Dollaghan, "She was a newspaperwoman through and through."[82] In St. Paul, Eleanor Ostman approached her work as any reporter would. She wrote that she actually appreciated when a recipe did not work out, as it made for a better story: "I am a journalist not a home economist. Therein lies all the difference."[83] Food editor Ann Criswell of the *Houston Chronicle* said of her career, "I am not so much a food editor or cook as I am a journalist. My job has never been to prepare outstanding meals, but to report on cooking and the fascinating world of food."[84]

FOOD JOURNALISTS AND THE USE OF PEN NAMES

A common practice of newspaper food writers was to use pen names, often at the request of management because they wanted to preserve the continuity of the columnist; after all, it was expected the female reporter would leave employment once married. Food writers were not the first women at newspapers to use pen names. As other historians have noted, female news reporters began using pen names in the late 1800s "because for a woman to work as a newspaper reporter was considered unsavory and disreputable."[85] Some of the most famous female journalists of that time were using pen names. Columnist "Dorothy

Dix" was really Elizabeth Meriwether Gilmer, and Elizabeth Cochrane was hired by Joseph Pulitzer to go undercover and to travel around the world in eighty days as "Nellie Bly." In 1905, the *San Francisco Chronicle* introduced a food writer with the pen name "Jane Friendly," supposedly for the sake of anonymity and continuity.[86] When Jane Gugel Benet became the *Chronicle*'s food editor in 1953, she continued the "Jane Friendly" moniker, even though she was no stranger to the newspaper, beginning first as a copygirl during World War II and eventually working in nearly every department.

The food editors at the Spokane (WA) *Spokesman-Review* used the pen name "Dorothy Dean" for decades, with several women sharing the continuous byline. The first woman serving in that role was Estelle Calkins, who eventually left not to marry but to become a college professor. The next, Edna Mae Enslow Brown, did leave after two years when she married and started a family. Emma States wrote as "Dorothy Dean" during the war years, from 1941 to 1946, before leaving for a job in Seattle. Verle Ashlock was the next "Dorothy Dean," leaving after one year because she married and went to work at the university while her husband completed his college degree. In 1948, home economist Dorothy C. Raymond took over the position of "Dorothy Dean" until she retired in 1957.

The Hearst newspaper chain used the pen name "Prudence Penny" for the position of food reporter at many of its papers beginning after World War I.[87] Because it would have been expensive to wire recipes across the country, there were different "Prudence Penny" reporters at the individual Hearst papers. Local journalists then took on the name in the manner that Aunt Sammy did in communities across the country. "Prudence Penny" began her reign in 1920 and was a quick success. During her first year on the job, Mabelle Burbridge of the *New York Daily Mirror* answered more than 70,000 letters addressed to "Prudence Penny." At least one man took on the role—Hyman Goldberg for the *New York Daily Mirror* in the 1960s—and he was described as "a crusty, cigar-smoking, girl-watching ex-police reporter" in his obituary.[88] In another example, home economist Cecil Fleming wrote as "Prudence Penny" while the food editor at the *Detroit News*. It was said of Fleming, "She knows why the jelly doesn't jell and why the meringue weeps."[89]

The byline "Mary Cullen" was used at the *Oregon Journal* by several home economists as early as the 1940s.[90] One of these was Beverly Robison Poling, who worked in the Mary Cullen's Cottage for Household Arts Service of the *Oregon Journal* in 1947. She earned a degree in home economics from Oregon State University.[91] A 2001 *Chicago Tribune* article indicated that five women had used the "Mary Meade" byline over the years at that paper; yet it is largely Ruth Ellen Church who was associated with the name during her four decades at the paper.[92] In fact, several of her cookbooks noted that Church was actually "Mary Meade." She did use her maiden name, Ruth Ellen Loverien, in her initial stories with the newspaper.

At other papers, the food editor remained employed longer than expected. Mary Sorensen graduated from the University of Minneapolis and was hired by the *Minneapolis Tribune* in 1945. At the time her name was Mary Engelhart. The newspaper shortened it to "Mary Hart" and made it her byline. The newspaper got the copyright for "Mary Hart" to use with the "Ask Mary" Taste column and planned to allow other women to use the name after she left, assuming she would leave the newspaper once she married. Engelhart did marry, taking on her husband's last name of Sorensen, but she remained as the food editor for forty-four years, writing as "Mary Hart" the entire time.

Other food editors who used pen names included Jo Ann Vachule, who penned the *Fort Worth Star-Telegram*'s culinary question-and-answer column, "C.U.P.S." (Cooking Up a Storm), under the name "Jacqueline Jones." She also wrote articles under her own name. Marion Olive Prior Ferriss Guinn was food editor at the *Seattle Times*, writing under the pen name "Dorothy Neighbors." Julie Duvac Bowes began her career of thirty years as the food editor of the *Times-Picayune* in 1949 under the pen name "Sue Baker." Virginia Harms and Clarice Rowlands at the *Milwaukee Journal* both used the pen name "Alice Richards" occasionally in the late 1940s and early 1950s.

By the 1960s, the female food editors were taking their names back and owning their bylines. Consider "Marian Manners," the original food editor at the *Los Angeles Times*. She made her debut in 1931 as the director of the *Times*' Home Service Bureau. The original Marian Manners was local cooking teacher Ethel Vance Morse. Publisher Harry Chandler created the pen name to honor his wife, Marian. Home economist Fleeta Louise Hoke took over the position in 1939. In addition to

producing a daily column and answering readers' letters, she demonstrated cooking techniques in the community. Her regular appearances
ranged from presentations in the *Times* building to the Shrine Auditorium, where more than 7,000 people attended a three-day food seminar
in November 1939.[93] Jeanne Voltz became the food editor at the *Times*
in 1960 as the section moved to the editorial side of the newspaper. In
the first few years, she used the "Marian Manners" byline occasionally,
but by the middle of the decade, she regularly used her own name.

"Jane Holt" was a pen name used briefly by *New York Times* food
reporter Margot Murphy McConnell in the early 1940s.[94] She also
wrote a cookbook during World War II to help home cooks with the
limits of rationing. She is listed by her actual name with a mention of
her pen name. She left the newspaper in 1943, replaced by Jane Nickerson, who wrote under her own byline until she resigned in 1957.

FOOD JOURNALISTS, CAREER, AND FAMILY

The use of pen names to accommodate what male editors expected to
be a revolving door of female journalists who would leave to get married
was largely unnecessary. Some journalists did leave upon marriage or
once they had children, but many took advantage of the new career
possibilities for women.

Several of the food editors balanced motherhood and a career. Ruth
Ellen Church raised two sons during her *Chicago Tribune* newspaper
career and wrote her cookbooks at night. While she was the food editor
at the *Arizona Republic*, Dorothee Polson raised a son and a daughter
who often appeared in her column, which combined food and local
news. She had some advice for working mothers: "Be grateful for small
things like teflon, heat-and-serve, permanent press and other miracles
of today's living that make it possible to even contemplate homemaking,
motherhood—and a career."[95] Eleanor Ostman often mentioned her
son in her recipe column at the *St. Paul Pioneer Press*. Readers knew
him from his birth to his wedding, thanks to her food columns.

Jeanne Voltz planned to be a stay-at-home mother when she and her
family moved to Miami following her newspaper experience during
World War II. But, after a minor health issue, her doctor said lifting and
chasing her children would be too much work for her.[96] So instead of

the taxing job of stay-at-home motherhood, she joined her husband at the *Herald*. Voltz first worked on the news side of the newspaper, running the city desk before moving to the women's news section. Becoming the food editor provided better hours for a working mother of two children.

It is worth noting that many of these food editors were working to support themselves and their families. *Orlando Sentinel* food editors Grace Barr and Dorothy Chapman were single mothers with children to provide for at home. After a divorce, Chapman asked management if she could switch from writer to copy editor because the pay was higher, but the request was denied: "The editor job was a night job and the newspaper wouldn't let women work at night in those days because they thought it was too dangerous for them to be in the parking lots late."[97] In one column, Chapman wrote about the difficulties of raising children on one paycheck: "Many of our Christmases were poor Christmases—a single mother on a Southern professional woman's salary in those days robbed Peter to pay the Christmas Paul. But there was always hope and joy and memories made."[98]

A few of the editors briefly left newspapers to raise their children and then returned to journalism. This was the case for Nickerson when she left the *New York Times* in 1957 to raise her young family. By 1973, she was the food editor of a Florida newspaper and had written a cookbook about the foods of her adopted state. In another example, Jo Ann Vachule, food editor of the *Fort Worth Star-Telegram*, earned a journalism degree from the University of Texas. She worked as a reporter at the newspaper, along with her husband, in the 1950s and then left to raise her children. She returned in 1963 when the newspaper needed a food editor. Helen Messenger Cass initiated the food coverage at the *Denver Post* and then left in 1955 to raise her children. When she returned to the newspaper, her replacement did not want to give up the position, so Cass covered entertainment instead.

FOOD SECTIONS AND THEIR READERS

While food magazines can cover trends and introduce new products, they have less of a direct connection to their readers. Newspaper food editors had local readers' needs to meet. For example, in 1957, Ruth

Gorrell reported back from the national food editors meetings about a new line of gourmet dishes from General Mills that represented the meals from different countries. She also wrote that the food would not be available in the St. Petersburg, Florida, supermarkets of her readers. "We'll keep you posted," she wrote.[99] Further, if readers requested cake and cookie recipes, the editors were not going to respond with recipes for vegetable dishes.

The readers of food sections wanted a mix of the familiar and the exotic. At the *Los Angeles Times*, Betsy Balsley noted that her "food section was aimed at the homemaker."[100] Barbara Dembski, the *Milwaukee Journal*'s assistant managing editor of features, said food editor Daum never abandoned her audience. "Despite her national stature in food journalism, she never forgot who her section was for. She wrote it for the typical, salt-of-the-earth, best cook on the block."[101] According to Janet Beighle French, her responsibility was to the entirety of her audience: "I believed that food copy could and should reflect every ethnic and racial group in the Cleveland area, and that we should cover food broadly. I think that food sections were an ideal way to showcase the everyday cultures of regular citizens in a community."[102]

Orlando Sentinel managing editor Bill Dunn said of food editor Dorothy Chapman, "I know of no other person on our staff over the years who has done more for readers. She has a real bond with them. To them, calling Dorothy to ask a question is like going next door to borrow a cup of sugar or an egg."[103] Denver food editor Helen Dollaghan's work has been described as a "conversation between people who love food." One of the readers contacted the newspaper upon Dollaghan's death. "I can honestly say I cried at the news," she related. "I felt I knew her personally, although we never met."[104]

The food editors wielded considerable influence over their audience, as *Time* noted in a 1953 article about that year's annual meeting of the food writers: "[O]nly the front page and the comics have a bigger readership. Last week 133 of these influential newshens (130) and newsmen (three) gathered at Chicago's Drake Hotel for their tenth annual meeting."[105]

The food sections were popular with newspaper readers. For example, when food writer Clementine Paddleford started at the *New York Herald Tribune* in 1935, her section received more than 78,000 calls and letters from readers.[106] In the 1970s, the food section of the *Detroit*

News received hundreds of letters a week.[107] In Spokane, Washington, according to a 1973 newspaper article, more than 20,000 calls came in each year to newspaper food editor "Dorothy Dean."[108]

NEWS VALUES

What makes it into the newspaper is based on news values taught in journalism school and reinforced by the tradition of newsrooms. Hard news values include timeliness, prominence, proximity, oddity, impact, and conflict. The more a topic or event connects to those news values, the more likely the newspaper would cover it. So, if a new product was introduced or a technology developed, it was more likely to be reported on. For example, when blenders introduced a second speed, Church devoted a new cookbook updating recipes using the improved blender. Timeliness was also an issue for some food editors because the deadline for food sections was several days in advance, meaning some events were ignored because the news was too old by the time it was printed or it occurred after the deadlines. If the news value dictated coverage, the news was then likely covered by a news reporter for the news section.

It is also worth noting that newspaper journalism was a competitive occupation. Journalists pride themselves on getting exclusive interviews and public relations people know that. When the famous French restaurant Maxim considered introducing frozen vegetables to its menu in 1953, owner Louis Vaudable debated whether he should be interviewed by the *New York Herald-Tribune*'s Clementine Paddleford or the *New York Times*' Jane Nickerson.[109]

While it has been assumed the food sections contained only soft news, food editors did not shy away from hard news. Consider a pivotal moment in food history that occurred in 1969 at the White House Conference on Food, Nutrition, and Health. According to a government report, several "landmark policy efforts with profound and lasting effects emerged from this conference." Some of policies included the expansions of the food stamp program, required food labeling, and an updated school lunch program.[110] Two Milwaukee delegates attended the conference and reported back about problems caused by poverty and hunger. Providing coverage of the meeting, Daum quoted a speaker who said, "There are still people who don't believe people go to bed hungry in this country." In the same article, she noted that hungry people were a local story—they could be found at 16th and Mitchell streets in Milwaukee.[111] Ultimately, the conference issued an official report, and Daum later wrote, "The ripple effect of that meeting is still being felt today. It has been referred to as the Vatican II of the food world."[112]

Jeanne Voltz also covered that White House meeting and reported back about the need to address malnutrition based on poverty,[113] topics food editors such as Voltz had already been covering. In several stories, Voltz covered the FDA as it prepared the first guidelines on nutrition for processed foods in 1971.[114] A few years later she covered the FDA-required nutrition labeling guidelines. She wrote about the various meetings with consumer advocates, scientists, and food industry representatives over what the requirements should be. In one story, she traveled to Houston to a meeting of food editors, where an FDA official addressed the group, describing the new recommended daily allowance guidelines that replaced the 1941 minimum daily requirement.[115] She described the new policy as "a mixed blessing—or at least [it] brought mixed responses."[116]

In 1972, Voltz wrote about a California law that would require enrichment in grains to improve nutritional value. About two-thirds of the states already had similar laws, and California was debating possible legislation. She quoted a home economist who had lobbied for passage of the bill: "Since so many people use highly processed foods without really knowing what they contain, this can be important in improving total nutrition."[117] For the story, Voltz also conducted an investigation of the foods in the local grocery store, looking for what was printed on the labels and then reporting the results. In the *Boston Globe*, Dorothy Crandall wrote about a new policy that would list vitamins and minerals on canned foods.[118]

Also in 1972 Voltz wrote about the problem of hunger in America as a follow-up to the federal study outlining pockets of malnutrition in the nation. She began by quoting a senator who noted there was talk about hunger but no action was being taken. "California's unwritten nutrition policy is at a crossroads," she declared. At risk were children who were hungry by noon and pregnant women who could not afford to eat properly.[119] During the same time period, a reporter at the *Los Angeles Times* investigated and wrote a budget column that compared prices for products in health food shops versus typical grocery stores. "She was astounded at the price differences," Voltz said of the reporter who conducted the investigation, "but she was even more astounded at the type of food and non-food that these people were buying at high prices." Examples included moldy pineapple, bread too hard to eat, and garlic tablets.[120]

For another story, Voltz interviewed a nutrition expert from the American Medical Association. He said malnutrition was a result of poor eating habits rather than a problem with the food supply. He also credited newspapers with providing information on proper nutrition.[121] With an emphasis on nutrition, she wrote about how to prepare vegetables in order to maintain the most nutrients: "The 'new' cooking, largely a return to Grandma's fundamentals, glorifies fresh vegetables. Young folk proudly proclaim they never use a frozen or canned vegetable."[122] In another article, she described nutritional and financial value of a particular vegetable: "Cabbage is that budget-pampering wonder, always available at a very low, low price and one of nature's most nutritious gifts to man."[123]

One of the most significant series of stories written by the *Milwaukee Journal*'s Peggy Daum compared local grocery food prices. This led to her being named a "Food Page Reformer" in the book *The Women's Book of World Records and Achievements*. The entry stated that Daum "contends that food pages should include controversy even when a story attacks a supermarket or product that contributes advertising to the paper."[124] In an example of this practice, her section included a chart that compared about a hundred prices every week at the five supermarket chains where nearly 90 percent of her Milwaukee readers shopped.

In the early 1970s, under Ruth D'Arcy's watch, the *Detroit News* published a list of local supermarkets that had violated various food regulations. Examples included excess fat in the ground beef and prepackaged meat not matching the quantities on labels. "Our advertisers undoubtedly prefer we not publish that list," D'Arcy said.[125] In fact, she noted that as a result of the publication of the list, local grocers were trying to prevent the Michigan Department of Agriculture from releasing the stores' names. "Despite all this pressure, we continue to tell who is guilty of breaking the law," D'Arcy said.[126] At the Omaha newspaper, Maude Coons ran a chart comparing food prices in her city with food prices in other American cities.[127] This is the opposite of the pandering-to-advertisers kind of journalism that US senator Frank Moss accused the editors of practicing.

RAISING THE STATURE OF SOFT NEWS

To point out that hard news occasionally was featured in the food pages is not to devalue the importance of soft news. History was a common theme for these editors when introducing new trends or foods to their readers. Consider that Jeanne Voltz once went so far as to debunk the biblical tale that Eve used an apple to tempt Adam. Instead, as Voltz wrote in the introduction to one of her many books, the tempting fruit was likely a mango, a persimmon, or an apricot, based on history, geography, and an evolving language.[128] When she addressed Indian cooking, she included this lesson of British colonialism: "Great Britain's almost 200 years of domination in India opened a flavor gateway for the world's gastronomes. Without the British military and trade missions in the East, curry powder and the aromatic heat of Indian cuisine might still be unknown to the West."[129]

Voltz was not alone in sprinkling history lessons throughout her content. In 1956, *New York Times* food editor Jane Nickerson wrote about the history of the elaborate cakes originally from Vienna. Like many of her stories, this article also included recipes and several pictures of the desserts.[130] In 1973, after she returned to food journalism in Florida, she wrote about what life was like in Lakeland in 1913—based on several interviews—and the dishes served that included hot biscuits served at every meal, greens that took two hours to cook, and homemade desserts for every dinner.[131] In 1957, *Boston Globe* food editor Dorothy Crandall wrote about the history of Thanksgiving meals and created an updated version that included pumpkin mince chiffon pie, potato balls, and hot-spiced cider.[132]

CONCLUSION

The field of food studies is just beginning to dispel some of the myths about the history of food journalism—namely, that early food sections were staffed with dilettantes and that real food journalism began with

Craig Claiborne's ascension to the *New York Times*. A closer look shows that serious female food editors and journalists were working in women's pages and elsewhere from the early twentieth century on. Some had home economics and journalism degrees, and all participated in a lively industry scene of conferences and travel.

These editors and journalists were some of the most important figures at newspapers, both because of the deep connection they had with their readership and because of the important topics that they covered, including poverty, nutrition, and the food industry. They covered hard food news and recognized the great value that soft news had for their readerships.

2

FOOD AND FOOD JOURNALISM DURING AND AFTER WORLD WAR II

In 2009 First Lady Michelle Obama launched an effort to encourage Americans to grow their own vegetables, supporting the effort with a cookbook spotlighting home gardening. But this was not the first time that the White House had promoted gardening. During World War I and more often during World War II, gardening was considered a political and patriotic act. Government-imposed rations limited Americans' ability to buy food, so the women left on the home front were encouraged to grow their own food, even as they entered the workforce in large numbers. When the produce was grown, they were encouraged to can the extra food. These messages were often delivered through the food pages of newspapers.

THE CHALLENGES OF FOOD PREPARATION IN WARTIME

World War II presented many challenges for food production in the United States. Rationing meant that many foods were unavailable or in short supply. Women were entering the workforce in record numbers to replace male workers who were now in the military. And new information about nutrition brought the importance of food choice to the forefront.

The US government and media worked to help address these new challenges for home cooks. As culinary historian Amy Bentley docu-

mented in her book *Eating for Victory*, when the government wanted
to win the war with food, it reached out to the homemaker. According
to Bentley, "Declaring the homemaker's kitchen a war zone made it a
public area. Cooking and shopping for food became, according to the
media, political and patriotic acts and thus subject to public scrutiny."[1]
Likewise, Joanne Lamb Hayes noted in her book *Grandma's Wartime
Kitchen* that after the bombing of Pearl Harbor, food was tied to patriotism, from victory gardens to meal stretching.[2]

Bentley and Lamb examined a wide range of mass media to document the changes to women's lives and the efforts to support food
production in the United States, including magazines, newspapers, and
advertising as well as government propaganda and industry publications. For example, the National Livestock and Meat Board published a
wartime pamphlet stating, "The American homemaker has an important part to play in the war effort. Her uniform is the kitchen apron and
she may wear it proudly."[3]

As Bentley noted, for the food supply to be managed during wartime, women had to be on board. Research from the time showed that
women were making the household purchasing decisions despite the
stereotype that husbands decided what meat would be served at a meal.
Psychologist Kurt Lewin described this role as "gatekeeping." Because
of their role as gatekeepers, "to change the kinds of meat families ate,
for example, it was necessary to influence not men or children but
women." The government reached women through neighborhood programs and media reports—including stories found in newspapers.[4] In
the *New York Times*, food editor Jane Nickerson noted that women
would be under extra pressure when men returned from war and expected better food than the military had provided.[5] Bentley noted that
by World War II, American "women's main role as consumer was clearly recognized, and cooking and child rearing had long been elevated as
the most important and rewarding domestic tasks for women."[6] This
was especially true for middle-class, white women with purchasing
power. They appreciated the help of the food editors who described
new products and how they would influence their recipes. Many of
these homemakers would eventually go into the paid workforce, which
would forever change the role of women in American society—even if
many briefly returned to the home in the 1950s.

A group of social scientists played an important role in educating citizens about the government's food plans through the Committee on Food Habits. Prior to entering the war, the government knew a food shortage was likely and that the food supply might have to be rationed. The CFH was concerned about the nutrition and morale of the American people. The group was headed by well-known anthropologist Margaret Mead. According to Bentley, "At a time when women social scientists found it nearly impossible to hold high wartime positions in the government, the number of women involved with the CFH was remarkable."[7]

NEWSPAPERS' ROLE IN THE WARTIME FOOD STRATEGY

Newspapers were a crucial part of the food strategy of World War II. One of the most important efforts of the government at this time was the 1942 campaign to encourage Americans to grow victory gardens, an effort that resulted in 16.5 million American planting gardens.[8] Newspapers were often the vehicles delivering this message. For example, in 1943, the editorial page of the *St. Petersburg Times* encouraged homemakers to create victory gardens.[9]

Newspapers participated in other ways as well. They covered new food-related topics ranging from food shortages to government rationing to nutrition concerns. As noted in *The Warmest Room in the House*, during the war "newspapers did their share to help Americans make the most of the foods in their kitchens."[10] Many newspapers included guidelines from trade groups like the National Livestock and Meat Board to help home cooks stretch the meat available to them. The newspaper food editors were no strangers to being creative with limited food options after living through the Great Depression; one Fort Worth food editor recalled eating squirrel that her father had caught while she was growing up.[11] *Houston Chronicle* food editor Ann Criswell wrote, "I grew up in East Texas during the days of the Depression, when the food was simple and Southern. We had brains and eggs for breakfast, hogshead cheese, catfish, dandelion greens, okra and other foods typical of the times that today might strike terror in the digestive tracts of diners."[12] These experiences helped food journalists convey important ideas about food during times of shortage.

Newspapers also served an educational role by using food as a way of understanding foreign cultures and trends. At the *New York Herald Tribune*, Clementine Paddleford wrote a weekly column during the war that included recipes for dishes representing the allied nations. Examples include *erwtensoep* (or snert), a Dutch sausage and pea soup, and *cochet à la contadine*, a chicken fricassee dish made by French home cooks. The columns would also include a history of the country and its people.[13] Cissy Gregg, food editor of the *Louisville Courier-Journal*, tied her interest in cooking to her collection of world maps that covered her kitchen walls. She said she could cook and analyze the war fronts at the same time.

Food was an easy way to normalize people who might otherwise seem different or unfamiliar. That societal conversation was made easier by using something that people in all of the nations had in common: food. In looking to normalize and understand the women of war-torn Britain, *Philadelphia Bulletin* food editor Mary Acton Hammond, who used the pen name "Frances Blackwood," traveled to the United Kingdom. The mission began with a February 7, 1942, letter to the newspaper's managing editor. She wrote:

> There is, I believe, a deep need in this country for a clearer understanding of what the war is doing to the homes of England. We do read and see pictures of women in war industries in England, but the most these seem to inspire is a wish to wear uniforms that look snappy. There has been nothing to give us a hint of the homes those girls left in the morning and will return to at night, or what those uniforms are costing in home-life.[14]

Her editor agreed and booked her a seat on a Pan Am flight for England. She would stay for six weeks and interview the women about their work lives, home lives, and the foods they prepared, sending back a story for her newspaper each day. She took notes describing the rationing system and the lack of food delivery trucks due to gasoline shortages. She told the stories of women who worked ten-hour shifts in factories, and then came home and cooked meals for their brothers and fathers. She also wrote about lack of fruit, the difficulty of matching ration books to local stores, and the need to swap or trade foods with friends and neighbors.[15]

World War II had a considerable impact on American menus, placing limits on available foods. Wanting to still provide healthy and nutritious meals for their families, homemakers looked to their newspaper food editors for help. For example, *New York Times* food writer Margot Murphy, who used the pen name "Jane Holt," helped readers plan their meals during the war. In fact, in 1942, she wrote the book *Wartime Meals*, which included both her actual name and her pen name as a byline. The book was a mix of recipes as well as advice on planning a meal and the process of canning. It also included an extensive explanation about vitamins.[16]

For food rationing to succeed, the US government needed American homemakers to get on board. After all, the two items most important to Americans' culinary identity—meat and sugar—were going to be severely restricted. The government also encouraged women to stock up by providing "victory specials" for readily available products such as frozen foods that were not rationed. It was meant to replace canned foods needed for the troops. It was a complicated message, balancing the country's new understanding about nutrition and health with the reality of the restrictions on available food. Commercial companies were also weighing in and targeting mothers. A Pillsbury Company ad featured a young girl who was sent home from school with the tagline "Dorothy sent home again! The school nurse says . . . 'Malnutrition.'"[17] It was a time when patriotism was linked to what a mother was feeding her children, as well as her later war-time job outside of the home.

Paddleford helped her home cooks deal with the challenges of war by suggesting an increased use of spices, which were not rationed, to help improve meals. She encouraged her readers to try the new bread and cake mixes because "war puts premium on leisure," and "war dips a deep scoop into sugar bowls."[18] At a time when desserts were served with each dinner, the loss of sugar was significant for homemakers. In Milwaukee, readers were encouraged to use cheese, the "victory food," as a substitute for scarce meats, with newspapers printing scores of cheese-based recipes.[19]

The end of the war did not mean the end of rationing. Many homemakers still had to stretch their ingredients. In 1946, Jane Nickerson described for her *New York Times* readers meals using "emergency" potatoes. The recipes featured potatoes in place of grain and flour. Examples included "eggs baked in potato cups" and "potato stuffing" for chicken. One recipe was for mashed potatoes with the butter removed because it was rationed.[20] Included at the end of her columns was a phone number so that readers could call Nickerson with questions about rationing.

After the war, the hungry nations in Europe still needed food, and America was ready to help. A 1947 wire story that appeared in the *Milwaukee Journal* addressed the response to President Truman's first meatless Monday as part of a food conservation program. An unnamed reporter wrote that restaurants and governmental offices respected the ban but the housewives ignored it.[21] Some newspaper articles argued that women were being unpatriotic by ignoring the call for meatless Mondays. Another story that year noted that, while the overall food supply was adequate, some staples were difficult to find.[22]

As news of the starvation in Europe spread, newspaper readers inquired how to help. During this time, Nickerson recommended that homemakers cut back on their food shopping and donate the savings to famine relief. "Substitute one like food for another that's more expensive—mackerel for swordfish, spinach for asparagus, oranges for strawberries," she suggested.[23] The following year, Nickerson followed up with information about a government program called CARE (Cooperative for American Remittance to Europe). "It is for the express use of individuals here who wish to help hungry persons in Europe," she recommended.[24]

WORLD WAR II'S EFFECT ON FOOD JOURNALISTS' CAREERS: MOVING BEYOND THE WOMEN'S PAGES

The war, of course, changed women's lives on the home front significantly. During World War II, women were hired in positions that had been reserved for men, a new role represented in popular culture through Rosie the Riveter. At newspapers, female reporters who had been restricted to the women's pages were allowed to cover other beats. For example, the United Press employed a hundred women during wartime, or 20 percent of its staff.[25] These women were typically fired in peacetime or returned to the women's pages—taking that hard news experience with them. Many of them went on to become food editors. For example, Jeanne Voltz began her career in journalism right out of college as a general assignment news reporter at the *Mobile (AL) Press-Register.* It was a busy time in the port city with its growing shipyard and increasing population. The impact of World War II was always near. "I lost so many friends," she wrote years later. "I did a lot of casualty stories."[26] She eventually became the food editor at the *Miami Herald* and then the *Los Angeles Times.* Polly Paffilas was hired at the *Akron Beacon Journal* during World War II. She worked in several areas before she became the food editor, remaining in the position for decades. Jane Gugel Benet started at the *San Francisco Chronicle* as a copygirl during World War II and worked in almost every part of the newspaper before being promoted to food editor in 1953 and writing under the pen name "Jane Friendly."

For other women journalists, the war meant a chance to join the military service. Ann Hamman had degrees from Oklahoma State University and the University of Chicago before enlisting in the Women's Army Auxiliary Corps at the beginning of the war. She spent two years in North Africa and Italy. Using the GI Bill, she earned a master's degree in home economics from Purdue University and became an extension agent for nutrition before becoming the food editor at the *Evansville (IN) Courier* in 1967.[27] Veronica Volpe served in the US Navy WAVES (Women Accepted for Volunteer Emergency Service) during World War II. With a degree in home economics, she went on to become the food editor at the *Pittsburgh Press* from 1961 to 1977.[28] In a third example, Bertha Cochran Hahn, who had a degree in home economics from Purdue University, became a second lieutenant in the Army Medical Corps stationed in Air Force hospitals. In peacetime, she earned a second degree in journalism and interned at the *Miami News.* She was hired full-time and became the newspaper's food editor in 1953.[29]

THE POSTWAR FOOD INDUSTRY

World War II had a lasting effect on US food manufacturing and consumption. Helping to feed the soldiers meant finding the right combination of product and packaging that would travel and be preserved. Those developments would later benefit consumers. Mass production of Florida orange juice began during World War II, but the quality of the beverage was questioned. The US Agriculture Department tested numerous oranges and grapefruits for their nutritional content. Nickerson reported on the findings that most of the vitamin C found in oranges and grapefruit was found in the rinds.[30]

Several new products came about because of the war, including caramel milk. It had been created by the Department of Agriculture for soldiers with poor appetites. The thought was that sweetness in the cans of milk would encourage soldiers on the battlefield to drink the dairy product. Manufacturers planned to introduce caramel milk to stateside consumers in 1946. Nickerson wrote about the product for her readers and questioned its potential for success: "Whether this product appears on retail markets depends on whether consumers come to realize its nutritive properties and are willing to pay a bit more than they expect to."[31] Clearly, the practical needs of wartime were going to change in a postwar consumer culture, and caramel milk never established a foothold in the public marketplace.

American soldiers had gone off to war with a can opener and canned goods. In 1941, New York–based newspaper food editor Marian Tracy, along with her husband Nino, published the book *Casserole Cookery*.[32] It was so popular that over the next decade, the book was reprinted thirteen times. Tracy came up with the idea after working at a bookstore and listening to customers constantly requesting a cookbook for casseroles, which was nonexistent. Also, as she told Associated Press food editor Cicely Brownstone, "I learned to take shortcuts in cooking because my husband took long cuts."[33] The continuing popularity of canned goods, bolstered by the new advertising possibilities of television, in turn generated the interest in an electric can opener. In fact, by the 1950s, one of every three food products available at the grocery store was in a can.[34] Ruth Ellen Church explained to her *Chicago Tribune* readers that canned foods would add variety to menus.[35] In another story, she explained that canned foods were economical.[36] Food production also became increasingly industrial in the 1940s and 1950s. Farming changed considerably with the consolidation of small farms and the introduction of new chemicals.[37]

Culinary historians often propose that American menus changed and became more exotic because the men had returned from World War II after being exposed to new dishes. Those stories also typically noted that prior to the war, American food was largely a country of meat and potatoes meals. Yet a review of food sections shows that, even before World War II, there was a more diverse palate. In part, this was a result of the World's Fairs, which introduced foods from foreign lands that the food editors covered. Hayes's *Grandma's Wartime Kitchen* confirms this, noting that, during the war, international dishes were prepared on special occasions. For example, the use of Creole sauce was popular in the early 1940s, even outside of New Orleans.[38]

The Postwar Rise of the Supermarket

Grocery shopping changed during the war and postwar years as well. For many years, just gathering the needed ingredients for meals was a taxing chore for home cooks. It often involved stopping at three places—the dry goods store, a produce shop, and the butcher. In many of these stores, the customer would request an item that the purveyor would then pick out and hand to her. The first store to move away from this paradigm was the Piggly Wiggly. Piggly Wiggly is largely credited with creating self-service stores in 1916, known initially as "grocerterias," in which customers would pick their items off of a shelf themselves and then simply take the items to the cashier.

The convenience of self-service was expanded in the 1930s with the first supermarkets, where some produce and meat was offered along with dried goods. The first supermarket is credited to Michael Cullen, who opened King Kullen in Queens, New York, on August 4, 1930. According to an article celebrating the seventy-fifth anniversary of the supermarket, "They popularized the idea of self-service. They spurred the growth of mass merchandising. They helped liberate women from the kitchen. They contributed to suburban sprawl. And they encouraged innovation, leading to the advent of the shopping cart and the bar code."[39]

Local food editors were important in educating homemakers about these new shopping paradigms. Consider Jane Nickerson's 1946 story about a new process used in the supermarket Food-O-Mat in Ridgewood, New Jersey. Thanks to the new system, 1,700 packaged and bottled products now took up 76 feet rather than the previous 225 feet. She described the process in this way: "When a customer removes a can or jar or package, a duplicate rolls down the slight incline into place, in somewhat the same fashion in which a Dixie cup dispenser works." She then included comments from several of the shoppers at the store.[40] Also that year, food editor Clementine Paddleford reported from a new supermarket in Syracuse, New York. She quoted the owner as saying that the women of that time might copy the style of Grandma's hat, "but you'll never go back to her way of shopping for groceries."[41]

These new food stores help create the thick food sections found in newspapers, as the number and size of advertisements sold dictated the number of pages. Editorial copy, like recipes and food columns, were then placed around the advertisements. Grocery stores advertised their weekly specials and food companies bought ads in the food sections, often with a coupon for a shopper to clip. In addition, some department stores included advertising for new kitchen appliances as technology developed and furnishing styles changed.

As homemakers did more and more of their shopping at supermarkets, store owners sought feedback. Meetings were regularly held with homemakers. For example, at one 1957 meeting in Milwaukee, grocery store executives met with a group of women and asked questions. They wondered if the women would buy prepackaged meat, rather than speak directly to a butcher for their needs. The women were quizzed about the importance of convenience, cleanliness, and the cost of food. A newspaper article about the meeting included the names and the opinions of the shoppers.[42] Similar kinds of meetings were held and covered by food editors in cities across the country during the 1950s and 1960s.[43] In Cleveland, food editor Janet Beighle French asked local supermarket executives why each market maddened consumers by using different names for the same cuts of meat. Her story appeared in a Sunday paper and featured color photos of the cuts with the differing names; the supermarkets responded by standardizing the names.[44]

1950s Food and Journalism

Some scholars have traced the change in eating patterns after World War II to the American soldiers' exposure to foreign cuisine. Other culinary historians argue that cookbooks that featured food from foreign countries were available in America prior to the war. The growth of the suburbs, increased kitchen appliances, and popularity of supermarkets changed life for homemakers. One researcher believed the 1950s and suburban tastes to be inherently linked. He wrote,

To describe suburban cuisine in the 1950s is to invoke images of hellish concoctions: day-glow Jell-O molds, insidious varieties of puffs and balls, international dishes that could as easily have been interplanetary. However, despite the apparent tastelessness which often characterized the suburban palate, fifties food was as much a product of the times as tailfins and television; in fact, the three were intimately related. [45]

The 1950s have also been characterized as a time of convenience foods, and clearly there was some truth to this. In 1952, the *New York Times* reported that by using canned food, American housewives had helped free themselves from 34 billion work hours annually in meal preparation time. [46] This change in cooking technique may have been best represented by food journalist Poppy Cannon's *Can Opener* cookbook, which was reissued regularly, as well as the popularity of Marian Tracy's casserole cookbooks.

From a different perspective, consider an essay about the food establishment in Nora Ephron's book *Wallflower at the Orgy*, in which she ponders that the beginning of the foodie movement may have been in the 1950s when cooking with curry became popular. She wrote,

> Historical explanations of the rise of the Food Establishment do not usually begin with curry. They begin with the standard background on the gourmet explosion—background that includes the traveling fighting men of World War II, the postwar travel boom, and the shortage of domestic help, all of which are said to have combined to drive the housewives of America into the kitchen. This background is well and good, but it leaves out the curry development. [47]

Kamp asserted that the curry craze was "instigated, or at least stoked," by Cicely Brownstone's recipe for Country Captain Chicken, which included the spice blend. [48] (When the recipe later ran in the *New York Times*, it included a typographical error, calling for one *cup* of pepper, [49] causing one reader to complain that he nearly died from eating the dish. [50]) Decades later, in the *New York Times*, food writer Molly O'Neill described Brownstone as the "Curator of Country Captain Chicken" and "a one-woman preservation society for this particular version of curried chicken." [51] Over the years, Brownstone had debunked the assumption that the dish was a recipe of the Southern United States. She found an early version of the recipe in the 1867 cookbook *Miss Leslie's New Cookery Book*, in which the author explained that it was an Indian dish. At Brownstone's urging, the dish was taught in James Beard's cooking school and was included in some editions of *The Joy of Cooking*. O'Neill wrote that over time, "The dish has gone in and out of style. One era idolized the dish's exotica, another loved its simplicity."[52]

Kamp attributed the 1950s development of a real American food establishment to "a small group of New York–based sophisticates who, via newspaper columns, magazine work, and cookbooks, had national even international reach." He included in this group Nickerson, James Beard, and *McCalls'* food editor Helen McCully, as well as Cecily Brownstone of the Associated Press and Clementine Paddleford of the *Herald Tribune*. He wrote that the members of this group "kept one another's counsel, exchanged gossip, and stood united in opposition to the quick-bake, canned-soup mores of the domestic scientists."[53] There was definitely something to this idea—although Paddleford likely did not socialize with the group very often. Nickerson and Brownstone had a long, personal friendship. They had met in New York City in the 1940s when Nickerson published a profile of Brownstone. "Our friendship flowered in Denmark during an assignment," Nickerson wrote. "Her modesty and magical sense of humor charmed me in the several days we sampled Danish cheeses, hams, beers, Cherry Herring and aquavit."[54] The two would go on to share several dinners together in Brownstone's New York apartment and dining in local restaurants that Nickerson was reviewing for her newspaper. Brownstone would later visit Nickerson when she relocated to central Florida.

Introducing Ethnic Food

Newspaper food editors were often the ones to introduce new kinds of ethnic dishes to readers. Sometimes they drew their inspiration from recently released cookbooks and other times from new local restaurants. In 1947, Jane Nickerson shared recipes for tempura (fish fritters from Japan) and bo-lo gai (pineapple chicken from China), both based on a recently released cookbook on Asian cooking.[55] Two years later, Nickerson wrote about Italian dishes, including frittatas and marinara sauce. They were meatless dishes recommended for the Lent season.[56] Also that year, she wrote about a classic French cookbook recently translated into English.[57] In 1953, Nickerson included recipes for creole jambalaya as part of a buffet supper—a popular trend at the time.[58]

In 1953, food editor Elinor Lee wrote a series of stories that explored different dishes based on the women—usually wives of government employees—who lived in Washington, DC. The series, titled "Baking 'Round the World," also ran in other newspapers across the country. In one story, Lee explored Chinese cooking and interviewed Mary H. Tan, who was married to a diplomat and taught cooking classes at the local YMCA. Included was a recipe for hang-yen-bang, or almond cakes.[59] In another example, Lee interviewed Señora de Java, the wife of an ambassador, about Chilean food. Lee explained the differences between meals in America and de Java's home country, and she included a recipe for a Chilean casserole called "Pastel de Choclo."[60]

The popularity of French food in America was due to a combination of elements. Most obvious, of course, was the publication of Simone Beck and Julia Child's *Mastering the Art of French Cooking* in 1961 and Child's subsequent television show. James Beard was a fan of the book and helped to promote it by introducing the women to his New York food friends and through his cooking school.[61] "I love your cookbook," he said to Child. "I just wish I had written it myself."[62] He went on to introduce Child to magazine and newspaper food editors,[63] and she spoke at the 1964 annual food editors meeting about cooking seafood in a French style. The event was covered by *New York Times* reporter Nan Ickeringill, who described Child as an "avid fish enthusiast."[64]

By the early 1960s, Child had a food column in the *Boston Globe* called the "French Chef." It first ran in 1963, and she updated her copy over the years. She explained that "a soufflé is nothing but thick sauce into which stiffly beaten egg whites are incorporated."[65] In another column, she wrote that potatoes "can be made wonderfully gastronomical when subjected to the imagination of the French."[66] By 1965, she wrote about quick meals and included a three-course menu that could be made in thirty minutes.[67]

The newspaper food editors regularly wrote about Child, often profiling her as she traveled the country promoting her cookbooks.[68] For example, *Boston Globe* food editor Dorothy Crandall, as well as thirty other food editors, covered a 1968 event during which Beard and Child cooked fish dishes together on a stage. During one demonstration, the two rather large people got in each other's way, Crandall wrote. "What we need, Julia, is not one stove but five," Beard said and laughed.[69]

The Kennedy White House has also been credited for inspiring interest in French cooking after First Lady Jacqueline Kennedy hired French-born chef René Verdon, considered the first professional chef in the position. His White House debut, a luncheon for British prime minister Harold Macmillan, made the front page of the *New York Times*. He continued on as the White House chef after the president was assassinated and cooked for Texas-born President Lyndon Johnson. The chef resigned in 1965 after being asked to prepare a cold garbanzo bean puree, a dish that he reportedly detested regardless of temperature.

French cooking also gained traction as early as the 1930s with the appearance of gourmet societies in several cities, including Boston, Chicago, New York, and San Francisco. Author David Strauss looked at these typically all-male organizations in his book *Setting the Table for Julia Child*. He examined cookbooks and cited newspaper coverage in several areas, including articles about fine dining written by Nickerson and Paddleford. For example, in one article, Nickerson wrote, "home dinners can never duplicate the luxuries of the Chevaliers du Tastevin."[70]

Dining in California was increasingly changing in the 1960s. At the *Los Angeles Times*, Jeanne Voltz combined traditional storytelling techniques with the basic elements of a recipe as she introduced new dishes, whether it was a European dessert or a curry recipe. In another story, she referred to the incorporation of curry in a meatball recipe as "adventuresome" because curry "creates excitement in the most ordinary foods."[71] Voltz also tackled an adventurous dish from Japan that is now so common you can buy it fresh in your local supermarket: "In Los Angeles they are called hors d'oeuvre or snacks. In Madrid they are tapas. Muscovites call them zakuski. In Japan they are sushi. Sushi is a savory tidbit of cold vinegared rice pressed or molded into any of several shapes and finished with tiny pieces of seafood or fish."[72]

The most common ethnic style of cooking Voltz wrote about in the 1960s was Mexican food. "The conversion of a Middle Westerner or Easterner to California cookery," declared Voltz, "usually is complete when tostada, tamale, taco, tortilla and taquito become part of the household kitchen vernacular."[73] In one story, she described a Mexican-themed party buffet at the pool,[74] and in another she introduced her readers to tamales.[75] Some of the most popular recipe requests from her readers were for enchiladas, mainly for the ease and inexpensive nature of the dish. "Mexican cuisine in general is low cost, since meat is used sparingly, with beans and corn and cheese supplying much of the protein," she explained.[76] She also introduced her readers to almendrado, a Mexican dessert, which she described as a tricolored, cold, foamy egg-white pudding.[77]

In 1968, the *Miami Herald* included several features with an exotic flare. One feature focused on the foods of New Orleans, with recipes for calas, French market doughnuts, and madeleines. Miami food editor Virginia Heffington described Creole food to her readers as combining "the French flair for subtle blending of flavors" (including Spanish seasonings) with contributions from Choctaw and Chickasaw Indians.[78] An article a week later featured Italian, German, and French recipes. One dish was "aquello e cannellini," or what Heffington described as "a tongue-twisting Italian for lamb shanks and white kidney beans. The shank is from the front leg of the lamb." There were also recipes for Sauerbraten, or German pot roast, and boeuf à la bourguignonne, the burgundy beef stew dish made popular by Julia Child.[79]

Not all meals were coming from American kitchens. The commonality of eating ground beef during the war meant that Americans were open to the idea of burgers as fast food. In 1947, Nickerson wrote about the popularity of burger bars in New York City and the introduction of cheese on the sandwich: "At first, the combination of beef with cheese and tomatoes, which sometimes are used, may seem bizarre. If you reflect a bit, you'll understand the combination is sound gastronomically. The Italians, for example, are famous for their veal parmigiana, which gourmets agree is good, and which consists of a veal cutlet with tomato sauce and cheese."[80]

Fast food was on its way. As families flocked to the suburbs, they were eager to eat out. Both McDonald's and Burger King were popular by the mid-1950s. As Gdula wrote, "There was an of-the-era aspect to driving up to the hamburger stand in your new car and placing your order at the shiny counter. In just a few minutes you were out the door with dinner in a bag."[81] With the acceptance of the hamburger came the introduction of mass-produced French fries. The process for flash-freezing potatoes was a result of keeping the military fed during the

war. It was only natural after the war that the developer of the technology used to dehydrate potatoes for the government, John Richard Sim-
plot, would strike a deal with McDonald's.[82]

THE RISE OF THE US FOOD ESTABLISHMENT

In the mid- and late twentieth century, food reporting and general
interest in cooking grew exponentially. New foods emerged, new cooking processes were popularized, and the profession of food journalism
itself began to thrive.

Cooking Celebrities

One sign of the growing interest in food journalism was the prolifera-
tion of stories in food sections about big names in food who were visiting the area or sometimes just a celebrity who liked to cook. Often these
celebrities would end up as a guest at the home of the local food editor.
In one example, Fort Lauderdale food editor Rita Ciccone invited Shel-
ly Winters over to the house to cook, and they went to the local Publix
grocery store and shopped before making dinner together, with the
grocer completely unaware of the celebrity in his presence.[83] In another
example, Wolfgang Puck was visiting Fort Worth on a publicity tour for
a new cookbook when food editor Jo Ann Vachule asked if he would
dress up as Santa Claus for a photo to accompany her article. His public
relations person declined, but when Puck arrived at her home, she
asked again and he enthusiastically agreed.[84] Paul Prudhomme and
Martha Stewart were also visitors to Vachule's Fort Worth home when
touring with new cookbooks. *Houston Chronicle* food editor Ann Criswell interviewed numerous celebrities in her career, including Paul
Bocuse, Julia Child, James Beard, Emeril Lagasse, Wolfgang Puck,
Alice Waters, Diana Kennedy, Martha Stewart, and Susan Feniger and
Mary Sue Milliken of the Food Network's *Too Hot Tamales*.[85]

In 1963, Jeanne Voltz profiled Helen Corbit, the director of the
restaurant in the Dallas Neiman-Marcus department store. The Texan
was on vacation in Los Angeles when Voltz interviewed her, gaining
some insight on how she thought about food and gender. Corbit said it
was a myth that men were meat-and-potato eaters whereas women

preferred chicken and salads. In her restaurant, she said, men were just as likely to order fruit salads and soufflés, while women ordered steak and hamburgers. Corbit also expressed disappointment in the Los Angles restaurants, saying, "I think with the wealth of fresh fruit and vegetables there is very little imagination here."[86] While in New York, Voltz cooked in her West Side Manhattan apartment for James Beard many times. On one occasion, Voltz cooked for *To Kill a Mockingbird* author Harper Lee.[87]

St. Paul food editor Eleanor Ostman was known for her lunch with Paul Newman in New York City's Rainbow Room atop Rockefeller Center. The lunch was a result of Ostman winning the food writers' division in Newman's annual recipe contest. Her entry was for Devilish Shrimp Bisque. She watched him taste the dishes and pick a top choice, which was not Ostman's soup. The actor still had his magnificent smile, she wrote, but her husband's eyes were bluer.[88] Over the years, she would refer back to the lunch in her columns.

One celebrity encounter with a food editor did not go so well. In 1971, Virginia Heffington was the food editor at the *Long Beach (CA) Independent Press-Telegram* when she covered a promotional event for the upcoming cookbook *Liberace Cooks*. She was kicked out of Liberace's kitchen when she objected to a photo being taken in his messy kitchen and openly criticized the singer's cooking. "I think we should forget the story because you're a better piano player than you are a cook," she told him. "Your beef stroganoff tastes more like canned beef stew." He asked her to leave and the argument was treated as a news story that went over the Associated Press wire service.[89]

Food Editors' Conferences

The growth of the field of food journalism was also evident in the appearance in the 1940s and 1950s of the first industry conferences for food editors and journalists. The most important of these was the annual conference known as the Newspaper Food Editors Conference. The meetings began in 1944 and each lasted a week. They included editors sampling new products and recipes, which often began at breakfast and continued through the night. There were also speakers—a mix of advertisers, food experts, and politicians.

The event was the brainchild of longtime *Atlanta Journal* food editor Grace Hartley. Tired of having to travel to the different food companies that were constantly producing new products, Hartley suggested that the American Association of Newspaper Representatives (later the Newspaper Advertising Sales Association) put together the annual event so all the food editors could learn about the new products and technologies at the same time. There was also an advisory committee made up of food editors.[90] The conferences eventually came under attack because they were sponsored by an association made up of newspaper advertisers. But the editors were smart enough to see through the advertisers' messages, and they found value in the conferences as a source of news and networking. As Ruth Ellen Church wrote in 1949, it was a "meeting of the people who write about food with the people who produce the food we write about."[91] A look at what was happening at the meetings reflects the changing American food marketplace and how journalists translated the importance and lack thereof to the advertising to their readers.

In the early decades, the meetings were usually held in Boston, New York, or Chicago. The post–World War II American culture was one of increased consumerism and changing dishes, with much of it documented at annual meetings for food editors. Most editors would report daily from the event with the latest news—similar to the technology reporters of today reporting on the newest gadgets. While there may have been a merry environment, there was also much reporting and typing to be done.

Jane Nickerson covered the 1950 New York City meeting, attended by what was described as about 135 "newspaper women." Included at the convention was the introduction of the new chef of the Waldorf Hotel, who oversaw a kitchen staff of 140 and presentations of new products and techniques by twenty-five food companies.[92] The new product highlighted was canned food, which was popularized during the war and commercially available after. Americans were also eating more macaroni, Nickerson wrote in one story, with Italian Americans consuming seventy-five pounds each of the pasta each year.[93] Four male journalists attended that year, according to Dorothy Parnell of the *Milwaukee Sentinel*. One of those writers, James M. Kahn, commented on the long days at the meetings and the women who attended them:

"Hardest working bunch of newspaper people I've ever seen—can't imagine men doing this."[94]

In 1952, Clarice Rowlands described a speaker at the meeting who recommended eating a good breakfast and included recipes for pancakes and baked French toast. Featured were recipes for barbecue sauce and corn pudding, which included cream soup with no brand name. "Hearty breakfasts, 4 and 5 course luncheons and sumptuous dinners in elaborate settings," she wrote. "All meals, held in conjunction with educational meetings, gave us a chance to taste foods prepared by some of the country's foremost chefs."[95]

Stories from the 1952 meeting show that, far from simply hawking recipes put forth by advertisers, the editors covered important industry and demographic trends. Food editor Maude Coons covered the meetings for her Omaha newspaper, at times sending back more than a story a day. In one story, she reported that the head of the grocery store trade group opposed price controls for food. She also wrote about a presentation from Frigidaire. She estimated that by 1957, 18 percent of American homes would have freezers.[96] Later, she wrote about a speech given by a doctor from the Massachusetts Institute of Technology who said that the biggest nutrition problem in the country was "weight control." He went on to declare the current diets in the news "dangerous, faddish, and silly." In other presentations, the editors learned that 75 percent of packaged ice cream was sold in grocery stores and that the home consumption of frozen orange juice had increased 400 percent in the past four years.[97]

Veronica Volpe continued this tradition of hard reporting when she wrote about Florida's fresh fruit shipping season in at the 1955 meeting. She was critical of some of the food companies' shipping tactics, writing that it "sounds just like the sort of thing that a publicity press release would say."[98]

In the 1950s and 1960s, the conferences continued to serve journalists as a source of information on trends and industry matters. In 1956, baby food originator Daniel Gerber spoke to the food editors. He said that while births had increased 11 percent in the past decade, the consumption of baby food had increased 43 percent. He believed the reason was that babies were developing increased appetites. Church disagreed in her reporting from the event and instead attributed it to the appeal of convenience food and its use in adult recipes. "They are beginning to be used a great deal in quick cookery for the average household," she wrote of the baby food used by her Chicago home cooks. She noted that a reader wrote to tell her that she commonly used banana baby food in cakes, cookies, and bread. Church also included information from a speech about the state of the industry delivered by a grocery store executive,[99] and the editors heard from zoologist Marlin Perkins about safaris and about new methods for preserving perishable food.[100]

The editors also learned about historical topics in food. For example, in 1956 the editors toured the United Nations' building and attended a brief by UN officials. They ate a Danish midnight supper and a dinner modeled after an English dinner from the early eighteenth century. Volpe reported on the re-creation of a 250-year-old menu served to royalty at Windsor. She also described a sampling of pheasant pâté, smoked bear ham, and wild duck slices.[101]

In 1957, the conference took place in Chicago. The editors watched as a famous New York chef prepared an omelet. *Miami News* food editor Bertha Cochran Hahn wrote about each step of the preparation: "Pan is hot enough when drop of water spatters in pan. Action is important, as is position of hands."[102] In another story from that week, Hahn wrote about how to cook with whiskey or gin. She also wrote about how much powdered milk had changed since World War II. Another speaker shared a survey of canned food and found that apple sauce was the most popular of canned fruit sales. She mentioned that the daily meetings at the conference began early and ended late and wrote of what the editors went through: "We exercised writing notes and rushing from one room to another as scenes changed, until we were loaded into busses for an hour's drive to the farm dinner provided by the American Dairy Association."[103]

Cookbook authors James Beard and Myra Waldo spoke at the 1958 food editors' conference about barbecue equipment. The editors learned about how tea was made and sampled drinks from India, Ceylon, and Indonesia. They tried an updated version of oyster stew and learned what was served in colonial days. Rowlands wrote of the conference for her Milwaukee readers:

> Although eating foods, simple and fancy, occupies a lot of the 16-hour days, we are busy, too, attending demonstrations, listening to

speeches and panels on new developments in the food field and visiting test kitchens. With notebooks in hand, we are constantly taking notes to pass on food news to readers now and after we return home. Our typewriters are clicking late into the night. [104]

The 1959 meeting also featured new food products and an update on consumers' food habits. Coons reported that Americans purchased two billion pounds of frozen and canned foods the prior year, accounting for 12 percent of the nation's total food supply. The most popular canned foods were peas, corn, beets, and tomato juice. In the frozen category, peas, corn, green beans, and strawberries were popular. The editors listened to a presentation from Ocean Spray about the use of cranberries as a topping on meatloaf and the juice for a basis for punches. Pillsbury presented its chocolate chip cookies and butter flake rolls. Coons also reported on the trend of "continental desserts" consisting of fruit and cheese. [105]

At the 1960 food editors' meeting, the speakers included novelist Gore Vidal, heart disease specialist Dr. Herbert Pollack, and food specialist Sylvia Schur, who presented the "Husband Saving Hors d'Oeuvre." [106] The editors also heard about an upcoming shortage of Florida oranges and grapefruit due to the damage from Hurricane Donna. [107]

Lowis Carlton covered the 1961 meeting for the *Miami Herald* and her stories were syndicated by the newspaper's wire service so it ran in numerous additional newspapers, including the *St. Petersburg Times*. She reported there was an emphasis on foreign food at the beginning of the week, particularly on French and Scottish dishes. Sara Lee introduced a new apple and spice cake with toasted hazelnut frosting, and the company representative explained that it was building a new plant with a twenty-four-hour workforce. The Kraft Company introduced new shredded and grated cheeses, pasteurized cheese and bacon slices, low-calorie Italian and blue cheese dressing, and flavored marshmallows. The editors also listened to research about a food process that would freeze-dry meat in cans, described as a "peek into the future." [108] And in 1964, the conference featured a lecture by Frederick Stare, the head of the Department of Nutrition at Harvard University, advising on nutrition and exercise, and a talk by the nation's agriculture secretary, Orville Freeman, discussing advances in production. "New equipment and methods have made it possible for today's farmer to supply the food and fiber needs of 30 persons besides himself," he said. "That is double what he produced 10 years ago."[109]

Not all of the coverage was industry related. Soft news and recipes were still the heart of food journalism and were of intense interest to readers. In 1964 Julia Child made an appearance at the conference, demonstrating how to make fish dishes.[110] Maude Coons covered the meeting and introduced recipes to her readers for topovers (with a mincemeat filling that could be served as dessert) and lasagna. Charleston food editor Charlotte Walker also covered the 1964 meeting and described a suggested method to save money—prepare enough party food for the initial event and leftovers. As an example, Walker wrote about a lamb party dish and a leftover recipe for lamp pilaf. She quoted a speaker who addressed the increased shopping savvy of young homemakers. "Each year about a million of them get married at about the age of 20," he said, "and all of our research shows that the young homemakers have greater shopping skills at an earlier age."[111]

The 1966 meeting introduced the first lemons ever grown in Florida, a self-basting turkey, and fish fillets with a crunchy coating that tasted deep fried but were not. There was a demonstration of a revolutionary "quick thaw" that allowed fruit cups to go from freezer to table in seven minutes, and a new kind of pouch that allowed onions and cabbage to be cooked without smelling up the house was introduced. The food editors tried Boston haddock and Maine lobster along with California wines.[112] Walker also covered the meetings and told her Charleston readers about butterscotch popcorn, a cheesy corn dish, and a blueberry relish meant to be served with chicken or ham.[113]

In 1968, the food editors attended a brunch sponsored by Libby foods and learned about new products, including a meatier barbecue sauce meant to be used in sloppy joe sandwiches. They learned about Libby's attempt to keep up with the competitive frozen vegetable industry by producing butter-seasoned peas, carrot, and succotash in cans. Also introduced was a low-calorie canned fruit. At a Kraft-sponsored event, the editors tried a new cheese called Bastogne—a pasteurized process cheese spread imported from Belgium. One of the featured meals was curried lobster, capon, and rice, served in the shell of a South African rock lobster tail. For *Miami Herald* readers, food editor Heffington adapted the recipe to include Florida lobster and chicken instead of the difficult-to-find capon. She also included recipes for dulce de leche con piña, cheese mousse with brandy sauce, and fiesta fruit compote.[114]

Clearly industry news, nutritional information, and the introduction of new product information came out of these meetings. While named companies provided recipes, the company's name generally would not be included in the recipe itself by a majority of the food editors. (The time a food editor was found naming a product in a recipe was when Mary Crum was covering the meeting for the *Miami News* in 1952.) No free publicity was being offered to the advertisers if the homemaker clipped the recipe for later use. And while the idea of eating interesting food all day seems appealing, the editors indicated otherwise. As Cleveland food editor Beighle French described it,

> Our long, long, calorific days involved listening to food manufacturer's spiels, and sampling frequently awful recipes, featuring old and new products, ad nauseum. Between three huge meals, we would be expected to run a gauntlet of samplings. I added up the calories in one dinner and described it. It topped out well over 3,000 calories. I got sick that night.[115]

Ruth Ellen Church concurred: "The settings are glamorous, the food and entertainment luxurious, but underneath all the fluff, there's a serious message in each gathering: new products, short cuts to better eating, easier ways for homemakers to work in their kitchen."[116]

The conferences continued from the 1950s into the 1970s, but eventually came under attack for their advertising sponsorship. In response, the food editors created an organization of their own with its own code of ethics. The Association of Food Journalists was created in 1974 as an independent body to provide the same kinds of opportunities for information and networking without the complications of industry sponsorship.

3

FOOD JOURNALISM AND THE RISE OF CONSUMER ACTIVISM

The 1960s spurred a new interest in consumer rights, with activists like Ralph Nader criticizing the American automobile industry, including appearing during Senator Frank Moss's Consumer Subcommittee hearings on the safety of General Motors' controversial Corvair sport car. According to one study, the consumer movement was born out of the campus protests, "when radicals tried to broaden their constituency by appealing to a middle-class public's vexation with shoddy material and service in the marketplace."[1]

The topic of consumer news increased in the late 1960s and early 1970s. At the time, the idea of supporting the consumer was considered suspect because, as described in one trade magazine, the consumerism movement was "waging this undisguised war on business."[2] In terms of food coverage, the safety of the food industry was a regular topic in Voltz's *Los Angeles Times* section, just as the topic continues to be part of news coverage today. California created the Department of Consumer Affairs in 1970, and while it exists today as an agency for professional services, in its original form it included food in its purview. Voltz highlighted the need for consumer protection in a story about the agency and quoted its original director, Leighton Hatch: "The consumer has the right to know that the goods he purchases are safe for himself. You may think of tires as being safe, but this applies to food, too."[3]

Food journalists supported the new interest in consumer-oriented reporting. Media critics began calling for more comparative reporting in the area of food, including price comparisons,[4] and journalists responded. At the *Milwaukee Journal*, Peggy Daum wrote a regular series that compared local grocery food prices. Her section included a chart that compared about one hundred prices every week at the five supermarket chains where nearly 90 percent of her Milwaukee readers shopped. By this time, the *Journal*'s food section was as large as thirty-two pages a week. This led to her being named a "food page reformer" in the book *The Women's Book of World Records and Achievements*. The entry stated that Daum "contends that food pages should include controversy even when a story attacks a supermarket or product that contributes advertising to the paper."[5]

The power of the consumer and the power of motherhood also made for a strong combination in food coverage. Voltz covered a panel in Las Vegas in which homemakers with children critiqued their experiences with the food industry in front of about seventy food scientists. The mothers accused the food industry of providing consumers with puffery about products rather than information about nutrition. The women, who included an African American mother at a time when minorities were often excluded from newspaper coverage, also questioned the rising costs of food and the high level of fat. They requested more nutritional information, especially for the contents of the snack foods their children craved.[6]

It is also worth noting that while experts were calling for more hard news in the food section, newspaper readers continued to request recipes in large demand.[7] For example, the *Los Angeles Times* reported that thousands of requests for recipes came in each year.[8] In Houston, Criswell said she did not receive requests for investigative or hard-hitting food news. "Many of these complaints about the food section totally ignore the reader," she said. "You can be idealistic, and that's wonderful, but if people aren't interested and don't read it, what good is it?"[9] Her point was backed up by a letter to the editor about the *Chronicle*'s food section: "As a graduate home economist, I would like to offer congratulations on the fine food section that appears in the *Chronicle*. I think that about half of my recipe file consists of *Chronicle* clippings."[10]

FOOD JOURNALISM COMES UNDER SCRUTINY

Food journalism was affected by the consumer rights movement in another way as well: greater scrutiny of journalistic practices, especially the relationship between advertisers and editorial content. An understood separation exists at newspapers between the departments of advertising and editorial. As explained in the first chapter, the magazine world often has a looser relationship between these two areas.[11] But if they wanted coverage of sponsor-influenced or corporation-based events in their food section, members of newspaper management often found ways for their reporters to provide it without violating the ethics of the profession. For example, the newspaper food editors would attend advertiser-sponsored conferences, but the newspaper would pay the airfare and lodging. What the journalists reported from the event would have to be news—copy editors would approve the information to verify that no bias was included, as was standard practice for all stories.

As seen in chapter 2, the food editors' conferences in the 1940s, 1950s, and 1960s were sponsored by an advertisers' group, the American Association of Newspaper Representatives, along with food companies such as the American Meat Institute. The conferences were the brainchild of Atlanta food editor Grace Hartley, but they were put on and paid for by the associations. Plenty of hard reporting was done at these events, but the sponsorship ended up being a point of contention.

The issue of advertising sponsorship came to a head at the 1971 conference, almost three decades after the initial 1943 conference. At the 1971 meeting, the food editors had invited US senator Frank Moss of Utah to speak. Moss, chair of the Consumer Subcommittee of the Senate Commerce Committee, used the opportunity to attack the professionalism of their field. He had charged them with being nothing more than shills for food companies and to succumbing to press agency practices. He questioned their ethics and even suggested the government should investigate the work of food and other consumer journalists—a thorny First Amendment issue.

Later that evening, the food editors gathered in the Chicago hotel room of *Milwaukee Journal* food editor Peggy Daum to discuss Moss's accusations. They had heard enough criticism about their profession. They set forth that evening to create an organization of their own, based on the journalism ethics that they knew they already upheld. A commit-

tee was created with Daum at the helm. Within two years, the Newspaper Food Editors and Writers Association (now known as the Association of Food Journalists) was up and running and would go on to have
its own conventions and awards program that continue today.

FOOD ETHICS

Journalism is largely guided by a separation between editorial and advertising, designed to encourage objectivity by making sure advertisers
do not influence the newspaper content. Food journalists, by the very
nature of their work, found themselves in an awkward position. In fact,
at some newspapers, the advertising department actually produced the
food section. For example, both the *Los Angeles Times* and the *Los
Angeles Herald-Examiner* initially had their food kitchens housed in the
advertising department. The relationship did not necessarily mean the
writers were influenced by advertisers. In the case of Grace Hartley at
the *Atlanta Journal*, the newsroom did not allow women, so she worked
out of the business office.[12] In many cases, the food editor was reporting on topics including nutrition studies and government regulations
regarding food.

In the case of a paper as large and as respected as the *New York
Times*, the question regarding the potential influence of local advertisers was not as much of an issue as it might be at other metropolitan
newspapers. According to *New York Times* women's page editor Charlotte Curtis in 1964, "The *Times* offered food news without having any
food advertising and the point is that with a city so enormous the grocery stores really couldn't deal with circulation. That advertising went to
neighborhood papers."[13] Regardless, internal letters between staff
members at the *New York Times* show that top editors were concerned
about advertising influencing the content of the food pages as early as
the 1950s—even if it was just a perception of advertiser influence. In
one example, a top editor complained to women's page editor Eleanor
Clark French about the name of a product appearing in a caption.
French, who went on to become a significant figure in the Democratic
Party and a New York City official, responded that food editor Jane
Nickerson made the call for an understandable journalistic reason. She
included the name because the company supplied the photo, and she

was a journalist naming her source, as was industry practice.[14] Another internal file about the food section of the New York Times dated September 6, 1956, showed that management was concerned about advertiser influence when an editor was critical about a photo that displayed the labels from cans of Rheingold beer, and registered this complaint: "Those cans could have been rotated just a trifle and the name would not have been legible. They would still have looked like cans."[15]

Furthermore, the food editors were aware that the goal of advertisers and food producers was to sell products. Because of this awareness, they were often critical of what was presented to them. In a 1968 column, food editor Charlotte Walker told her readers that she and her fellow food editors attended the annual meetings to learn about new products and new ways of using typical products. "This sometimes calls for considerable fortitude," she wrote. Such was the case when Henry Heinz II, of the Heinz food company, attended a meeting to introduce an apple pie dish that included ketchup. When Heinz took a bite of the dessert, Walker noted that a Chicago food editor whispered to her, "I hope he chokes." Then it was time for the editors to try the dish. "This is above and beyond the call of duty," a Richmond food editor said to Walker.[16]

FOOD EDITORS UNDER FIRE

A public concern over the role of advertisers' influence on food sections came to fore in the early 1970s, prompted by two events. The first was raised by Senator Frank Moss when he was invited to deliver a speech about consumer safety issues at the 1971 national conference of food editors. The second was a highly critical article about the ethics of food editors published in Columbia Journalism Review that appeared shortly after the Moss speech. Moss, who served in the senate from 1959 until 1977, was no stranger to taking on consumer issues and enjoyed being in the media's eye during this period. At one point, he became known for going undercover as a Medicaid patient to expose wrongdoing.[17] As a guest of the food editors at their conference, Moss took an accusatory tone in his remarks toward the entirety of the event when he hinted at the impropriety of an advertising group's role in arranging the conference, despite the fact that newspapers paid for the editors' travel and lodging.

The senator from Utah began his speech by clarifying the gender of those who wrote the news of food: "It is indeed a pleasure to be here with you ladies this evening. I suppose we might say this conference is an example of female chauvinism and I am the men's liberation speaker at your conference."[18] He went on to make parallels between the women's liberation movement and the consumer revolution. He focused on recently implemented government regulations that were meant to ensure automobile safety and truth in labeling acts. Not until the twenty-fourth page of his speech did he get back to the reason for his appearance—the cereal and snack food industries and the "huckstering being done through the advertising medium."[19]

At one point, he veered off script and referred to the women as "whores of the supermarket industry," according to an editor who heard the speech.[20] He took the women to task for not taking on issues of advertising and nutritional claims. Of the limited coverage, he asked, "Who did the reporting? Who did the ferreting out of nutritional problems? If I may be pardoned, not the food editors."[21]

The debate over cereal quality was an old one, even in the 1970s. The first issue of what is now *Consumer Reports* featured an investigation over cereal quality in 1936 and what families were looking to put on the table with limited budgets. The article noted that the cost of daily breakfast cereal for a family of five ranged from 45 cents to $3.85. The reporter noted, "The main virtue of the breakfast cereal is in its cheapness as an energy food." The magazine looked at the thirty-one different brands available, and two-thirds were for hot cereal. *Consumer Reports* looked at breakfast cereal again in 1961. By then, there were 109 different kinds, and two-thirds were cold cereal, featuring the sugary cereals such as Cocoa Puffs, Alpha Bits, and Trix that are familiar today.[22] These cereals employed marketing campaigns aimed at young children, with cartoon characters in advertising and small toys inside the cereal box.[23] By 1970, Senator Moss was chairing government hearings about both the quality of children's cereal and how the product was marketed to the youngsters. The *New York Times* considered the hearings to be a news story rather than a food story.[24]

After encouraging more consumer reporting by the food editors, Moss concluded with a series of accusatory questions: "Ladies, are you the pawns of your advertising managers? Is your food section just a form of promotional device, or are you journalists? Have you ever found fault with the food industry and its product? Why is it so often that hard news about food is in another part of the newspaper, not authored by anyone from the food desk?"[25]

The journalism industry publication *Editor & Publisher* covered the senator's talk and the reaction, describing it as "a highly explosive speech." The writer noted that as Moss spoke, there were "cries of anguish from the audience" and some asked that he stop speaking. When he ended, he did not take questions and instead said he had to catch a plane. According to the reporter from *Editor & Publisher*, "The women literally jumped into action, demanding that the Congressman 'be set straight.'" Moss's public response was as follows: "Write me and I'll read all your letters."[26] Food editor Jeanne Voltz, who was in the audience, said later, "I really wonder what Senator Moss would think if the newspaper crucified him so without any attribution or without any proof at all."[27]

Milwaukee Journal food editor Peggy Daum did not duck the negative charges levied by Moss toward the food editors and wrote a story disclosing the allegations. "Newspaper food sections in general and their editors in particular came under attack here Thursday," she stated.[28] Other inflammatory comments from Moss included in her story charged that "Too often our food pages are first rate press agentry," and "How much of your reporting (from the conference) is hard news and how much is plugging?"[29] Her article also featured an element often left out of the reporting of this particular conference—the discussion of feminism. Gloria Steinem was a speaker at the event, at a time when women's liberation was still trying to find its place in newspaper coverage. In fact, *Ms.* magazine was still a few months away from publishing. Steinem's opinion of the food sections was not favorable and she did not pull any punches when asked about them, stating that "the most destructive thing about them is that they make women feel their self worth depends on being a cook."[30]

In addition to the comments Moss made at the conference, he was also critical of food editors in separate interviews he gave to newspaper reporters. "It seems to me that the automotive reporters, the food editors and other specialized reporters who operate in a rarified atmosphere clouded with smoke blown by industry press releases have simply lagged behind the healthy growth of responsible consumer journalism," he is quoted as saying in one interview. He asserted that these journalists were not living up to their First Amendment obligations, subsequently calling for formal hearings to look into the matter.[31] These hearings never took place, likely because courts have made it clear that the First Amendment does not allow the government to make decisions regarding newspaper content—regardless of ethical questions.

While Moss offered no proof of impropriety, it was at this time that the respected industry publication the *Columbia Journalism Review* featured an investigative article about food reporting titled "Newspaper Food Pages: Credibility for Sale" with the subhead, "The food section is the cash register of the newspaper, a happy hunting ground for advertisers."[32] The article, written by a freelance reporter named Richard Karp, featured numerous allegations about conflicts of interest by food editors. The article was written with a slanted tone and made broad accusations based on a few narrow examples. "Most food editors, leery of controversy, simply bypassed the front-page news story," Karp alleged, demonstrating a lack of understanding of gender politics in the newsroom. What Karp should have known and noted was that if a topic was worthy of the front page, it is highly unlikely that the female food editors would have even been given the opportunity to write the story. Instead, a male news reporter would likely have covered the issue.

In addition to accusing the food editors of shirking the front page, Karp also claimed that they ignored the news about the government's hearings in 1970 about the lack of nutrition in children's boxed cereals. The ensuing uproar involved the fact that the Harvard University department where one of the government's experts, Dr. Fredrick J. Stare, worked received $1.5 million from cereal companies. The implication was that the donation colored the findings of the cereal studies. In writing about the cereal hearing, Karp made the claim that only food columnist Marian Burros, then at the *Washington Star*, wrote about Stare's supposed complicity with the cereal industry. However, Daum clearly did write about the issue in the pages of the *Milwaukee Journal*,[33] as did Voltz at the *Los Angeles Times*, and likely others.[34]

BRAND NAMES

Karp also was critical of the use of brand names in recipes, claiming this was a common practice of food editors. For proof, he wrote that he found four or five articles in the *New York Times* that included brand names in recipes. His accusation is that the use of the brand names was a form of advertising—a violation of journalism's standards. According to an academic study of newspaper food journalists, editors may have depended on public relations materials from food companies for information "they were not spoon-fed by business."[35] The study's author noted that newspapers had policies that forbid the use of brand names in recipes. Instead, food editors had a list of generic terms to use in place of the brand name. She wrote that while some food editors used photographs provided by food companies, most made sure that it was not used in a way to promote the product. Other editors only used images from industry groups rather than a photo from a food company. One of the editors said she "only uses public relations photographs that illustrate a general theme such as breads and cheeses. Those that pertain only to a particular recipe are thrown out."[36]

Food editors were often in a difficult position when it came to images, a central issue for food sections. Research in the 1950s found that readers were more likely to read a food story if there was a prominent illustration with it. For example, a study cited by the industry group American Press Institute found that 61.6 percent of food page readers would read an article that included a photo.[37] At the *Courier-Journal*, editors found that female readers preferred menus and images of complete meals while male readers preferred close-ups of a single dish.[38] At some newspapers, such as the *Los Angeles Times* and the *Chicago Tribune*, there was a photo studio next to a test kitchen. This way, photos could be taken of the food. At other newspapers, images were harder to come by, prompting the editors to use images supplied by industry groups. Others debated if this was an ethical breach. When Marjorie Paxson was at the *Philadelphia Bulletin*, she recalled, "We had a tremendous argument over two illustrations. I wanted to take colored photographs of Coca-Cola and Kellogg's corn flakes, because it seemed to me the readers would relate so much more to an actual photograph of bottles of Cokes. But our management's a little bit squeamish about this, so we had to go with sketches instead."[39]

While the use of brand names was not a typical journalism practice, a culinary reason to do so did exist: sometimes the use of a particular product impacts the taste of a dish. In one of their cookbooks, *At Blanchard's Table*, Melinda and Robert Blanchard include a specific name brand of mayonnaise, although most ingredients are listed by generic terms. "We don't usually recommend many name brands, but when it comes to mayonnaise we always use Hellmann's," they explained. "The flavor is better and it has more body than other brands."[40] In another example, *Orlando Sentinel* food editor Dorothy Chapman often collected recipes for favorite dishes featured at local restaurants, including those at Walt Disney World's Epcot Center, for her popular column "Thought You'd Never Ask." For the recipe of warm artichoke dip, she included in the ingredient list "dry Good Seasons Italian Dressing mix."[41] Rather than a form of advertising, the ingredient was included in order to be true to the original recipe used by the restaurant's chef, but also because there was a particular flavor profile associated with the product. There also was likely no sufficient generic substitute for the ingredient.

Journalists use the *Associated Press Stylebook* as an industry-wide guide for use of language, including best practices regarding brand names. The *Stylebook* recommends, "When they are used, capitalize them." It then notes that brand names "normally should be used only if they are essential to a story."[42] In following that guide, it is expected that when a specific name brand ingredient was needed to make a dish turn out correctly, that name would be used in a recipe.

Likewise, Indiana food journalist Ann Hamman, who earned a master's degree in home economics from Purdue University, stressed that the typical practice of food editors was to ignore brand names unless there was a particular reason to include them. Hamman wrote a full-page letter to the editor to the *Columbia Journalism Review* as a direct rebuke to Karp's story, and in it she stated she would need a specific reason to include a brand name:

> I do rewrite the recipes completely to comply with my own notion of what makes a recipe easy to follow. I use the brand name only when that is the only product I know of that will answer the purpose. (I would never think of saying to use a "tomato-based hot sauce" I say Tabasco.) Otherwise, I defy Karp or anyone else to say what brand-name product was called for in the original.[43]

However, several of the more famous cookbook book authors of the time period often endorsed products, and some of these same people wrote syndicated newspaper columns. James Beard endorsed Green Giant frozen products. Poppy Cannon, Myra Waldo, and Peg Bracken also endorsed food products and appeared in advertisements over the years. It is hard to imagine that a newspaper food editor would engage in such practice, as it would be a clear violation of journalism. Julia Child noted that she was appreciative of the face that her television program was on public television, so she did not have to be associated with sponsors.

FOOD EDITORS RESPOND

While Karp did appear to have spoken to several food editors in researching his story, he did not define "most," as used in his allegation about the food editors having questionable ethics. On the contrary, several food editors questioned whom he talked to and his motives. In an industry organization magazine article, *Akron Beacon Journal* food editor Polly Paffilas questioned Karp's intentions and noted that he had lied about the publication he was writing for when he phoned her. She wrote of the conversation,

> After talking to Karp for only a few minutes, it was obvious from his caustic degrading comments about our profession that he had already made up his mind what he was going to write. He waived aside my suggestion to interview Janet Beighle of the Cleveland *Plain Dealer*, one of the many food editors in the country who does what Kamp accused us all of not doing. [44]

In Karp's article, he quoted the then *Los Angeles Times* food editor Jeanne Voltz—a woman with a college degree in journalism and a background in hard news. According to Karp, she said she had become dependent on freebies such as aluminum foil. Yet, according to Voltz, the two never spoke, and she said other food editors had reported never being interviewed. In a 1972 speech, she said only one person in the article was quoted correctly. "I never met Mr. Karp, or talked to him," she declared. "Yet he quoted me." [45] Furthermore, it is unlikely that free aluminum foil would have impacted her reporting about food. She further said that the accusations of Karp and Senator Moss certainly did not apply to most of the newspaper food sections she was aware of, citing the specifics of her newspaper as well as newspapers in Chicago, Detroit, Milwaukee, and Philadelphia.[46]

In an industry magazine article, Church said she interviewed each of the food editors whom Karp had written about. She created a report, "What Richard Karp Said She Said and What She Actually Said," in which she described "fantastic discrepancies" between what she found and what he wrote. Apparently, the errors were many, including misquotes, incorrect names, and titles. "The comments attributed to these ladies are unbelievable and, in fact, untrue," Church wrote.[47]

The majority of the active food editors also had journalism degrees, which would have involved ethics education. Further, most newspapers had policies preventing undue influence. Hamman's *Columbia Journalism Review* rebuttal defended the ethics of her colleagues: "The food editors I know are an extremely conscientious lot. Naturally they are concerned about the financial well-being of their newspapers. Does Karp think they should not be? But they are not about to promote something they think is not good just because the manufacturer is an advertiser."[48]

The food editors, however, were aware of the perception that they were pandering to the whims of the advertisers. Indeed, at some newspapers the food sections initially had been produced by the advertising department. But many newspapers, particularly by the 1950s, did not operate this way. Newspapers such as the *Chicago Tribune, Milwaukee Journal,* and *Miami Herald* had long had food editors with journalism educations. In 1960, the *Los Angeles Times* moved its section from advertising to the editorial side. However, the *Los Angeles Examiner*'s food editor was still on the advertising payroll until at least 1971. But in the words of one food journalist, the editors were smart enough to see through the advertisers' messages, and as long as the *New York Times* was sending a reporter to the food editor meetings, other newspapers would also send a reporter.[49] This is not to say that all reporters were immune to the lure of accepting freebies. Several food editors said they knew of at least one common unnamed colleague who had her kitchen redone for free by a newspaper's advertiser. Other food editors also reported they had fired reporters when they learned that freebies had been accepted.[50]

At the *Arizona Republic*, food editor Dorothee Polson said no one interfered with the material that she wanted to put in her section during her twenty-seven-year career. She said it was largely based on the management style of managing editor J. Edward Murray, who said, "When you hire creative people, just let them alone; you get much better work out of them that way."[51]

At the *Los Angeles Times*, food editors Betsy Balsley and Barbara Hansen, who worked with Voltz and Cecil Fleming, said advertisers never pressured them. "Ethics was always a very important matter," Hansen said. Balsley said there was no connection between editorial and advertising at her newspaper. "The food section was completely autonomous," she said. "Nobody told me what to put into it. Nobody told me what to leave out."[52] Regardless, the food journalists were not immune to the fact that their sections made money for the newspaper. The week before a 1970s Thanksgiving, the food section of the *Los Angeles Times* was ninety pages thick. The day after the section ran, Balsley happened to be in the elevator when the advertising manager got on and bragged to her that the section had brought in a million dollars. "I tell you, I wanted to slug him," Balsley said. "We made money for the *Times* and we had an awful lot of fun doing it."[53]

In terms of the cereal controversy, mentioned by both Moss and Karp, Hamman's response in that 1972 letter to the editor published in the *Columbia Journalism Review* defended coverage of the issue by food sections. In particular, she found it ludicrous that any of her colleagues would push the notion that cereal could provide the daily acceptable amount of nutrition, as advocated by a representative of the cereal industry. "I have not seen any food section that said the minimum daily requirement for total nutrition could be purchased in a box of oats," she wrote. "If Karp were really investigating, he would document such a charge."[54]

A 1972 *Houston Journal Review* article by reporter Linda Ambrose informally examined the food section of the newspapers in that city as a response to the Karp article. She began by stating that she found several factual errors and undocumented claims in the Karp article. She also appeared shocked that despite the criticisms leveled against the food editors, readers reported that they had a "high degree of confidence" in the food sections. "There is apparently little reader demand for investigatory reporting or consumer news on the food pages," she wrote. In fact, *Houston Chronicle* food editor Ann Criswell, a graduate of Texas Woman's University, said she was lauded by readers for being the one section of the newspaper with good news.[55] Ambrose did report, however, that she found several images in the local papers carrying no attribution, which led her to believe the material was provided by an advertiser. And while she praised the section for not including brand names in recipes, she also thought that was actually a potential problem because by "avoiding specific plugs" they were "at the same time making it harder than ever to determine the source of information."[56] Regardless, neither food editor of the Houston newspapers, when interviewed by Ambrose, said they had ever been pressured by advertisers to ignore a topic or slant their coverage in a particular way.

HOUSTON FOOD MEETING

Even though most food editors disputed the allegations of both Moss and Karp, the nation's papers reacted with an "unprecedented" meeting, according to one account, at the University of Houston to address the charges and the state of food journalism.[57] A congressman, a journalism professor, and several male managing editors spoke at the meeting, and several newspaper food editors presented examples of their sections, with the record being preserved by members of Theta Sigma Phi, who transcribed the speeches. In one newspaper story about how the criticisms may have impacted policies at individual newspapers, an unnamed food editor responded that instead of her usual marginalization, "the editor of my paper spoke to me for the first time in several years."[58]

One of the speakers at the meeting was *Detroit News* women's page editor Ruth D'Arcy, who answered Karp's accusations of advertising pandering. "I suggest the answer may not be various kinds of payola-paid food editors, as Mr. Karp concluded, but timid newspaper managements," she said of the perceived influence by advertisers. "I don't say this lightly. The readers' right to know versus the advertisers right to withdraw their advertising is not a comfortable dilemma for any newspaper management to face."[59] She noted the heavy workload of her food editor and her role meeting public needs including answering several hundred questions a week. The weekly food section was twenty-six pages, with sixty columns of editorial space. The editor also judged cooking contests and wrote an annual cookbook. It was her newspaper's consumer section that was more likely to take on issues of food safety.

Her newspaper's crosstown rival at the *Detroit Free Press*, Dorothy Jurney, agreed with the need for management support. At the same seminar, Jurney posed the question to the food editors, "How far does your manager want you to go in consumer reporting?" She posited that the advertising manager might actually have more pull with the publisher than the women's page or food editor. "I think Knight Newspapers are a very progressive group of papers," she said, "and yet one of the advertising directors of one of the KNI papers told the publishers that he wished editors would play down coverage of consumer issues."[60]

Marjorie Paxson noted the battles that she waged with management and referenced the argument over using Coca-Cola and Kellogg's corn flakes in images. It was her opinion that the pictures would be more relatable for the newspaper readers, an approach that was covered by the Associated Press guidelines: "Sometimes the use of a brand name may not be essential but is acceptable because it lends an air of reality to a story."[61] However, management rejected the idea and instructed that sketches of generic products be used instead, and these were for purposes of accompanying or illustrating content that included a column by a woman who ran a local gourmet cooking school, a news story about the business of school lunches, and a health story about chubby babies not being the healthiest.[62]

Despite the Associated Press guidelines allowing a sponsor's name to be mentioned in an article, such as "Pillsbury" in the Pillsbury Bake-Off, some newspapers found the use of the sponsor's name in stories about the bake-off to be advertising. For example, at the *Louisville Courier-Journal*, the contest was covered as newsworthy because of the size of the monetary prize, but the name "Pillsbury" was not used.[63] That editor was not alone. Another food editor revealed she was not allowed to cover major bake-offs because it would be seen as advertising.[64] Food editors were allowed to write about the competition when there was a news value, such as proximity of the contestants. For example, one Milwaukee food editor covered a bake-off event because 10 percent of the finalists were from Wisconsin.[65]

ADVERTISING AND PUBLIC RELATIONS INFLUENCE

Some research regarding food journalism and the journalists' interaction with food advertisers has generally found that editors are resistant to the idea that advertisers could successfully influence content. In one 1973 academic study, food editors denied that they were pressured by the food industry to run a positive story or kill a negative story. "They wouldn't dare," one editor said. Another editor said of an advertiser, "If they try to dissuade us, it's a sure way to get us to run it. We won't be influenced."[66] One editor noted that when concerns were being publicly raised about the quality of commercial baby food, she ran a story about how mothers could make their own baby food. That led to a nasty letter of complaint from a baby food manufacturer, but it did not change the editor's approach to the topic or bring punishment from upper management.[67]

Sometimes it was the food companies' public relations firms that provided the pressure. In one example, when a war was brewing over butter versus margarine, an editor received a letter from a public relations person asking specifically that the editor use the term "margarine" in her recipes. The request was not heeded.[68] Another editor noted that a public relations person applied pressure by explaining how many full-page ads the food company placed in the newspaper and implied there should be special treatment. "It's a sure way for their information to land in the wastebasket," the editor responded.[69]

Other examples of the food industry attempting to influence the press exist. In 1962, Paul Willis, the president of the Grocery Manufacturers of America, boasted of "harnessing the power of the press" in a talk to magazine editors. In a newspaper example, attempts to pressure *Cleveland Plain-Dealer* surfaced in April 1970 when the newspaper published an editorial criticizing the Thomas J. Lipton Company for informing its distributors—but not the public—that there might be salmonella bacteria in its products. Dan Pensiero, a Cleveland-area food broker, was bothered by the editorial and advised his clients that it was "not in their best interest to advertise in the *Cleveland Plain Dealer*." The loss was several hundred dollars, and the newspaper's advertising department complained to editor-publisher Thomas Vail. This was not an isolated incident. Congressman Leonard Farbstein of New York said he had uncovered more than twenty cases of supermarkets and food manufacturers attempting to use advertising to eliminate negative coverage in the news section.[70] One industry suggestion was to be transparent about incidents of advertiser pressure and the newspaper's response. As a writer noted in the *Columbia Journalism Review*, "No self-respecting editor would knuckle under to a politician's threats."[71]

When it came to accepting free promotional items, the position of the food editors was that they did not accept them unless the item had a particular news value. For example, if the editors were testing a new product before it was available in grocery stores, a news value existed. In another case, a food editor accepted free samples of freeze dried foods for a story she was writing about food for safaris. It was a matter of convenience—for both time and monetary reasons. "It would be more objective to purchase the foods ourselves," she said in an interview. "But we lack the time and the staff to do this thoroughly. It is easier if the product is sent to us."[72] Overall, food editors reported that they followed the same ethical policies as the other editorial departments and could not accept gifts.[73]

PUBLIC SERVICE VERSUS NEWS

It is worth noting that advertising and public service are not the same. In his job interview for the food editor position at the *New York Times*, Craig Claiborne was asked by editor Lester Markal whether his approach to food was as news or service. He responded by calling his work service. "There's very little news of food that is all that interesting," he said. "Recipes are." Markal said he disagreed.[74] It is safe to say that most newspaper food editors saw their roles as both news and service. They wanted to report food news and they wanted to help their readers with their cooking questions.

When looking at the operation of a newspaper, it is important to separate the advertising or funding of the publication from the publicity department, which serves to promote the publication. Several food sections originated in the publicity department, some with test kitchens and some with classes held to teach local homemakers how to cook. It was often a part of an editor's responsibility to engage with the community—a kind of public relations on behalf of the publication rather than an advertiser. For example, food editor Cissy Gregg spoke to women's clubs in Kentucky about once a week. According to her newspaper, "The *Courier-Journal* finds all this worthwhile because it makes friends for the newspaper."[75] This was at a time when there were often around a hundred women's organizations in a typical metropolitan area.

FOOD EDITORS AND TRAVEL

International travel was important for the food editors to both learn more about food and understand if a dish created in America was authentic to its home country's taste. However, few, if any, food editors had a travel budget. Management was unlikely to authorize the expenses to allow the editors to travel abroad. At the Houston meeting, Voltz wrote about the complexity of the junket issue. One issue was the question of who the reporter would be loyal to in her reporting. The other was the scarcity of available travel money. Her advice was to find any means necessary to travel: "I say go on as many trips as you can go on, and I don't care if you have to borrow or steal or anything, but preferably at your company's expense so that you're not beholden to anybody. I think you learn mighty little sitting at your desk."[76]

Some food editors, such as Clementine Paddleford, regularly traveled. Arizona food editor Dorothee Polson wrote that she traveled to more than fifty countries "in search of recipes" and news. In one example, she was in Kenya to try cow blood pudding when the president of the country died. This led to an interview with the president's son for a story that ran in the newspaper along with the recipe for a Kenyan dish.[77] Associated Press food editor Cicely Brownstone noted that her wire service's policy following the quiz show scandal was that she could travel abroad if a country formally invited her. For example, she went to Denmark three times after being invited, each trip funded by dairy companies. "They got very little for their money," she said. "I wrote two or three pieces about Denmark, but not the products. A.P. would not have allowed that. And I was smart enough not to want to do it."[78]

In 1967, Ruth Ellen Church spent several weeks in Europe to report on the foods of various countries, including Sweden, Denmark, Belgium, Austria, and Hungary. As she did in Chicago, Church interviewed the home cooks of Europe and included their recipes. The series, which included pictures, ran under the following headline: "Ruth Ellen Church Reports What's Cooking in Europe."[79] It was a sign of progress that the story ran under her own name rather than the "Mary Meade" pen name. The *Milwaukee Sentinel* food editor Rosa Tusa often traveled with Poppy Cannon, sampled local foods, and then wrote about the experience.

Soon after the Association of Food Journalists was established in 1974, trips abroad were planned. More than thirty trips were made to foreign countries where new foods were sampled. The food editors were spurred to action by the words of Barbara Bush, who spoke at the 1978 Pillsbury Bake-Off about China: "Food writers better get to China before there's a McDonald's on every corner." AFJ president Eleanor Ostman began planning the trip. The following year, they were the first American food writers to enter the country. Subsequent years featured trips to Italy, France, and Ireland. By the time the women made their fifth trip to China, McDonald's could be found.[80] *St. Louis Post-Dispatch* journalist Barbara Ostmann, who traveled with Ostman, said, "We just ate, cooked, and drank our way through every country. Then we wrote about it and got some fantastic stories. Now it is called culinary travel but that is what we were always doing."[81]

All that travel meant a mix of high cuisine and local dishes that made some of the writers squirm. During her career as food editor at the *Houston Chronicle*, Criswell traveled widely and sampled chocolate-covered ants, fried parsley, raw tuna, quail eggs, black rice, and rattlesnake. She wrote, "Despite our adventurous nature, even some food editors occasionally turn squeamish. When a group was touring France a few years ago, several editors refused to try the eel, a world-famous specialty in the St. Julien region."[82]

4

COOKBOOKS, EXCHANGING RECIPES, AND COMPETITIVE COOKING

As women's changing roles in society were being discussed in the late 1960s and early 1970s, traditional expectations were often under fire. Concepts like cooking and home economics were considered ways of keeping women in the home—an enemy of feminism. Yet, in more recent reexaminations of cookbooks, some scholars have found that the act of producing the publications was more feminist than originally thought. For example, a study of the "Lutheran Church Women" in Iowa found distinct feminist actions in gathering information and producing a cookbook. The researcher wrote of the women:

> They entered the economic sphere both to produce and to sell their cookbooks, and they negotiated and developed a corporate process that gave them an important voice in the community. Of course, they did so in the service of a domestic ideology that feminism opposed, but their methods were closer to those of contemporary feminists than either side was then likely to admit: a politics of celebrating women getting together, creating collectively, valuing women and women's work.[1]

HISTORY OF COOKBOOKS IN AMERICA

The publication of cookbooks goes back far in American history. One culinary history project notes that the first cookbook printed in America was the *Compleat Housewife* printed by William Parks in Williamsburg, Virginia, in 1742—a reprinting of a British cookbook.[2] According to another history of cookbooks, the first book aimed at Americans was published in 1796: Amelia Simmons's *American Cookery*.[3] The recipes featured ingredients indigenous to America such as corn meal and recipes named for the native people of the land such as Indian Slapjacks. The first cookbook by a black American was published in Boston in 1827, although it was aimed at running a wealthy white household rather than cooking the food prepared in black households.[4] The next few decades offered American cookbooks about ethnic dishes, frugality, health, and desserts. By 1870, there was what has been described as "three major cookbook explosions," with books produced by women's charitable organizations, promotional materials published by food companies, and the growth of the cooking school movement.[5]

Cookbooks are sources of practical information, but they are also historical documents "supplying information about the publishing practices, available ingredients, food fashions, or household technology of the past—cookbooks reveal much about the societies that produce them."[6] And food journalists helped determine if the authors were successful in their missions. After all, hundreds of cookbooks are published each year and authors hope for positive reviews. In 1941, so many cookbooks were published that the *Chicago Tribune* simply listed them by topics, such as cooking for large groups and nutrition rather than reviewing each book individually.[7]

MID-CENTURY COOKBOOK TRENDS

According to a 1947 *Publishers' Weekly* article, the postwar consumer climate helped to produce a "cook book boom."[8] By 1955, publishers were complaining about the glut in the market: "In the usual frantic pattern of the publishing business, since cookbooks have become popular and profitable, everybody has started publishing them, the market has become highly competitive."[9] In 1947, Nickerson reviewed a cookbook written by a woman who had spent fourteen months traveling around the world. The recipes focused on *Far Eastern Cookery*, which included Hawaii—more than a decade before it would become a state.

Included in the book was a chart to substitute American ingredients for unavailable native ones.[10]

An academic study of cookbooks in the 1950s era (roughly from 1945 through 1963) found the books "as a whole, imposed certain limitations on convenience and speedy meal preparation." An increase in ornamental cooking also occurred—think of the fruit found in Jell-O molds. This was a form of showing the impression of time and trouble taken by the homemaker, according to the study. While convenience, quick meals, and presentation were popular topics, other themes can be seen in the cookbooks of this era, especially the importance of regional food and the growing presence of men in the kitchen.

Regional Food

The food editors and their readers regularly debated the question of regional food. One thing that was clear was food certainly defined communities. When the *Rocky Mountain News* asked readers for the dish that most defined their community, the newspaper received more than 11,000 entries.[11] Another interesting example of this was the 1952 publication *Coast to Coast Cookery*, which contained recipes from newspaper food editors, who included stories about the recipes' regional roots. It was funded by the American Association of Newspaper Representatives (an advertising group) and published by the Indiana University Press. A reviewer wrote, "The book gives a good picture of what most of America eats. It will appeal especially to the thousands who clip recipes regularly and regularly lose them."[12] The book was divided into dishes by state, similar to the cookbook produced by Clementine Paddleford a decade later. (Paddleford contributed recipes to the *Coast to Coast* cookbook.) The book's editor Marian Tracy wrote, "The recipes in this collection have been gathered from all sections of the country by those local and vocal experts, the newspaper food editors, who have put these traditional and often half-forgotten recipes into a workable idiom for the present-day cook, unfamiliar with the terse and sometimes cryptic instructions of our ancestors."[13]

The book included dishes based on the local ingredients and traditions of the people who had settled there. In South Florida, for example, citrus recipes were popular: lime-flavored meringues, green mango pie, and lime chiffon pie. *St. Petersburg Times* food editor Diana Rowell wrote of the mango, "It may be considered the tropical equivalent of the apple of the diet." [14] In Detroit, recipes included smelt, described as "tiny, scaleless, silvery fish that run in Michigan streams every spring." A recipe was also included for a specialty of the state's Upper Peninsula: Cornish pasties. *Detroit Times* food editor Ruth Gorrell (later Ruth Gray of the *St. Petersburg Times*) wrote that the dish was pronounced with the "a" as in "mast," not as in "mace." [15]

Regional tastes are also defined by the people who settled in an area. Iowa food editor Naomi Doebel wrote that the state's most distinctive dishes were a result of two groups of early settlers: Czechoslovakians and Germans. Its featured dish was kolasky—sweet rolls filled with poppy seed, fruit mixtures, or Dutch cheese mixed with eggs, milk, and sugar. It was recommended that they be served for breakfast or dessert. [16] Considerable food history was sprinkled among the recipes as well. The food editor of the *Atlanta Constitution*, Agnes Reasor Olmstead, a trained home economist, shared two recipes for hush puppies—one intended for home cooks and one from an Atlanta tearoom. She also wrote about a possible history of the dish:

> When General Sherman was making his flight through Georgia to the sea, back in the days of the War Between the States, the pursuing gallant boys in gray had trouble carrying enough supplies, and the dogs that invariably follow armies were going somewhat hungry. Each time mess would be prepared they would surround the cooking places and howl dismally. Cooks usually would hurl them scraps of corn pone and admonish, "Hush, puppy." [17]

Newspaper food editors regularly published cookbooks that included recipes from the women in their communities, thus bringing them into the public sphere. For example, in Jane Nickerson's *Florida Cookbook*, she wrote about reader Catherine Stereos of St. Petersburg, who contributed a recipe for Kourambiades, or Greek butter cookies. She had spent her early years in Athens, Greece, and had made more than 3,000 of the cookies for a recent benefit. [18] A 1964 recipe pamphlet published by the *Rocky Mountain News* included not only the names of local women who contributed recipes but also their home addresses. [19] The 1970s cookbook published by the *Milwaukee Journal* included the names of local cooks—along with photographs of the chefs. [20]

In the 1960s, a debate broke out over whether there were any re-gional dishes anymore. *Miami Herald* food editor Virginia Heffington noted that cooking in Florida was now the same as the rest of the country. For example, Floridians were now buying shrimp and spiny lobster in frozen form. "The days are gone when you catch your own or buy fresh," she wrote.[21] *Chicago Tribune* food editor Ruth Ellen Church said that, by 1958, there was no more regional cooking. She cited the example of what is now called German chocolate cake. In 1957, a homemaker had sent a cake recipe to her local newspaper food editor, Julie Benell of the *Dallas Morning News*, for the Recipe of the Day column. The reader called the dessert Texas German Sweet Choc-olate Cake. In reality, it was German's Chocolate Cake, created by the Baker Chocolate Company and named for Sam German in the mid-1800s.[22] (In later years, "German's" became "German.") When Benell told Church about the new cake sweeping the South, Church replied that the cake was popular in the Midwest, too. "I think what used to be distinctive regional cookery in the country has all but disappeared," Church concluded.[23] This conversation would change, of course, in later years as regions embraced their local dishes.

Men in the Kitchen

The 1950s era slowly brought changes to gender roles in American households, and the role of cook was no exception. As one researcher noted, "Recipes and rhetoric from the 1950s cookbooks illustrated the anxieties of a middle class caught in the throes of huge cultural change."[24] In 1956, *Boston Globe* food editor Dorothy Crandall wrote that men were beginning to pitch in with kitchen duties, based on information she learned at the annual food editors' meeting. It caused her male colleague at the paper to title a column "Men-in-the-kitchen era horrifies columnist."[25] On the other hand, *Milwaukee Sentinel* food editor Rosa Tusa learned to cook from her father.

The idea of men cooking in households seemed to start with grilling, or what James Beard described as "fireside cooking" in his 1949 cook-book.[26] Miami food editor Jeanne Voltz noted that she initially played a supporting cooking role to her barbecuing husband. "In the fifties all husbands barbecued," she wrote, "with wives as chief assistants and errand girls."[27] She soon increased her role in front of the grill, proclaiming that "a woman can barbecue as well as a man."[28] Years later, she would write one of the most significant cookbooks on barbecue—*Barbecued Ribs, Smoked Butts and Other Great Feeds*.

Women have long been considered the cooks in families but men have also been in the kitchen. Beginning in the 1940s, Morrison Wood had a food column in the *Chicago Tribune* that was also syndicated in other newspapers. It was called "For Men Only." In one 1947 column, he answered a woman's request for "pizza pie" and noted that he had not yet tried to make the dish himself.[29] In 1954, he wrote about making lobster dishes.[30] He noted that the primary difference between men and women was the constant pattern of cooking that women had to do, which took away creativity: "I do believe it is true that most men approach cooking in an adventuresome spirit, simply because they are not obligated to cook day in and day out. To most women who have to cook three meals a day, cooking is likely to be a sorry bit of drudgery."[31] Morrison Wood wrote the 1949 cookbook *With a Jug of Wine* and one for gourmet cooks in 1957.

Dallas Morning News food editor Julie Benell published a cookbook in 1961 with the title *Let's Eat at Home*. Benell was a former concert pianist who switched to the stage and later to performances on radio and television; she had a daily television show about food and fashion for fifteen years while she was at the newspaper. Her cookbook included some of her recipes and some from home cooks, such as Mrs. Frank Krusen's "Liptauer Spread." It included a chapter titled "Be Daring," which featured elaborate dishes, and another that featured low-fat and low-cholesterol recipes. In her introduction, Benell wrote, "Once upon a time a charming woman told me that she hated food, that she couldn't stand to cook, and that she would be glad when we had different colored pills to take for the three meals a day." About a year later, Benell ate at the woman's house and found the meal delicious. She concluded that the woman had "fallen into a dull routine in meal preparation that of course is fatal to any creative ability." She hoped that her cookbook would inspire her readership of home cooks.[32]

FOOD JOURNALISTS AS COOKBOOK AUTHORS

Connected as they were to their readership, food journalists and editors felt motivated to help their audience reconnect with cooking as a pleasure as well as a duty. Their combined efforts, both as cookbook authors and as reviewers of new cookbooks, had a substantial impact on the cooking habits of Americans.

While food editor at the *Washington Post*, Marian Burros wrote several cookbooks independent of her newspaper. She had a degree in English from Wellesley College and became a cooking instructor after graduation. In 1967, she published *The Elegant But Easy Cookbook* along with her friend Lois Levine. The book sold more than 500,000 copies. When *The Elegant But Easy Cookbook* was reissued in 1998, the convenience foods from the 1967 edition had been deleted.[33] In 1965, Burros and Levine published *Freeze with Ease*. It began with a description of freezers and how to defrost them. The food writers noted, "Home freezers, whether freestanding or in combination with a refrigerator, have revolutionized home cooking."[34]

By 1972, an Indiana food editor, Ann Hamman, pondered the need for so many cookbooks. "It is a mystery to me why recipe books are so popular, in view of the fact that so many newspapers, magazines and handouts are full of recipes," she wrote.[35] One explanation may have been a renewed interest in healthier, natural foods. Initiated by those in the counterculture movement, it had gone mainstream by the 1970s. By 1973, Voltz published the *National Foods Cookbook* for the *Los Angeles Times*. She wrote that while home cooks had enjoyed the use of processed food in the 1950s and 1960s, the trend had run its course by the 1970s. Instead, homemakers were now interested in making their own bread, cooking soups from scratch, and baking their own pies. "We plain food people who have never lost our touch and taste for fresh things hail the revolution," she wrote.[36] At the *Milwaukee Journal*, Peggy Daum profiled Frances Moore Lappe, the author of *Diet for a Small Planet*, which Daum compared to Rachel Carson's influential book about the environment, *Silent Spring*. Lappe championed "eating food directly from the earth rather than as it is processed through livestock." To make her point, Lappe argued that it took twenty-one pounds of protein to feed a steer to get back one pound of meat protein.[37]

The popularity of cookbooks was often a result of the reviews written by newspaper food editors. For example, Voltz's *Natural Foods* cookbook was hailed by wire service food editor Gaynor Maddox in a review that ran in many newspapers across the country. He quoted Voltz at length in the article and wrote that she "believes that the current passion for unadulterated and fresh foods among the young will upgrade everyone's diet."[38] Wood wrote a glowing review of *Mary Meade's Blender Cookbook*: "In my opinion, it is worth many times the modest price of $3. Anyone who doesn't own it is not only missing a lot of grand food, but a lot of fun."[39] Church dedicated a later edition of the book to Morrison, "whose enthusiastic review of this book thirteen years ago launched its successful career."[40]

The success of the classic cookbook *The Joy of Cooking* was in part a result of the strong reviews that newspaper food editors gave it. Associated Press food editor Cecily Brownstone was a central figure in the New York food community beginning in the 1950s. She became a good friend of St. Louis, Missouri, resident Irma Rombauer—author of *The Joy of Cooking*. Their friendship predated Brownstone's wire service career; she was a food editor at *Parents* magazine when the cookbook first came out. She traveled to St. Louis to meet Rombauer. As they sat on a bench at the St. Louis Zoo, Brownstone asked the cookbook author, "Did you vote for Roosevelt?" The answer was "yes," and the two fans of the New Deal became friends for life.[41] Brownstone said she was one of the few editors to interview Rombauer because the cookbook author would not come to New York initially. In later years, Brownstone would finally get the chance to introduce Rombauer to the "foodie community in New York,"[42] and she would write the foreword for the fiftieth anniversary edition of the cookbook, describing Rombauer as a "great and good friend."[43]

The Joy of Cooking was first introduced in 1931 and was revised several times over the decades. Written in a conversational tone, the book mixed simple dishes with complex cuisine. Church wrote in the *Chicago Tribune*, "If this book has too wide a circulation, there will be little for us food editors to do."[44] Nickerson also positively reviewed *The Joy of Cooking* for the *New York Times* in 1951, explaining that it was a time when there were fewer servants and thus cooking was encouraged by being a "joy" to do.[45] Fifty years later, the *New York Times* described the cookbook as "the most fabled of all American cookbooks, although not always the most fashionable."[46] Burros said she developed her sense of recipe writing from reading *The Joy of Cooking*.[47] The introduction in the 1953 edition encourages readers to forge on after failure: "Your first efforts at cooking may result in confusion, but soon you will acquire a skilled routine that will give you confidence and pleasure."[48]

Brownstone hosted a party in her home for Rombauer when the 1951 edition of the cookbook was published, and a photo from the event, found in her papers at the Fales Library, shows well-dressed women gathered on a garden balcony. Nickerson was fond of that 1951 edition, writing that the book was a classic with a personality: "Mrs. Rombauer summed up her lively, intelligent approach to the table arts as the New Deal of the American household."[49] Anne Mendelson, who chronicled the story behind *The Joy of Cooking*, stressed, "The cachet of the *New York Times* food coverage under Miss Nickerson was already considerable." Thus, her endorsement of the book meant "an authoritative announcement that *The Joy of Cooking* could stand as the American cookbook of its era."[50] An un-bylined *New York Times* review of the 1950 edition appreciated the use of instructional photographs and easy-to-use recipes with accompanying variations (though the writer did criticize the use of sugar in a recipe for French dressing).[51] At the *Chicago Tribune*, Morrison Woods wrote that the book was "the finest basic general cookbook that has ever been published." He praised the recipes for breads, cakes, and pastries.[52]

Julia Child, the cookbook author who became a television personality and household name, knew that for her publication to be a success it had to be well reviewed. Her first cookbook, *Mastering the Art of French Cooking*, was embraced by American newspaper food editors; but before that success, she worked for years to get her book published with several stops and starts along the way. In 1954, she received a letter from her publisher with the following advice on getting good press for her book: "Want big splash on household page of either *Herald Trib.* or *Times*. *Trib.* as you know is that dame Paddleford, knows a lot, ghastly (for me) style, but the big noise in the newspaper food world. Dorothy or I must sound her out very carefully. Don't know if she ever writes about cookbooks. Have a hunch if she knew about it ahead of time she wouldn't be beyond swiping credits and ideas. Know less about the dames at the *Times*—Nickerson or Casa-Emellos. But we must walk carefully and find out which is the best pitch for absolutely the right publicity for the book."[53] The letter reveals an interesting aspect of Paddleford's reputation and also shows the power that food editors had in reviewing a book.

The *Can Opener Cookbook* would make Poppy Cannon a household name by 1960s, but she was a much more complex character and her background in food more nuanced than her cookbook's title might imply. She was also the author of other cookbooks of more significant cuisine. She traveled widely, often with *Milwaukee Sentinel* food editor Rosa Tusa. Cannon dined in the top restaurants and had connections through her second husband, Claude Philippe, a big name at the Waldorf-Astoria. But she also had connections in the newspaper industry and had spent time in advertising and as the food editor of the *Ladies' Home Journal*. In these roles, and as the mother of two children from different marriages, she knew what middle-class homemakers needed. A book that capitalized on the need to produce a quick dinner was one that women would buy—and they did in droves. Cannon's initial version of the *Can Opener Cookbook* was published in 1951 and went on to at least three additional printings. "At one time a badge of shame, hallmark of the lazy lady and the careless wife, today the can opener is fast becoming a magic wand," Cannon wrote in the introduction to the 1968 edition, "especially in the hands of those brave young women, nine million of them who are engaged in frying as well as bringing home the bacon."[54] In Nickerson's review of the book, she acknowledged the book's relevance to American kitchen culture. "This is the country of the can-opener; we are, so it contemptuously is said, 'tin can cooks,'" she wrote.[55]

Cannon's other cookbooks also were critically popular among the food editors. In 1961, the *New York Times* positively reviewed her book *Eating Abroad*, observing that there were no other cookbooks like it. The book included recipes as well as background material on dishes. "Did you know that Dublin Bay prawns are tiny lobsters, not shrimp?" the reviewer marveled. "She tells you how hard the English work to spoil vegetables—and to make wonderful marmalade."[56] The most revealing of her cookbooks was written in honor of her third husband, Walter White, whom she described as a "Gentle Knight."[57] The *Bride's Cookbook* included her devotion to the NAACP leader and the long path it took for them to come together at a time when interracial marriage was considered sensational and sometimes dangerous.[58]

While Cannon has received some recognition in recent culinary histories,[59] Marian Tracy, who wrote numerous cookbooks during those decades, is often left out of histories chronicling the cookbook craze. She was the food editor for *New York World-Telegram* and *The Sun*, and her most popular cookbook, *Casserole Cookery: One-Dish Meals for the Busy Gourmet*, was reissued at least ten times by the 1950s. (Her coauthor and husband, Nino, died in 1942 shortly after the book was first issued, but she continued to list him as the coauthor in the updated editions.) In one version, Pulitzer Prize–winning poet and social critic Phyllis McGinley wrote the introduction and described the book's author as "the prophet of a new gospel—immensely stylish."[60] Cannon also reviewed several of Tracy's cookbooks in her newspaper column, "30-Minute Meals." Her review of *The Art of Making Real Soups* was an enthusiastic endorsement. "Every so often there comes across my desk and into the kitchen a book that makes me want to clap and sing for the pure joy and discovery," she wrote, concluding the review with a recipe for black bean soup with white grapes.[61] In another newspaper column, Cannon praised the 1970 edition of the *New Casserole Cookbook*, aimed at brunches. She wrote, "The foods are not exotic. The combination is not strange—just potatoes and eggs. But the look is dramatic—the taste most delectable."[62] A 1978 review in the *Chicago Tribune* of another Tracy cookbook lauded the author's lifelong interest with "real food."[63]

Advertising copywriter Peg Bracken was having lunch with several professional female friends when the topic of cooking came up. The busy working women complained of the task of making meals. That discussion eventually resulted in the witty 1960 *The I Hate to Cook Book*—which would lead to other humorous advice publications and cookbooks. The newspaper food editors enjoyed both the recipes in the book and the tone it set at a time when there was a lot of pressure on home cooks. A reviewer at the *St. Petersburg Times* wrote that it was a funny book that also included "marvelous recipes."[64] Bracken was appreciative of those who did enjoy cooking. Of those women, she wrote, "Invite us over often, please. And stay away from our husbands."[65] In reality Bracken was a good cook—after all, she had to test all of those recipes. The Bracken book was a mix of food advice and wit. She began by explaining, "This book is for those of us who want to fold our big dishwater hands around a dry Martini instead of a wet flounder."[66] The dishes were a mix of yummy-sounding dishes and mocked recipes. Take her recipe for "Cheese Rice." The ingredients were for three cups of hot cooked rice, one-third cup of grated Parmesan, three tablespoons of melted butter, and a dash of pepper. The instruction: "Just toss these items together."[67] Bracken said she credited her success to "admitting what other women would like to but can't."[68] The success of her book led to a newspaper column called "I Try to Behave Myself" and more books.[69] The book was updated and reissued in 2010 with a foreword by Bracken's daughter.

Cookbook author and newspaper food columnist Myra Waldo traveled the world to gather recipes. In 1953, Church encouraged her *Chicago Tribune* readers to buy Waldo's latest book about beer and good food. Church endorsed the cookbook and told readers that she had tested two of the dishes in the newspaper's test kitchen: one for beef kidneys and the other for roast goose. The recipes for both were included in the column.[70] Waldo wrote more than forty cookbooks beginning in 1954 and soon became well known in the New York food world. A 1963 review of her cookbook about barbecue referred her to "the world-famous gastronomist."[71] Eventually she took over the position of food editor for *This Week*, which ran in several Sunday newspapers including the *Baltimore Sun*. (It was the position held by food editor Clementine Paddleford prior to her death.) Nora Ephron reported it was a job that everyone else in the New York food establishment had applied for. Ephron wrote of Waldo, "Shortly afterward, she went to the Cookbook Guild party, and no one except James Beard even said hello to her."[72]

NEWSPAPER COOKBOOKS

In addition to the cookbooks written by food journalists singly, newspapers themselves began to produce cookbooks. Occasionally these would be thematic cookbooks, like *The Cartoonist Cookbook*, a collection of recipes from the all-male newspaper cartoonists. In his introduction to it, James Beard gives value to the smaller, regional books: "I have often remarked that the small cookbooks published by various ethnic and professional groups have done more to stimulate our food traditions in this country than most of the major collections."[73]

Most cookbooks of this type, though, were published by a single newspaper. One of the first was the 1905 version of the *Los Angeles Times Cookbook*, which was actually the *second* edition of the book produced by the newspaper. The publication was the result of a recipe contest—a common feature of the newspaper food sections since their inception—that allowed newspapers to reach female readers and for female readers to appear in the newspaper in a socially acceptable manner: as good cooks. A culinary historian describes the Los Angeles book as regional and ethnic, with recipes for alligator pear salad, which originated in Mexico, and Spanish asparagus. The book cost 35 cents and included 957 recipes submitted by readers.[74]

The *San Francisco Chronicle* published several cookbooks over the years. The newspaper's food editor Jane Benet wrote the *San Francisco Chronicle Cook Book* in 1958, which identified her as the "nationally acknowledged food editor" writing as "Jane Friendly." In that book, Benet wrote, "The women of San Francisco are good cooks (so are a large number of the men)." She recommended a simpler form of entertaining, writing that "the days of the nine-course dinner are gone," because "servants are nearly a thing of the past." In 1973 she wrote the *San Francisco Cook Book*. There were a few earlier cookbooks from the newspaper. For example, in 1922 *Chronicle* food writer Belle De Graf published *Mrs. De Graf's Cook Book*, which was reissued five years later.[75]

Dallas Times Herald food editor Dorothy Sinz wrote a 1964 cookbook (more like a thick booklet with advertisements between the recipes) called *Recipe Book*, which was included with a Monday edition of the newspaper. It included a section about game cookery and a spice chart. It also included the recipe for the popular Perfection Salad. Sinz wrote, "The recipes have come from foreign countries during recent travels, from readers who have, in many cases, had them in their families for many generations." It concluded with prayers to bless food—with Catholic, Jewish, Protestant, and Orthodox versions.[76]

In 1971, *Arizona Republic* food editor Dorothee Polson published her columns and recipes in the cookbook *Pot au Feu*. The title refers to a French term for "pot on the fire," which was a dish that included meats, vegetables, and everything else. A little bit of everything was also the philosophy behind her column, which included recipes, stories about her two children, and local gossip. "All of the recipes have been family tested," Polson confessed, "the most significant result being that my husband and I gained a combined total of 14 pounds. The children, of course, only grew taller."[77] One of the columns in the book is titled "Working Mother Makes Rules." "I happen to be one of those statistics," she revealed, "the 1-of-every-3 homemakers who hold jobs; the 1-out-of-5 mothers who juggle careers." In the column, she offered advice on her rules for combining family with work: "Forget schedules. Take it one crisis at a time."[78]

The *Milwaukee Journal* published a cookbook in the mid-1970s based on the column "Best Cook on the Block," and it produced 275 recipes in its first year. Photos appeared with each recipe, and while there appeared to be a lack of cultural diversity, more male faces were featured than might be expected. Her introduction focused on the familial meal: "In a city where family ties are still strong and three or four generations still live in the same neighborhood, this means holiday feasts for relatives, Sunday dinners for family, Saturday night suppers for friends."[79] Neighborhood cook Alex J. Linder contributed a recipe for kluski (Polish potato dumplings) with pork. "From a family of seven boys, Linder got interested in cooking when he helped his mother in the kitchen," Daum wrote. "Now retired, he does all the cooking at home."[80] Another example was Tom Radoszewski, who contributed a Polska kielbasa, or Polish sausage, recipe. "As a boy, Radoszewski watched his grandfather make sausage," Daum wrote. "Later, he evolved his own recipe from his father's recipe. A Milwaukee cookbook couldn't be complete without such a recipe."[81] In the book's introduction, Daum wrote about the importance of preserving the regional traditions practiced by the home cook:

> Milwaukee with its strong ethnic tradition is known for the good food of its restaurants. But that's only part of the good food in this area. Some of the best meals are served in the homes, where the tradition of good food fosters a tradition of good cooks. There are those who learned from their mothers and grandmothers, discovering the feel of a dumpling when the mixture is light, the taste of a sauce when the seasoning is right, the elasticity of a strudel dough when it's ready to stretch without tearing.[82]

For other newspaper editors, it was their own experiences that led to cookbooks. At the *Charlotte Observer*, food editor Eudora Garrison wrote *It's Not Gourmet—It's Better*, spotlighting a collection of 270 recipes spanning fifty years of what she made in her own kitchen. She explained that the title was derived from an encounter when someone asked her if the dishes were gourmet, which she quickly rebuffed with the answer, "They're better than gourmet."[83] In the cookbook, she rejected the idea of exotic dishes and unusual ingredients and instead embraced simple recipes. "They're basic. They're nostalgic. Most are easily prepared," she explained. "Not many are complicated or fancy. And they're familiar. I've made them all. That's the test—they're repeats in my kitchen."[84] The cookbook included sections on hot fruits as well as fish and fowl. While her obituary highlighted her brimmed hats and swept-up hairdo, the cover of her cookbook featured a smiling, hatless Garrison wearing a polo shirt and looking into the camera.

In 1968, *Miami Herald* food editor Virginia Heffington wrote *Food with a Florida Flair*. The introduction took a swipe at Peg Bracken, known for *The I Hate to Cook Book*. "This should be called the I Like to Cook Book," Heffington wrote, "as we disagree with the lady who hates our favorite pastime." She described the long history of the mango and the allergies that some suffer when touching the fruit. Another section was devoted to the avocado and to Florida lobster. She warned readers not to compare Maine lobsters to Florida lobster, sometimes called spiny lobster. One of the differences was that the Maine lobster was cooked live, while the Florida lobster was not.[85]

In some cities the commonality was culture rather than the ethnicity of the people who resided there. At the *Washington Post*, the big political names of the city clearly read the food section. An article about seafood led to a call from a prominent senator to the food editor asking where he could buy fresh Dungeness crab. In another case, the food editor received a message to call "Ethel" and an unfamiliar phone number. This led to a conversation with Ethel Kennedy about the best venue for a rehearsal dinner.[86] It was not just the power players who got food editor Elinor Lee's attention. Her articles were described as "pragmatic." According to later *Post* food editor Bonnie S. Benwick, "Lee created a deep smorgasbord, interviewing the city's home cooks and enlisting a corps of society hostesses to write about what they served."[87]

Two DC cookbooks in particular exemplify the culture of power and prestige in the city and also the trend of cookbooks as fundraisers. The first was the 1955 cookbook *Who Says We Can't Cook!* by the Women's

National Press Club. The members stressed the book was not a defense of their culinary talents but rather a fundraising venture so they could rent space for a clubhouse. A story by the journalists accompanied each set of recipes. One contributor was Henrietta Poynter, the editor of *Congressional Quarterly* and mentor to many of the reporters in the women's page section of the *St. Petersburg Times*, the newspaper owned by her husband. She offered recipes for heavenly hamburger and cheese wafers and described her kitchen experiences as a young girl:

> I learned to cook at about 14 when my mother went on a three-month speaking tour for suffrage and left me to keep house. Whatever I saved out of the budget was mine, so I specialized in recipes for making cheap cuts of meat delicious and managed, without starving the family, to indulge in new clothes, theatre tickets, and other things not covered by my allowance.[88]

The initial cookbook had a press run of five thousand copies and they were all sold in the first week. For the next three years, the cookbook was regularly reprinted with requests coming as far away as Australia.[89] Elinor Lee, who contributed a recipe for oatmeal refrigerator rolls, noted that she collected recipes the way others collect stamps or coins: "It's my hobby as well as my job."[90]

It is worth remembering that women journalists were excluded from membership in the Washington, DC–based National Press Club until 1971. Important politicians and significant celebrities delivered speeches at the press club, and prior to 1955, women were not even allowed in the club building to cover the speeches that made the newspapers. That year, the male members came up with a plan that allowed women journalists to cover speakers from the balcony of the ballroom, but they had to stand—because the balcony was too narrow for chairs—while their seated male colleagues ate and drank below. According to Bonnie Angelo, chief of the *Newsday* bureau in Washington,

> Here were the people in the balcony, distinguished journalists treated like second-class citizens. I *had* to cover the stories there. Some people equated the balcony with the back of the bus, but at least the bus got everybody to the same destination just as well. We could not ask questions of the speakers. All this standing—it was like a cattle

car. And all the time you were really boiling inside. You entered and left through a back door, and you'd be glowered at as you went through the club quarters. It was discrimination at its rawest.[91]

The cookbook of the Washington press women proved so popular that a second edition, called *Second Helping*, was released in 1962. Lee shared her recipe for "Whipped Butter," which included brandy and finely chopped blanched almonds. "The recipe, I was told, is a specialty of the Kansas City Club," she explained, "but I sampled Whipped Butter for the first time at a breakfast given by the American Institute of Baking during the 1961 Newspaper Food Editors' Conference."[92] The second edition of the cookbook did contain a rather embarrassing error for the precise journalists—the cooking time for Mrs. John F. Kennedy's *Poulet à l'Estragon* was omitted. The error was included in newspaper coverage of the book.[93]

Some of these newspaper cookbooks were produced through a partnership of the editorial side and the publicity side as a form of public service. In an undated Eudora Garrison booklet, it states that it was prepared by the promotions department at the *Charlotte Observer*. Regardless of which department funded the publication, the recipes stayed true to the personality of the food editor, as Garrison noted in the foreword: "In this little book of favorites from my kitchen, I had a real struggle to get some down on paper. There are certain older familiars I prepare by using a pinch of this, a handful of that and cooking until it's done."[94] She also wrote a booklet about foods for holiday celebrations, which was a mix of her recipes and reader contributions; hers were labeled "My Own" and those of readers as from "Martha" or "Mrs. Carr."[95]

In 1962, the *Detroit Free Press* food editor Kay Savage published the cookbook *Secrets of Michigan Cooks*. The book included an interesting set of chapters, beginning with "Just a Housewife." Savage clarified, "But our Mrs. Homemaker is much more," as she was also a purchasing agent, community worker, and dressmaker. A chapter called "She Cooks with Her Hat On" was devoted to women who worked outside the home. Other chapters were devoted to male cooks, teen chefs, and food contest winners. Of the collection, Savage explained, "Some belong to the cook-on-the-run school, some to the dedicated gourmet class, some to the mathematically precise groups and then there are the freewheelers who cook by instinct."[96]

Grace Hartley, food editor of the *Atlanta Journal*, wrote one of the first cookbooks to raise the status of Southern cooking, and it was well received by most reviewers. The 1976 book was a result of more than forty years of recipes from her newspaper. "Many of them are heirlooms passed down through several generations," she wrote. "I have visited in many of the homes they came from." She began with breads and recipes for corn pone, hoe cake, and spoon bread. Some recipes included the names of the home cooks who volunteered their creations, such as Mrs. Phyllis Hairr's Creamed Eggs New Orleans and Mrs. Robert Mouk's Barbecued Rib Roast. A few recipes were from male cooks, such as Rod Carlyle's Creamy Hot Buttered Rum and chef Manuel Filotis's recipe for South Carolina peach slump—a kind of pie.[97] The recipes with alcohol were a more recent addition. In her early years at the newspaper, she rarely included recipes with liquor because of some of the readers' reactions. "I was really chewed out by some WCTUers and a couple of ministers," she said. Her response was that in her Bible, Jesus turned water into wine.[98]

Several cookbooks celebrating Southern food were penned by Cissy Gregg of the *Louisville Courier-Journal*. Gregg had a college degree in agriculture and home economics and an interest in maps. In her 1953 cookbook, she wrote that she had selected her favorites from a collection of more than 12,000. She included Country Captain, stuffed pork chops, and spaghetti rings. The dishes were meant to inspire the home cooks as "cooking the two to three daily meals for the family represents a constant drain on a cook's imagination."[99] In the 1960s, she noted that the American diet included too much meat, bread, and potatoes and not enough green vegetables.

When *Orlando Sentinel* food editor Grace Barr retired in 1969, her friends pushed her to write a cookbook. Barr had long been a good cook and had helped support her family during the Great Depression by selling baked goods. The financial difficulties of the time led to divorce, and with her teenage twins in high school, she became a society reporter and eventually food editor at the newspaper. Barr decried the rationing of World War II and was known to begin a recipe with "Take a stick of butter." Her cookbook *Cooking with Grace* came out in 1970 to rave reviews, with one reviewer remarking, "The overall flavor of the book is Deep South."[100]

Near the end of her career, *Denver Post* food editor Helen Dollaghan published a compendium of *Best Main Dishes*. The variety of dishes in the cookbook represented Denver as a highly mobile city, which she said meant a continuous introduction of new recipes to the area. She wrote that it was without gimmicks and presented "the kind of cooking that is actually going on in today's best home kitchen." She included beef chapters and another for meatless entrées. Other chapters were called "Off the Beaten Path" and "High Country Cooking." She also addressed the challenge of cooking in high altitudes. The problem is decreased atmospheric pressure and a lower boiling point, which means water boils at about 202 degrees Fahrenheit at 5,000 feet, compared with 212 degrees at sea level.[101]

In 1972, Associated Press food editor Cecily Brownstone published a cookbook that included 400 recipes from her vast collection (later donated to the Fales Library at New York University). In the introduction to the book, she wrote that when she began as a food writer, she was bothered by the fact that all recipes seemed to stem from the same place. Her friend and *Joy of Cooking* author Irma Rombauer responded that she should just be a "good pirate." "To me a good pirate means eschewing what I call typewriter-cooking," Brownstone wrote in the book's introduction. "I find it easiest to write out my own experience and background."[102] The cookbook was included in the compilation *101 Classic Cookbooks* published by New York University in 2012.[103]

Newspaper food editors also commonly wrote their own cookbooks independent of the newspaper. Often it was because these women had such regional expertise. In between her jobs as food editor at the *New York Times* and the *Lakeland Ledger*, Jane Nickerson raised her children and wrote a cookbook about Florida foods, published by the University of Florida Press. "Florida is a good cook's dream come true," she wrote of her adopted state, "where anyone fascinated with the kitchen art can find an abundance of ingredients almost without going to market." She wrote about the abundant and varied produce available in the sunny state, and the seafood was also plentiful, with "a wider assortment of fish than is caught in any other state."[104] Readers learn as much about history and culture as recipes in the book, as she includes information about chopped chicken livers, popular at Miami Beach bar mitzvah luncheons, and a carrot salad recipe her teenage daughter brought back from a trip to Guadeloupe.[105] Brownstone's review of the book for the Associated Press was positive, declaring that Nickerson knew the culinary history of the state, and Brownstone had tested all the recipes in the book—including the directions for Cuban bread, which was listed in the story.[106]

Milwaukee Sentinel and *Palm Beach Post* food editor Rosa Tusa authored a recipe booklet about Southern food called *True Grits*. With President Jimmy Carter in the White House, she claimed there was a need to understand dishes from the South. The recipes were aimed at Yankees "who don't know a Limpin' Susan from a Hopping John." Most of the recipes included a history of the dishes. She included a recipe for Brunswick stew that she labeled "a Southern classic dating back to colonial times." A recipe for Kentucky burgoo included the notation that the dish was "well known in Kentucky, where early settlers made it with wild game." A third recipe was for oysters Rockefeller, invented in the 1880s at Antoine's in New Orleans.[107]

While many of these examples illustrate how the food editors were preserving regional traditions in their cookbooks, a few food editors took a more continental approach to their cookbooks. Most notable was Church, who wrote numerous cookbooks—some connected to her newspaper and some written on her own. One of her most well-known cookbooks was *Mary Meade's Magic Recipes for the Electronic Blender*. Originally published in 1952, it sold 209,000 copies. The book needed to be updated in 1956 because blenders were then manufactured with a second speed. According to a questionnaire for her publisher, "I wrote the book by working late at night after I'd gotten my children to bed and the household settled, for the most part. Fortune smiled on me when it gave me a handyman husband whose activities in his basement workshop or at his drawing board could be carried on while I was at my typewriter."[108]

In fact, her husband, Freeman Church, designed the covers of several of her cookbooks. The blender book was republished for a third time in 1965. Among her other cookbooks were *Mary Meade's Kitchen Companion: The Indispensable Guide for the Modern Cook* (1955), *The Burger Cookbook* (1967), and *Entertaining with Wine* (1970).

Another example of a food editor catering to a more national audience would be Clementine Paddleford, who published *How America*

Eats in 1962. It took her twelve years to gather the material, traveling more than 800,000 miles. She personally interviewed more than 2,000 cooks and tried all of the dishes in the 479-page book. Even then, however, Paddleford made the case for regionalism. "The pioneer mother created dishes with foods available. These we call regional," she wrote. "It is to these, perhaps, I have given the greatest emphasis here."[109] She traveled the country to collect the recipes—including a three-week visit to New Orleans. This chronicle was similar to the 1930s America Eats! project for the Works Progress Administration and was described in Pat Willard's 2008 book of the same name.[110]

Voltz wrote numerous cookbooks, sometimes for her newspaper and sometimes on her own. She wrote recipes from Los Angeles restaurants, Southern food, and dishes from California and later Florida. She won two Tastemaker Awards, which recognized the best regional cookbooks, in 1970 and 1978.

HONORING HOME COOKS AND RECIPE EXCHANGE COLUMNS

A case could be made that the recipe columns and the cookbooks that came from the newspaper food editors were an early form of social media, linking the food journalists with the home cooks of their communities. After all, women often communicate with friends and family by sharing recipes. *New York Times* food writer Amanda Hesser observed in 2010 that newspapers "are really in the business of community building"—particularly in the food pages, where "readers had always been integral," whether they contributed recipes or were featured in news stories.[111] Church wrote to her *Chicago Tribune* readers in 1950, "You, dear readers, are always losing your recipes! That's all right. Go ahead and call us or write. We'll find the recipe for you if it was ours. That's what we are here for."[112]

The newspaper food editors received dozens of letters each week. Mary Hart's column "Ask Mary" in the *Minneapolis Tribune* was so popular that a 1978 tabulation of mail received by *Tribune* columnists listed advice columnist Ann Landers with 763 letters, while Mary Hart racked up 1,056. Food editors' phones rang regularly with food questions. According to Carol Haddix, who worked in the food sections of the *Detroit Free Press* and the *Chicago Tribune*,

> Of the calls, many were asking basic questions about "can I freeze this?" or "is it safe?" Occasionally, I would get calls asking for a whole menu for someone's dinner party! It would amaze me that after running so many articles on food safety or basic cooking techniques, the questions on those topics would keep coming. I had to continually remind myself that, no matter how often we run that chart on the safe thawing of turkey, there is a whole new generation of cooks out there that has no clue.[113]

At the *Omaha World-Herald*, food editor Maude Coons answered between sixty and seventy-five questions each day, she estimated. Some were about fashion and etiquette but most were about food. With her home economics background, she could answer most questions on her own. Yet she was stumped by some queries—such as how to grill rattlesnake, turtle, and blackbirds. Sometimes the questions veered into other areas, as some callers "really were just lonely and wanted to talk."[114]

The newspaper food sections needed to appeal to both foodies who appreciated gourmet cuisine and those who simply wanted a quick and easy way to get dinner on the table each night. As a result, newspaper food sections typically featured three kinds of recipe columns: (1) those in which a reader is looking for a long lost recipe and the newspaper asks readers to help; (2) those in which a reader is requesting a recipe for a dish in a local restaurant that the food editor then tries to imitate; or (3) those for which readers contribute favorite recipes—such as a call for Christmas cookies. Top recipes often were reprinted because of reader demand. For example, Marie Dugan, food editor at the *Journal* in Lincoln, Nebraska, said she had to reprint the recipe for spiced peach jam nearly every year.[115] In 1962, Kay Savage wrote that her "At Your Request" column had resulted in 365 recipes each year for the past twenty-five years. She explained that the recipe for chicken poulette was requested about once a week.[116] These popular recipe exchange columns in the 1960s and 1970s were published in newspapers across the country and provided appreciation and understanding of the home cooks and their regional dishes.

In the 1950s, *Denver Post* food editor Helen Messenger initiated the popular food column that ran in the newspaper's Sunday publication

Empire Magazine called "Munching Through Denver with Messenger." *Charleston News and Courier* food editor Charlotte Walker wrote a column for readers looking for misplaced recipes called "Loved, Lost . . ." In one 1968 column, a reader was given a recipe for vanilla French toast while another reader requested recipes for gingerbread.[117] Jo Ann Vachule began penning the *Fort Worth Star-Telegram*'s culinary Q&A column in 1963 called "C.U.P.S." (Cooking Up a Storm). In 1966, *Houston Chronicle* food editor Ann Criswell started the column "Looking for Cooking" in 1966, which she described as a "backyard type of discussion about cooking."[118]

St. Paul Pioneer Press food editor Eleanor Ostman initiated a recipe column in 1968 called "This Sunday" that ran for more than twenty-five years. She wrote about her family's love of a dish or a disaster that she had in the kitchen. Her readers wrote in often, and Ostman quickly learned what they wanted to know about. "Readers, I soon learned, loved my flubs," she wrote. "I didn't promise to be scientific, and I didn't promise to be perfect." Some residents later complained that they missed hearing about her mistakes as she became a more proficient cook over the years.[119]

The recipe exchange column "Dear S.O.S." began in the *Los Angeles Times* in 1961. The intended audience was "mostly homemakers who were curious and innovative, but limited by the foodstuffs found in the markets at that time." Thousands of requests for recipes came in each year, ranging from old favorites to restaurant dishes to childhood memories from Los Angeles cafeteria desserts. Cecil Fleming answered the requests in the 1960s, and later it was Rose Dosti.[120] The column is still running in 2013 with the name "Culinary S.O.S." Several cookbooks have been published based on the column, including one book that was based on recipes from Los Angeles restaurants.

The *Kansas City Star* food column "Come into My Kitchen" turned fifty years old in 2005. At the time, the newspaper's food editor wrote, "From suet to sun-dried tomatoes, *The Star*'s popular column chronicles the home cook's ever-changing tastes." Food editor Erma Young began the column in November 1955, and scrapbooks of the weekly column reflected the changes in food trends and technology over the years. For example, a 1970 column included the recipe for a six-can casserole.[121]

The *Philadelphia Bulletin* had an early food column, "Between Neighbors," that appeared for decades. The section's editor was Frances Blackwood, who began in 1929. She was at the paper for so long she eventually admitted that she no longer tested the recipes from the readers she knew so well—she trusted their culinary skills. And some recipes she received were from grandchildren of her first readers.[122]

COMPETITIVE COOKING

Televised competitive cooking programs have become increasingly popular in recent years—from *Top Chef* to *Cupcake Wars*. Yet a long history of competitive cooking exists, and many of them were connected to newspapers' food sections. At times, the newspapers themselves held the competitions. As early as the 1940s, Church ran a recipe contest in the *Chicago Tribune* each week with a $5 prize and publication of the recipe. Readers were advised to test the recipes and be specific with the measurements and directions.[123] Most winners were rather simple, such as a recipe for orange sweet potatoes. This was typical of many newspapers at the time, since food sections served as both news and service to readers.

Food celebrities were sometimes asked to judge contests when they were in town. Many visited the local newspaper when they were traveling on book tours. The *Chicago Tribune* asked Julia Child to help judge the newspaper's annual holiday cookie contest in the newspaper's test kitchen. She accepted the offer, but after sampling twelve finalists' cookies, she said, "I wouldn't make any of these cookies." Haddix said, "Admittedly, it WAS an ordinary group of cookies that year and luckily the finalists weren't present to hear her. We didn't use her quote in the article." Another memorable visitor to the *Chicago Tribune* was New Orleans chef Paul Prudhomme, who helped judge the newspaper's gumbo contest in 1986. There were six finalists who were told to bring their best bowl of the gumbo to the *Tribune*. According to the food editor, the event was held in the *Tribune*'s elegant twenty-first-floor dining room and the hefty chef sat at one end of the massive oak dining table like a king: "Unlike Julia, he had good things to say about all the bowls of gumbo brought for sampling, but finally picked a delicious chicken and andouille sausage version as the winner."[124]

In other instances, the food editors served as judges of the competitions or covered the competitions as news. The Pillsbury Bake-Off always included newspaper food editors as judges, and the Great American Cook-Off—a contest restricted to male contestants—also was judged by food editors. News from that particular contest ran in *Sports Illustrated*. *Houston Chronicle* food editor Ann Criswell judged several national cooking competitions, including the National Beef Cook-Off, the National Chicken Cooking Contest, and America's Cookout Championship for men in Hawaii.[125] Violet Faulkner of the *Washington Post* judged the same competitions. Food editors also judged local pie and cake competitions, as well as state fair competitions. "I've helped distribute nigh into a million bucks judging recipe contests," said Eleanor Ostman of the *St. Paul Pioneer Press* of the judging, which she described as "a fulfilling task, a huge responsibility and sometimes a very funny experience." Ostman recalled a food editor judge who once awarded a first prize to an apple pie during a cherry pie contest because "All the cherry pies were so bad."[126]

Competitive cooking was not only women's domain. Men and women both competed in the chili cook-off circuit. The initial chili cook-off was held in October 1952 at the State Fair of Texas in Dallas. It was the idea of Joe E. Connor as a way to promote his book *With or Without Beans*. Fifty-five cooks made chili that day, with Mrs. F. G. Ventura taking home first prize. For many years, it was assumed that the first chili cook-off was in Terlingua, Texas, in 1967, but a newspaper clipping clarified the original competition.[127]

Another of the well-known cooking competitions was the Delmarva three-day chicken cooking contest, which began in 1947, according to *Cooks, Gluttons and Gourmets*.[128] (The *New York Times* reported that the first chicken cooking competition took place in 1949.) The name of the region, known for its poultry farms, is a combination of the states Delaware, Maryland, and Virginia. Cooking divisions existed for entrants under age twenty, barbecue, and "patio cookery." In 1965, a twelve-year-old St. Petersburg, Florida, girl defeated fifty-two competitors, earning $2,000 and an electric range. The US Department of Agriculture encouraged poultry eating, as huge flocks could be raised in a small area. By 1958, Americans were consuming about two million chickens a year.[129] The large-scale competition lent a news value to the event that caused many of the food editors to cover the contest, such as Clementine Paddleford, the *Philadelphia Bulletin*'s Frances Blackwood, and the *Washington Post*'s Elinor Lee.[130]

Of course, the most famous of the competitive cooking events is the Pillsbury Bake-Off. It began in 1949 as the Grand National Recipe and Baking Contest and was covered in newspapers across the country where food reporters deemed it the more headline-friendly "Bake-Off." Held at the New York Waldorf-Astoria Hotel that first year, former first lady Eleanor Roosevelt handed out the top prize to a Detroit homemaker, Mrs. Theodora Smafield, who entered No-Knead Water-Rising Twists—a recipe handed down by her mother. Nickerson wrote that the winner had "only been cooking for six years."[131] Several years later, *Detroit Free Press* food editor Kay Savage tested the original recipe and discovered it did not quite work as described. The problem was with the recommended technique of putting the dough in a cloth bag and letting it rise in a bowl of water. "We tried it in the Test Kitchen without much success," Savage wrote. "Sticky dough was everywhere."[132] Ostman, food editor at the *St. Paul Pioneer Press*, was a judge at the 1969 Bake-Off. She wrote that soon after the $25,000 check was presented, "it was discovered that a similar concept was in a Betty Crocker cookbook, which made the folks at Pillsbury very uncomfortable."[133]

Recipe plagiarism was a common problem for recipe contests. After the winning recipe for the 1974 Pillsbury Bake-Off ran in the *St. Paul Pioneer Press*, editor Ostman's phone started ringing and letters started coming in. The recipe was for a chocolate cherry bar, which included four ingredients plus frosting. The readers told Ostman that the recipe had been printed in Minnesota's Kandiyochi County Electronic Co-Op newsletter the previous August. As a judge in the contest, Ostman said she was concerned that the recipe was too simple and she asked Pillsbury personnel if they were sure the recipe was an original. They responded that their home economists had researched cookbooks and found nothing like it.[134]

The publicity of these contests and the subsequent publication of the winning recipes in newspapers introduced dishes and techniques to readers and cooks in communities across the country, thus creating national dishes and crazes.[135] In 1954, for example, the Pillsbury grand prize recipe was for Open Sesame Pie, leading to a rush on sesame seeds at grocery stores. And, in 1966, a second-place recipe for Tunnel of Fudge Cake led to a rush on Bundt cake pans. The exotic-for-the-time pan forced NordicWare into overdrive to meet customers' needs.[136]

In 1968, there were 150 food editors—of both newspaper and magazine writers—who attended the contest. Another ten food editors would actually judge the finalists, including Benet of the *San Francisco Chronicle* and Volpe of the *Pittsburgh Press*. As in previous meetings, this meant a chance for advertisers to share their products or technologies and a chance for the editors to learn about local foods among the intended propaganda. The women learned about new General Electric products and a new Pillsbury campaign to develop a protein-rich drink for the El Salvador market as a way to combat malnutrition.[137]

Carol McCready Hartley was the longtime food editor at the *Phoenix Gazette*. Armed with a degree in home economics, she oversaw one of the largest food sections in the country at fifty pages. At the time, Phoenix was popular with food companies as a city to test products because it was a rather isolated market. In 1969, she was a judge in the national Pillsbury Bake-Off when her group chose a recipe that involved rolling a marshmallow in butter and then wrapping it in a Pillsbury crescent roll and baking it.[138] The winning entry became a "landmark recipe in the history of the bake-off," as culinary historian Laura Shapiro described it. "People made them and made them and made them."[139]

There were cooking contests for high school students, too. While these competitions were aimed at the idea of a girl eventually becoming a housewife, the prize was often a college scholarship. It was in this way that honoring a traditional skill helped women gain a hold in the public sphere. For example, consider the Betty Crocker Homemaker of Tomorrow contest that ran in the 1960s and 1970s. In 1970, the winner in Nevada was Joyce Kay Nelson. In her application she wrote about an exciting trip she had taken to Mexico, where she learned about the culture and the people. She described what she thought was important in a homemaker: "By keeping the home as clean and comfortable as possible, the homemaker can provide an escape from the growing pressures of the outside world." Upon winning the prize, she used the scholarship to attend veterinary school.[140]

COLUMNS, COOK-OFFS, AND THE PUBLIC SPHERE

The recipe exchange columns and the newspaper cooking competitions were important ways for publications and readers to interact. Most of the food section editors received piles of mail and had a phone that rang constantly, in ways that other editors did not receive. As women's roles in society changed, the food section provided a way of entering the public sphere in a traditional manner. It has been said that for a proper woman, her name should only appear in the newspaper three times: her birth, her marriage, and her death. It is safe to say that a fourth acceptable reason for a woman's name to be in the newspaper would be to recognize her role as a cook.

5

HOME ECONOMICS

The Study and Practice of Domestic Science
in Food Journalism

Over the past decade, scholars and historians have begun reevaluating
the history and role of the home economics field. Once looked at as a
field of study that only reinforced a woman's place in the home, home
economics has been reassessed for its role in nutrition, consumer news,
and household budgeting. What was discovered was a more complex
and often empowering position—at least for those within the industry.

Three significant books have offered a new way of looking at the
female-centered profession. In *Perfection Salad*, culinary historian Laura Shapiro outlines the beginning of the domestic science movement
and its evolution into home economics. "They wanted to create a profession for themselves and a creed for women at home," she writes,
"and they wanted to do so by charging ahead into the future."[1] The
book *Rethinking Home Economics* included a collection of essays that
demonstrated the value of the field in terms of health, technology, and
women's roles. It also chronicled how the women's liberation movement challenged the value of home economics. "The feminists of the
1970s cast off their aprons long before they burned their bras," an
editor noted.[2] The third book, *Creating Consumers*, was a scholarly
study focusing on the role of home economics in creating a consumer
culture.[3] While these books are helpful in understanding home economics, there is almost no reference to home economics journalism or

the journalism classes that were common within the home economics curriculum.

A recent Cornell University online history of home economics— "What Was Home Economics?"—documents the significance of the field and uses new scholarship to suggest "that home economics was a progressive field that brought science to the farm home and women into higher education and leadership positions in public education, academia, government and industry."[4] Again, little of the material includes references to journalism classes in the curriculum, but reporting was included in a list of professions available to home economics majors, and journalism would have been part of the curriculum.

Before becoming a target of some feminist activists and its public image problem in the early 1970s, home economics courses were a significant part of many high schools and universities. For decades, the programs not only helped teach girls how to be wives and mothers but also created employment opportunities for them. The government, education agencies, and domestic industries all employed home economists for decades. By the 1960s, change was on the horizon as society began questioning tradition. Historians of women's history have been leery about giving the field recognition. Home economist historian Carolyn M. Goldstein put it this way:

> For feminist historians seeking to understand the forces and factors that conspired to limit women's opportunities in the public sphere, home economics was an easy target. In blaming home economists for confining women to the domestic sphere, this type of analysis reinforced assumptions that home economics was concerned only with private matters of the home.[5]

THE HISTORY OF HOME ECONOMICS

The female-dominated field of home economics, initially called domestic science, was a significant career path for women for decades. In 1871, the first college class in domestic economy was offered at Iowa State University, and by 1873 Kansas State began a domestic economy curriculum. One scholar noted that the emphasis on applied science for largely Midwestern male students created a place for female students: "In many ways, household equipment studies developed as a feminine parallel to agricultural engineering."⁶ At several conferences in Lake Placid between 1899 and 1909, women defined their field and debated what it should be called. By 1909, the American Home Economics Association (AHEA) was officially named. It aimed to improve "living conditions in the home, the institutional household and the community."⁷ Creating domestic science or home economics allowed women into the public sphere without threatening traditional roles. As Shapiro explained, "The women who chose domestic science had no quarrel with women's rights, but neither did they have any desire to call themselves feminists. They wanted to have a career and they needed a cause, but they weren't interested in breaking very many rules, reordering society, or challenging men on their own turf."⁸

Congress passed the Smith-Lever Act in 1914, which created the Agriculture Extension Service to provide farm women with an education in home economics. During World War I, home economists taught the nation about rationing and substitution, such as replacing meat with beans. They also worked for food conservation programs and promoted victory gardens. The idea was to win the war through food. Following the war, the USDA created the Bureau of Home Economics in 1923. Its mission was to research consumer behavior and to modernize rural homes.⁹ For example, many home economists were employed by the Household Refrigeration Bureau to educate "Mrs. Consumer" about the need for refrigerators. The information campaign utilized advertising, presentations to women's clubs, and pamphlets with such advice as "When a baby's health hangs in the balance, the intelligent mother will see to it that the ice supply never runs too low."¹⁰

By 1920, the objectives of home economics shifted from an emphasis on housework to parent education, which sometimes included fathers taking an active role. The research on familial roles would provide a significant counter to the post–World War II government propaganda espousing the dangers of working mothers. The Purnell Act of 1925 offered federal money for the scientific investigation of vitamins and rural home management research. Granted exclusively to women, Cornell awarded its first master's degree in home economics in 1922 and its first doctoral degree in 1930. Food preparation was becoming central to the mission of the field, and the mass media and food companies were employing home economists during this time to create and test recipes.

By the 1930s, federal legislation created even more positions for home economists and increased funding for home economics programs. In addition to food preparation, consumer education was long a part of the home economics curriculum. After all, new products and inventions for the kitchen were being introduced all the time. A review of scholarship produced by home economics students shows an emphasis on the scientific understanding of the new appliances. For example, a 1923 master's thesis examined the efficiency of stoves.[11] A 1948 article in the *Journal of Home Economics* explained the results of a study of dry versus steam irons.[12] A trustee at Iowa State University, which helped establish home economics as an academic field of study, explained equipment studies this way: "We must teach the girls to acquire by practice a thorough knowledge of the art of conducting a well regulated household."[13]

An emphasis on journalism was present within academic home economics programs by 1923. A study published that year found that of the twenty-six leading home economics programs at American universities, twenty-two offered classes in journalism. After beginning to see an increase in the number of home economics stories published in newspapers, the author recognized the possibilities of media job opportunities and called it a "most unworked and fertile field."[14] She also noticed the success of home economics programs producing their own publications, such as the "Iowa Homemaker" at Iowa State University, which Ruth Ellen Church wrote for while a student. Some of the programs offering classes in home economics journalism included the University of Arizona, where students could combine a minor in home economics with a major in journalism, as Peggy Daum did. Other universities, such as at Kansas State University, the University of Wisconsin, and Iowa State University, offered a major in home economics journalism. These programs were often marketed as places for women to be trained to work as food advertising copywriters, women's magazine editors, or newspaper women's page journalists.

As described in chapter 2, home economists were in high demand during World War II. They were needed to help the country by operating canning kitchens and encouraging victory gardens. While it could be argued this was part of a governmental propaganda campaign, the efforts were grounded in research to help women. During the war, some home economists left their positions as food editors. For example,

Grace Hartley, who was the food editor at the *Atlanta Journal* from 1936 to 1970, worked for the War Production Board during World War II. Further, home economics departments at newspapers were helping local housewives. Marion Olive Prior Ferriss Guinn was food editor at the *Seattle Times*, where she wrote under the pen name "Dorothy Neighbors." During World War II, when events were held in Victory Square, Guinn presented a number of "Housewives Go to War" programs.

While images of Rosie the Riveter and her sisters had proved powerful in getting women into the workforce, the intent was always to return those jobs to men when the war ended. The government needed a new strategy to encourage women to return to the home, so it funded research to show that the children of working mothers would become juvenile delinquents. This was countered by research in the home economics field. Consider a speech given in 1952 by Elizabeth Sweeney Herbert, president-elect of the AHEA, to the Congress on Industrial Health, which was sponsored by the American Medical Association. Titled "Occupation Housewife," her speech was a roundup of the research that had been conducted about mothers who worked outside of the home. She said family relationships were more important than a clean house and that how time was spent with children was more important than how much time. Finally, she stressed that mothers need some time for themselves—away from the children.[15]

Some of the women who worked in the army during World War II returned to the United States and used their GI Bill funds to earn home economics degrees. One example was Ann Hamman. She served in the Women's Army Auxiliary Corps and spent two years in North Africa and Italy. When she returned, she earned a master's degree in home economics and wrote a thesis focused on cost per hour saved by the use of vacuum cleaners, washing machines, and electric dryers.[16] She then served as an extension agent for an Indiana agency before becoming the food editor at the *Evansville (IN) Journal*.[17] Her columns addressed food and consumer issues, with an emphasis on the quality and price of food products.

THE WORK OF HOME ECONOMISTS AS JOURNALISTS

Introducing Appliances and Technology

Women who had entered the workforce and fed their families in the war years were in for a pleasant surprise at the dawning of the 1950s. After being urged by commercial advertising and governmental propaganda to return to the home, they discovered their kitchens were becoming nearly self-sufficient with the new appliances.

Those home economists who had entered the field of journalism were among the first to test and introduce these modern kitchen luxuries to their readers. Food editor Grace Hartley had one of the first electric ranges in Atlanta, and likely the first microwave in the city. In 1946, Jane Nickerson explained to *New York Times* readers how dishwashers worked, describing the latest in kitchen technology in a very process-oriented manner:

> Soiled dishes are scraped, stacked on a wire tray and lowered into the machine, the lid is closed and the water, sprayed from eight jets, is then turned on. This hydraulic pressure causes the tray to revolve on its roller bearings, permitting water to reach every part of every dish. After thirty seconds of this, the soap is poured in the dishes, washed for three minutes, then the drain opened and the final rinsing takes place. Drying is accomplished by continued revolution of the tray after the water has been turned off.[18]

St. Paul Pioneer Press food editor Eleanor Ostman recalled being the first person on her block to have a microwave. After she tested a few recipes using the microwave, she realized that few of her readers could use the information, as they did not own the machine. She ended up having to use two sets of instruction—one for a microwave and another for conventional ovens.[19] She did not believe in recipes that used a breadmaking machine, so her husband, Ron Aune, tested those recipes.[20]

Before *New York Times* food editor Craig Claiborne introduced American cooks to the Cuisinart, the basic blender was a new and exciting product but aimed more at bartenders than cooks. Church wrote two versions of a blender cookbook after the appliance was introduced with a second speed. Before long, home cooks figured out that it would make food preparation easier. Soon recipes appeared for everything from baby food to sauces. The 1965 edition of her blender cookbook began with an explanation of what a blender could do:

> A blender is an electrical appliance that makes daily meal preparation and entertaining less work and more fun. It takes the nuisance and clutter out of chopping, grating, pureeing and mincing. It does something no other appliance can do—liquefies fruits, vegetables and other solid foods, thus making possible an entirely new kind of cooking.[21]

For all the technology being introduced in their pages, food editors still found stories that went back to the basics, like camping stories. Dorothy Crandall wrote about an overnight bean recipe that used coals from the cookout the night before and tortillas intended to be cooked over a fire.[22] And each Thanksgiving the editors would re-explain the basics of a turkey dinner.

Writing Recipes

Home economists still worked at the basic task of writing recipes. Certainly this was a part of the job description for home economists working at newspapers. At the heart of any newspaper food section are the recipes, whether elaborate dishes meant to show off culinary expertise or quick, budget-conscious meals. Newspapers appeal to a wide and varied readership but the readers share an interest in local issues. While sometimes serving as an introduction to new meals based on unusual ingredients or innovative techniques, the recipes published in the local newspaper's food section also reflected the community's demographics and ecosystem, sometimes even by what it left out. For example, in Milwaukee, Wisconsin, with its rich German heritage, the newspaper rarely received letters or phone calls about how to make German potato salad. "If you are making German potato salad, you already know how," according to *Milwaukee Journal* food editor Peggy Daum. "The right way to make it is the way your mother and grandmother made it. You may argue about it with someone down the block, but you don't call me."[23] Her point is proven in that not a single recipe for the popular staple was included in *The Best Cook on the Block Cookbook*, a collection of recipes submitted by Milwaukee home cooks as part of a weekly column in the *Milwaukee Journal*. Daum, who was born and raised in Milwaukee, shared a childhood story regarding the dish in the 1984 cookbook *Food Editors' Hometown Favorites Cookbook*: "I was eleven or so before I knew that any other kind of potato salad existed," Daum revealed. "That's when I saw an egg-and-mayonnaise version at a Girl Scout potluck supper and said: 'What funny potato salad.' Unfortunately, I was speaking to the Scout whose mother had prepared it. I've learned to like a number of potato salads since, but German Potato Salad is still my favorite."[24]

As happens under deadlines and with newspaper copy, there are sometimes mistakes. Those errors are amplified when the mistake is in a recipe carefully followed by a reader. Cleveland food editor Janet Beighle French admitted that these mistakes happened because the journalists were rewriting recipes while answering a constantly ringing phone. "I wrote one story about a missing ingredient, the result of such a rewriting, interspersing the cook's demands for the completed recipe with actual phone calls we received," she said. On another occasion, she and her staff sampled every crumb of a minimal-ingredient dessert recipe that contained cake mix before publishing it. "Then we started getting calls," she recalled. "One reader memorably said it was so hard after refrigeration that she could throw it against the wall and it didn't crumble. It turned out cake mixes vary quite a bit."[25]

Some errors could be rather comical. At the *Houston Chronicle*, Ann Criswell published a recipe that called for two bags of camels (rather than caramels) and an Impossible Pie recipe that omitted sugar (it was "truly impossible" without the sweetener, she wrote). Another recipe called for "4 eggs, strained." Most puzzling was a recipe for cake frosting that required two 14-ounce cans of stewed tomatoes. "To this day, I don't know how that error occurred," she recalled years later.[26]

Ostman published her share of recipe errors during her several decade career, explaining, "It was hard to escape typos in those pre-computer days of typewriters and hot type."[27] In one 1969 example, a recipe for fruitcake ran without the needed amount of butter. So many phone calls came into the newspaper the following morning that the staff in the women's department skipped a greeting and began answering the phone with "half cup of butter." A colleague grumbled, "I never knew so many people started baking before 8 a.m."

Sometimes the errors were not the fault of the food editor. At the *Denver Post*, Dollaghan had a favorite recipe for apricot brandy chicken that she had prepared before with great success. But a couple of days after printing the recipe in the newspaper, she started to get phone calls. The oven doors were being blown off in the kitchens of a few readers who had prepared the dish. Members of newspaper management were concerned about what had happened and began an investigation. They interviewed the home cooks who had experienced the explosions and inquired with experts from chemistry departments at local universities. It turned out the readers had modified the recipe by adding extra brandy, then covered the casserole with foil—in essence, constructing a tiny bomb in the oven. "We, as a staff, including the legal department, were relieved to know it wasn't our fault," a columnist wrote.[28] Nevertheless, the incident led editors at the newspaper to come up with new names for the dish: Chicken Flambe, Coq au Blam, and Chicken Cacciatora, Tora, Tora.

Managing Test Kitchens: The Art and Science of Testing Recipes

The Iowa State College Press issued a textbook for home economics journalism in 1949 called *How to Write for Homemakers*. Although clearly aimed at female students, the preface used the male pronoun: "The factual writer, or journalist, deals with facts. His basic job is to inform—to pass along news, ideas, discoveries, and results of research." The authors then instructed the students to write in an interesting way to keep the attention of the homemaker. They concluded that they should approach their jobs in the same way any other journalist would: "As a writer of home economics material, you are a factual writer, a journalist. Your primary job is to pass along useful, factual, technical information to homemakers in a nontechnical way."[29]

Including recipes in the food sections meant involving an editorial decision-making process that generally involved a testing process of some sort, and then writing about the food and recipe in a way accessible by the average reader. Some of the recipes that were tested came from readers and others from food companies or industry groups. A 1973 master's thesis investigated the relationship between public relations practitioners and food editors at Midwestern newspapers regarding recipe use. The scholarship revealed varying approaches to testing recipes. Half of the editors responded that they did not test recipes before printing them. One said that she used a syndicated recipe column—which was likely Cicely Brownstone's Associated Press column. Another said that 90 percent of the recipes that she ran came from readers who she assumed they had tested in their own kitchens. Another said, "Our food editor tests two recipes at home each week for a Sunday recipe column. We run these regardless of how they turn out, explaining why they were a success or a failure."[30]

As early as the 1920s, newspapers and women's magazines were creating test kitchens that employed university-trained home economists. These testing centers were also called "bureaus" or "institutes." Magazines such as *Good Housekeeping* were known for testing and then endorsing products, though *Good Housekeeping* was investigated in 1939 for its testing practices. The Federal Trade Commission found that the claims made by the magazine were exaggerated. Publisher Hearst admitted that 40 percent of the tests were in error.[31]

The *Milwaukee Journal* began a test kitchen with its Housewives Institute in 1928 that was operated by the public relations' side.[32] As the impact of the Depression reached Milwaukee like the rest of the country, the institute's emphasis shifted to the economics of food. The institute partnered with the Marquette University sociology department and the Milwaukee Association of Commerce to describe a method to live well on $1,500 a year.[33] This was typical of metropolitan newspapers across the country. Following the Great Depression, food rationing became the reigning food topic as housewives were forced to use stamps to purchase many food items. Newspaper food editors were crucial in explaining the programs to home cooks.

The *New York Herald Tribune* had a Home Institute by the 1930s, located on the ninth floor of the *Herald Tribune*'s building, which included a test kitchen. The kitchen, equipped with the latest appliances donated by the manufacturers, was used to test recipes and create food to be photographed. It was overseen by Eloise Davison, who had earned a master's degree in home economics from Iowa State University. In March 1936, the *Herald Tribune* hired famed food writer Clementine Paddleford, with her journalism degree from Kansas State University and extensive food writing experience, as food editor.[34] While Paddleford collected recipes, it was the test kitchen cooks who made sure the recipes worked. The kitchen also tested new products, such as sixty-two dehydrated food products during World War II.[35] The paper published a cookbook in 1937, which included meal planning, based on recipes created in its test kitchen. The text included charts for issues such as how long to boil vegetables and explained which foods contained vitamins and the role of proteins. The introduction noted that access to foods such as strawberries, oranges, avocados, and fresh asparagus were now taken for granted by the American public. "During the past 25 years the United States has become a great food country," trumpeted the book.[36]

The *Los Angeles Times* has long had a test kitchen and once was a public place where touring groups would come by to watch the women cook. There were some downsides to having a test kitchen in the building. In the 1970s, Barbara Hansen was preparing an Indonesian dish using a shrimp paste that smelled so bad the facilities crew came up because they thought there was a gas leak. "No, it's just the shrimp," she responded.[37] Jeanne Voltz cited the need for a test kitchen as one of the reasons she left the *Miami Herald* for Los Angeles in 1960.

The *Cleveland Plain-Dealer* also had a test kitchen and a team of home economists to test recipes. In 1968, the food section published a cookbook devoted to meat and included recipes as well as educational information including where each cut of beef came from.[38] Cissy Gregg oversaw the test kitchen at the *Louisville Courier-Journal* with two assistants and a photography department. In 1951, the setup included a new experimental kitchen, a dining area, a food bar, an electronic kitchen bay, a gas kitchen bay, and a storage pantry. Gregg's biggest project was preparing a four-color layout for the Sunday magazine, and she would spend an entire day planning and preparing the meal for photographs.[39]

As the food editor of the *Chicago Tribune* for four decades, Church oversaw the largest food department of any newspaper, with five home economists and a kitchen assistant. The *Tribune* test kitchen opened in April 1949 with the newest kitchen equipment of the time and included a special space for food photography.[40] In what appears to be unique for the time, there were plenty of pictures of a meal being prepared step-by-step in the style of today's cooking blogs. She described these features as a "picture recipe."[41] The room was also lined with bookshelves to hold the many cookbooks needed for inspiration and reviewing, and the filing cabinets were brimming with letters and clippings. She noted that readers were regularly requesting recipes that had run years prior. A news editor commented in a 2007 *Tribune* article that the test kitchen's role in accuracy "reminds me that a newspaper's credibility may be measured more by the common place than its major stories and investigations."[42]

Some food editors tested recipes in their own home kitchens, such as Barbara Ostmann, Grace Hartley, and Jo Ann Vachule. In Palm Beach, Rosa Tusa had two kitchens in her home to test recipes. For newspapers that do not have test kitchens, there was still some recipe testing done. Later, at the *Milwaukee Journal Sentinel*, journalists tested recipes from home cooks and restaurant chefs, as well as cookbooks, if there was a suspicion that they might not work as written. Various *Journal Sentinel* staff members, both current and former, test a recipe in their own kitchen and are reimbursed for the ingredients. Current food editor Nancy Stohs wrote, "Most newspapers I know test at least some of the recipes they publish. The processes vary widely."[43]

Carol Haddix headed newspaper food sections in Detroit and in Chicago where both newspapers had a test kitchen. She described the testing process in her 2011 speech to the Culinary Historians of Chicago, listing the factors that needed to be considered with each recipe:

> Does it list all ingredients needed, in the order that you need them? Are the measurements standard and precise? Do the directions seem logical and clear? Are the steps numbered in the correct order? Is the cooking time and temperature accurate? Is the yield of the recipe (in cups, quarts, or number of servings, for example) right on? And most important, once the recipe has been followed exactly, does the final dish taste good? And would we make this recipe at home? The best recipes meet all these criteria and also have something extra, a "wow" factor that lasts in your memory.[44]

In her talk, Haddix said what many other food editors had echoed—the most difficult recipes to test came from restaurant chefs. Trying to translate their measurements and techniques so home cooks could make their recipes was a challenge, calling for testing and retesting again—not to mention making allowances for the processes that a home cook would likely not do, such as creating large batches of homemade stock.[45] At other times, it was a matter of translating portions, a common challenge for Dorothy Chapman at the *Orlando Sentinel* and the theme park restaurants in her city. "She would request a recipe for the column and our yield would be for hundreds, not a household of four," recalled former Disney publicist Suzanne McGovern. "I would have to break it down with the chefs and she would grill me until I got it right."[46]

HOME ECONOMISTS AND MID-CENTURY FOOD STYLES

The recipes from the 1950s and 1960s are sometimes criticized as simply not producing anything good to eat. Clearly, a lot of Jell-O was consumed and soup-based casseroles were prepared. While the purpose of this book is not to debate the quality of the food, the reality of what was on America's kitchen tables was more complex than a series of Jell-O molds, and that is reflected in the food sections.

In 1954, the *Milwaukee Journal* had a color food section that appeared every Thursday, as did many other American newspapers. And the section was large—up to twenty-two pages—thanks to those numerous full-page grocery ads. Regardless of whether they had access to a test kitchen, the journalists in the women's section were testing recipes in their own kitchens. The typical stories were about food preparation, such as Peggy Daum's 1956 story about creating holiday meals.[47] Others were about entertaining, like a 1957 Daum story clearly aimed at stay-at-home mothers busy with their club work.[48] Another story about entertaining appeared the following year based on family customs.[49] Food news included a story about the 1954 milk price wars, when a gallon of milk cost 68 cents,[50] and a 1956 story about the introduction of fortified bread.[51]

A look at what was recommended for homemakers in Miami in the late 1960s demonstrates a mix of foods. A fall-themed food feature was about recipes with a "foreign accent." Virginia Heffington included the dishes Aquello e Annellini (lamb shanks and white kidney beans),[52] Boeuf à la Bourguignonne (Burgundy beef stew), and Sauerbraten (German pot roast). She reassured her readers, "Food with a foreign flair does not have to be highly seasoned, hard to fix, or even overly expensive."[53] Another feature recommended various kinds of "Hawaiian Chicken" that were aimed at budget-minded cooks. Heffington also recommended recipes such as Chicken à la Grape, Cherry Chicken, and Plum Chicken to be served over rice.[54]

Elinor Lee wrote in 1970 that popular foods for March included peanuts, canned pears, rice, and broiler-fryers. Chicken was no longer an austerity dish, she wrote; rather, it was becoming a standard meal choice:

> The fact that plentiful poultry is reasonably priced is a boon to bud-get-conscious homemakers. But you know it hasn't been too many years ago when chicken was considered quite a luxury, to be served for "company" or Sunday family dinners. Chicken was used as a symbol of prosperity in Herbert Hoover's presidential campaign. A "chicken in every pot and a car in every garage" was the slogan.[55]

A popular cookbook during the 2012 holiday season was *Tiny Food Party*,[56] a return to a style of food that was popular in the 1960s and into the 1970s—the hors d'oeuvre. In 1968, Heffington wrote about "mini-bites" as part of her appetizer party scene, all intended to be served in small portions, and included recipes for London Broil Bites, Mini-Chicken, and Marinated Vegetable Patch.[57]

Steak Diane was a popular dish in the 1950s and 1960s that often appeared in food sections under several variations. Nickerson's 1953 story about the dish, which included three different recipes made by different restaurants, was a good example. She contended that while there was no official American meal, steak came close.[58] She also wrote about the origins of the favorite New Orleans dish, jambalaya. The dish was a popular suggestion for buffet dinners, a trend of the time. In the story, she even recommended the proper beer and wine to be served.[59] Seafood was a focus of another Nickerson story in 1953, a long piece about the seafood industry in America that included several kinds of fish, mussels, and shrimp. In addition, she wrote about local fish markets in New York City.[60]

The popular Thanksgiving soup-based green bean casserole had its beginning thanks to Cecily Brownstone. In 1955, she attended a dinner at the home of wealthy Floridian John Snively. The meal was a replica of a dinner prepared earlier for Iranian royalty that included a green bean casserole made with sauce and mushrooms. She took notes about it and asked the test kitchen at Campbell Soup to create a version for home cooks. Her story ran under the headline "Beans Fit for an Iranian

Queen" and included the recipe. *Saveur* included an article about the origins of the dish in 2007.[61]

American meals in this era almost always ended with a dessert, usually made from scratch, a sign that a wife and mother cared. In 1948, a recipe feature "Cake of the Week" was introduced at the *Chicago Tribune*. Ruth Ellen Church was quoted, "My staff and I have known for a long time that women love cakes, but we were somewhat surprised at the popularity of this weekly cake presentation." As proof, she noted that two hundred readers called the newspaper on the day that the recipe for Orange Lemon Sunshine Cake appeared too blurry to read.

After the war, advances in food preparation led food companies to find easier ways to make a cake, but that was the difficulty with mixes. Did this mean a homemaker loved her family less? A 1950 study looked at the quality and efficiency of cake mixes versus those made from scratch. Researchers found a variety of opinions in taste and texture among the two styles,[62] but by 1958 the cake mixes were considered a success story.[63]

Despite the increasing popularity of mixes, readers still requested original recipes for cakes. In fact, according to Brownstone, the most popular requests for recipes were for desserts—usually cakes and cookies. Specific requests came in for brown sugar brownies, carrot cake, and fruitcakes. At the *Detroit Free Press*, readers requested recipes for both a white fruit cake and a dark fruit cake. Other requests came in for a Mystery Chocolate Cake with coconut-pecan frosting, Wacky Cake, and Tell-Your-Neighbor-Cake with butter frosting. A 1974 informal poll of food editors found that Los Angeles was unique in its ten-year love affair with carrot cake.[64]

Thanks to investigative reporting, Marian Burros of the *Washington Times* learned that the wedding cake for President Lyndon Johnson's daughter was eight feet high and had to be carried to the White House by the Secret Service through the back roads of Washington. She said, "I had two scoops that drove [press secretary] Liz Carpenter right up the wall."[65] In 1971, the Nixon White House found itself in hot water with the food community when the recipe for Tricia Nixon's wedding cake did not turn out for home cooks.[66]

Cakes made with alcohol also were common in food sections in the 1950s and 1960s. Recipes with liquor were heavily promoted by the industry. Cecily Brownstone of the Associated Press said that liquor companies would regularly send samples as encouragement or offer trips as incentive, and while she never used brand names, she regularly wrote about whiskey and cognac as a recipe additive. "I think food editors increased the consumption of cognac in this country, no doubt about it," Brownstone said.[67] The publicity people were not always so savvy. Ostman recalled receiving a recipe for Kentucky Bourbon Cake from the Bourbon Institute. The only problem was that it did not include bourbon. She called and was told that the cake needed one cup; a week later she received a revised version and this time the recipe included two cups of bourbon.[68] In 1962, *Washington Post* food editor Lee shared a recipe for Kentucky Bourbon Pecan Cake that she took from her grandmother's ancient cookbook.[69]

There was one dish that never went out of style—pancakes, along with its cousins waffles, crepes, and omelets. Paddleford wrote about pre-packaged blintzes in 1949.[70] In 1962, Ruth Ellen Church of the *Chicago Tribune* shared the story of Shrove Tuesday, which took place the day before the beginning of Lent. It is also known as Pancake Day, and on that day in Liberal, Kansas, women ran a race while holding a skillet in which they had to flip a pancake three times. She wrote her pancake cookbook because pancakes were becoming increasingly popular as a food choice, and she cited a survey that found the favorites were buttermilk, blueberry, buckwheat, and crepes. The recipes and stories came from her newspaper column.[71] In Boston, Dorothy Crandall wrote about men making pancakes a part of a competition.[72]

HEALTH AND NUTRITION

Numerous research studies regarding nutrition and health were published in the 1940s and 1950s and food companies were quick to respond with new products. Likewise in the mid-century decades government research produced vast amounts of data regarding nutrition. Home economists helped homemakers make sense of the new items on their grocery shelves and the new information coming from government and researchers alike.

In one 1946 story, Jane Nickerson addressed the trend of adding vitamins to ice cream. Nickerson included interviews with experts who questioned the practice.[73] In another 1946 story, she addressed the

nutritional value of Florida grapefruit and orange juices, based on research by the US Department of Agriculture. The study found that
making the juice in advance would not reduce the amount of vitamin C
in the drink.[74]

The work of the federal agencies, along with the food research being
conducted at Los Angeles universities, meant that the content of Voltz's
food section in Los Angeles went well beyond including only recipes. In
several stories, Voltz covered the FDA as it prepared the first guidelines
on nutrition for processed foods in 1971.[75] A few years later she covered
the FDA-required nutrition labeling guidelines, attending various
meetings with consumer advocates, scientists, and food industry representatives over what the requirements should be. In one story, she
described the new recommended daily allowance guidelines that replaced the 1941 minimum daily requirement[76] as "a mixed blessing—or
at least [it] brought mixed responses."[77]

In 1972, Voltz wrote about a California law that would require enrichment in grains to improve nutritional value. About two-thirds of the
states already had similar laws, and California was debating possible
legislation. She quoted a home economist who had lobbied for passage
of the bill: "Since so many people use highly processed foods without
really knowing what they contain, this can be important in improving
total nutrition."[78] For the story, Voltz also conducted an investigation of
the foods in the local grocery store, looking for what was printed on the
labels and reporting the results, exactly the kind of reporting that Senator Frank Moss had called for the previous year.

In an article the following year, Voltz questioned the overconsumption of sugar in Americans' diets. She researched the problem by examining the ingredients list on different packaged foods and noting the
often hidden ingredients.[79] For another story, she interviewed a nutrition expert from the American Medical Association, who said malnutrition was a result of poor eating habits rather than a poor food supply; he
credited newspapers with providing important information on nutrition.[80] Voltz also trumpeted the "new cooking" that emphasized the use
of fresh vegetables to maximize their nutritional content.

The content of commercial bread was also a hot topic at this time.
People were still baking bread at home during the Depression and
leading up to World War II; the *Chicago Tribune* published a booklet in
1939 with ninety-nine bread recipes.[81] But by the 1930s and 1940s,

Americans were consuming more calories from industrial white bread than from any other food. Home economists and nutritionists were concerned.

The answer seemed to be enriching bread. Home economists had been attempting to educate Americans about vitamins since the 1910s. Yet a Gallup Poll taken in 1940 found that only 9 percent of Americans knew what vitamins were. A poll taken a year later found that only 16 percent could distinguish between calories and vitamins.[82]

A 1947 story by Nickerson in the *New York Times* addressed a group that was against buying enriched bread. Instead, the group advocated for homemakers to bake their own bread using whole grains. Decades before the term would become popular, Nickerson wrote about the amount of gluten in the bread dough. Included with the story was a recipe for Rolled Oats Whole Wheat Bread.[83] By 1953, the bread debate involved the addition of vitamin D to increase the absorption of calcium. She began by writing about the companies that were now using the practice. She went on to quote a nutrition expert on the subject and wrote that although "he was not opposed to it, he could not see any real reason to do it."[84] A 1956 *Milwaukee Journal* story explained the introduction of fortified bread.[85]

In the 1960s and early 1970s, a mix of the counterculture and a health food movement led people finally to return to making their own bread. In the *Cleveland Plain-Dealer*, nearly twenty stories about bread were published in 1966.[86] In 1970, Voltz wrote in the *Los Angeles Times*, "For a time, home bread baking almost disappeared from cookery. At best, it survived only as a grandmotherly anachronism, about as practical and practiced as crocheting pillow-slip edging or churning butter. Today, bread making is enjoying an enthusiastic revival."[87] That same year, Daum profiled Tom Farley of the food division of Milwaukee Public Schools, who was being honored for forty years of service. His program was ahead of its time in terms of quality. "We buy locally," Daum quoted Farley. "We believe in quality. We do all our own baking of breads, rolls, cakes, pies, cookies. We haven't bought a loaf of bread in 10 years."[88] James Beard wrote about bread in his newspaper column, "Beard on Food," declaring, "The disappearance of the neighborhood baker and the pushing of those abominable, tasteless, elastic loaves that fill the supermarket shelves are warnings that the day is coming when we will be forced to make our own bread."[89]

FOOD PRICES

Household budgeting had always been an important topic in home economics. Homemakers were the key readers of the food sections, and food journalists tackled the economics of homemaking on a regular basis. For example, in 1947, Nickerson reported that beef prices were on the rise but that the cost of vegetables dipped toward prewar levels.[90] One common way to track the cost of food was through the annual cost of Thanksgiving turkeys. For example, in 2012, the cost of Thanksgiving dinner was estimated to be $50.[91] In 1955, it was estimated that a family of six could eat a Thanksgiving dinner for between $6.10 and $10.73, and that included the pumpkin chiffon pie for dessert.[92] Food editors also regularly cited government and industry reports about food prices—the economist role of home economists.

Beighle French wrote that to determine the credibility of food prices, she took a food stamp user to a Cleveland supermarket, with a calculator, to see if she could figure out the most nutritious buys within her budget. When Ostman wrote about the popular dish Beef Wellington, she provided two versions in a 1969 column. One was for classic Wellington with beef tenderloin, and one was for an economical Wellington with a boneless chuck roast. Years later, she suggested that readers could make the dish even easier with Pepperidge Farm frozen puff pastry.[93]

In the 1970s, the country was experiencing a recession and women were encouraged to take extra care while shopping at the grocery store. As a potential solution to the hunger issue, Voltz published stories addressing how to prepare a nutritious meal on a budget, including one about the ease of preparation and economic value of meatballs. "For only a few cents a serving, you can offer an epicurean treat," she wrote.[94] Other stories also noted how cooks could save money and cut corners on groceries.

An Indiana newspaper provided many examples of the focus on budgeting. Articles might suggest using low-cost ingredients like grapefruit and cottage cheese in dishes.[95] Ann Hamman told her *Evansville (IN) Courier* readers about particular produce that was cheaper such as peaches and cucumbers.[96] She explained to readers that buying in bulk might be more inexpensive in the long run.[97] In other cases, she wrote that packaging was the reason behind different prices.[98] In Las Vegas, food editor Ann Valder worked with a local nutritionist to plan low-cost meals based on commodity foods and foods in season. She explained why she developed this series: "With the price of food making it almost imperative that family interest in budget meal be increased."[99]

HUNGER ISSUES

The Food and Drug Administration was active in the 1960s and 1970s as more research on nutrition was conducted and the interest in consumer issues grew. Most noticeable was the 1969 White House Conference on Food, Nutrition and Health, which would change the course of food policy in the country. According to a government report based on the meeting, "Several landmark policy efforts with profound and lasting effects emerged from this conference, including expansions of the food stamp program, food labeling, and the school lunch program."[100]

Dorothy Crandall wrote a 1969 story about what was contained in the average school hot lunch in Boston. She described the meal as a hamburger, a tossed salad, beans, and a glass or two of milk with either fruit or a cookie for dessert. In addition to speaking to local school leaders, she also interviewed state and national hot lunch experts, and quoted one expert as saying, "You can't teach a child who is too hungry to listen."[101] In 1972, Voltz wrote about proposed legislation in California that would have required healthier school lunches. One of the most progressive laws in the country at the time, the bill ultimately passed so that students would have hot lunches. The story examined food as an educational issue, noting that students would be more able to learn if they were well fed.[102]

At the *Philadelphia Bulletin*, the food editor followed up on the White House meeting by going to the local schools and investigating how the menus were developed. According to women's page editor Marjorie Paxson, they "really got what turned out to be a fascinating story about how they stretched pennies." They learned that the school district sought surplus foods from other places to include in the lunch program. For example, a New Jersey company had extra cranberries and they were given to the Philadelphia schools.[103]

Voltz wrote about the problem of hunger in America in 1972. Her story was a follow-up from a federal study that outlined pockets of malnutrition in the nation. She began by quoting a senator who complained that there was talk about hunger but no action being taken. "California's unwritten nutrition policy is at a crossroads," she declared. At risk were children who were hungry by noon and pregnant women who could not afford to eat properly.[104] Another story Voltz reported on was from Mexico City about a meeting of the International Congress of Nutrition on malnutrition. In examining the problem, she interviewed a professor at the University of California who pointed out the common misconception that "the poor generally select foods more wisely than the affluent."[105] In another article that year, Voltz examined food deficiencies on the nearby Havasupi Indian Reservation. Voltz began with the story of Gene George, a coordinator with the Food Advocates, who rode on horseback to the reservation to explain the details of the food stamp programs and the problem of hunger in the community.[106]

ORGANIC FOOD AND THE HEALTH FOOD MOVEMENT

Concerns about the quality of food and the impact of chemicals on food stretches back decades. The counterculture movement helped create the interest in natural foods, and by the 1970s the conversation reached mainstream masses. Food journalists brought their training and expertise to bear on what was not only a cultural movement but an important and complex nutritional topic. Jeanne Voltz's stories on natural foods preceded the current organic food revolution by a few decades, making several references to organic food in the early 1970s, especially in relation to food safety. Voltz advised that food consumers demand organic foods at their supermarkets for better value and safety.[107] Later in the story, she asked a question that remains a conundrum within the food industry: How is "organic" defined? "What is organic, organically shipped or organically grown food?" she asked.[108] There were no clear guidelines at the time, and they remained ambiguous until the passage of the Organic Foods Production Act of 1990. The question of what the term "organic" meant was also raised in a story about grocers facing off with angry customers.[109] At a local meeting, the shoppers accused the businesses of having poor-quality foods and not weighing food honestly. The theme of the meeting was opening communication with the consumers and also requesting that the media take the topic of food safety seriously.[110]

Voltz also covered the results of a three-year study about the health food movement and organic food. Central to the research was the question about the sociological aspects of the movement. The researcher found tensions between the old-line health food advocates and "hippies." The growth of the counterculture community in Berkeley clearly had an impact on food in the state. Voltz noted that decades earlier the increase of health food stores was a reaction against the massive US food industry. Experts believed the trend of health food would continue in the future.[111]

Voltz capitalized on this wave of interest and wrote the *Natural Food Cookbook* in 1973 based on her newspaper reporting about natural foods, stating in the introduction that "the home cook who bakes good honest bread, makes a fragrant soup or stew from scratch or prepares her own homemade pie is regarded as the culinary genius of the 1970s."[112] In the book, she criticized the growing trend of loading up processed foods with sugar, especially breakfast cereal. She cited a new product called Breakfast Squares that was supposed to be a cookie intended to take the place of a bowl of cereal. "It contained more sugar than any other ingredient," according to Voltz, "and hydrogenated shortening, the hard type implicated in cardiovascular disease, was the second most predominant ingredient."[113] Voltz's expertise in the growing health food movement was a significant one at the time.[114]

THE DECLINE OF HOME ECONOMICS AS A FIELD

Home economics had made important contributions to American culture on many fronts: nutritional, technological, and social. And food journalists were often the ones who brought the study of home economics to everyday readers. But as traditional gender roles for women were beginning to be questioned in the late 1960s and early 1970s, the field increasingly came under attack. Betty Friedan's *The Feminist Mystique* was published and aimed at middle-class homemakers—the same ones who read the food pages. Friedan, who got her start in the women's pages of newspapers, wrote about the lack of respect for women's roles. She examined the lack of fulfillment that a college-educated wife and mother could find in a spotless house. In these and other writing, feminists began to question the role of home economics and its emphasis on the domestic arts in limiting the opportunities for women.

It was a perfect storm that led to the end of home economics as it had been known for decades. According to historian Goldstein, "Reacting to both feminist cries against domesticity and attacks from male administrators, many college home economics programs took steps to eliminate the word 'home' from their names." This transition began in 1960 and within twenty years, there were thirty different names for the field. A committee was created after realizing that they needed to make changes in response to the awareness spread by feminists. Academic Virginia Trotter said, "We've really had our heads in the sand and haven't been listening."[115]

In 1972, influential feminist Robin Morgan addressed the Home Economics Association Conference in Denver. It may have seemed an odd choice given her anti-establishment views. Yet it is clear that the home economics group was looking to address the changing gender roles. In the letter regarding her contract, it is explained that she was invited because of her interest in daycare centers on college campuses. While that familial role was part of the invitation, she was also intended to be the "radical" voice on the panel.[116] In going through Morgan's papers, it is clear that she gave the kind of address that was expected. Morgan said she was there "addressing the enemy" and that to help end the oppression of women, they should quit their jobs as home economists. "You run the risk of becoming obsolete," she warned the women. "Those institutions that home economics has been hooked into are dying, and they are dying even without the feminist revolution."[117]

The organization took her message seriously. In a personal letter to Morgan, the organization's public relations person thanked her for her talk. The spokesperson also indicated that she was frustrated, as "I feel I didn't really communicate very effectively on what home economics really is."[118] A task force was created to examine the field's reputation, and a copy of Morgan's talk was included in the organization's journal, as was a response from the task force. It was the beginning of the end of home economics as it had been known. It was something that women's page editors would also experience by the early 1970s.

6

THE RESTAURANT REVIEWER
AS JOURNALIST

In the decades of the 1950s through 1970s, restaurant reviews remained a gray area for women journalists. On the one hand, reviews were often featured in the women's pages. On the other hand, newspapers often preferred male reviewers, and even some restaurants excluded women during certain times of the day (and occasionally at all times).

THE EARLY DAYS OF NEWSPAPER
RESTAURANT REVIEWS

Many hotels in metropolitan areas had quality restaurants by the 1940s and reporters were there to write about them. During that decade, the *Houston Post*'s gossip columnist set up a desk in the Shamrock Hotel. In addition to writing about the people, what they ate was also reported. That included baked Alaska and French-inspired vichyssoise.[1] According to *New York Times* food editor Jane Nickerson, there were more than 21,000 restaurants in her city by 1949. She wrote, "They serve to the city's residents and guests foods in so many languages as to rob the city of any one set of distinctive dishes." She went on mention Polish, French, Italian, Chinese, and German restaurants.[2]

Women's page editor Marj Heyduck noted that in Dayton, Ohio, residents ate at a variety of restaurants in the 1950s. Eateries included seafood, Chinese, Hungarian, and Italian specialties.[3] Washington, DC, had its first sushi restaurant in the 1950s and had numerous Vietnamese restaurants in the 1970s.[4] In 1951, Nickerson wrote about the menu on the popular Baltimore & Ohio railroad's dining cars for the *New York Times*. In the article, she profiled a colorful character in Colonel White, who oversaw the railroad's kitchen and shared his opinions about how his cheap patrons ate their meals. For example, he noted Americans' interest in free items such as rolls: "I always say that if you were going to give an American a free passport to hell, he'd probably take it because it was free."[5] She wrote a 1957 restaurant review of Chateau Henry IV, located in the Hotel Alrae. She described the Venetian stained glass windows, said to be about four hundred years old, and the prices of the various dishes. She also recommended the thin pancakes served hot with seafood as an hors d'oeuvre and, for the main dish, filet of sole meunière, veal kidney, and brains in black butter.[6]

In Orlando, the growth of the restaurant community was largely the result of Disney World opening in 1971 and the development of a culinary community built on international foods. It was in that year that *Orlando Sentinel* food editor Dorothy Chapman started reviewing restaurants—the first time it was done at the newspaper. She was influential, according to chefs in the city. "We [chefs] gave her a lot of respect because she gave us a lot of respect," said longtime Orlando restaurateur Major Jarman. "She was fair. Everyone took her comments as constructive criticism and learned from them." Fellow chef Johnny Rivers agreed: "I think Dorothy was more than just a food editor. She was a mentor to many of us and raised the bar of expectation in Central Florida."[7]

Duncan Hines: Before the Cake Mix

The reviewing of restaurants has a lengthy history in America. Likely the first restaurant reviewer was Duncan Hines—in the years before he went on to help found the cake mix company that bears his name. A traveling salesman, he would take notes about where he ate while on the road. In 1935, he and his wife included the short reviews on the back of their Christmas card. The following year, he published a booklet of his reviews in the booklet "Adventures in Good Eating," which went on to be published in forty-six editions. The reviews were brief and focused on the food. For example, in 1939, he wrote about Colonel Sanders's café in Corbin, Kentucky. (This was before Sanders began his Kentucky Fried Chicken franchises.) Hines said it was a good place to eat "sizzling steaks, fried chicken, country hams and hot biscuits, 60 cents to $1." He collected recipes from the places where he dined in that led to a three-times-a-week syndicated newspaper column, "Adventures in Good Eating at Home."[8] In 1952, Duncan Hines's bread and later cake mixes were introduced and his work in the bakery field would overshadow his reviewing fame.[9]

Hines liked both fancy food and everyday diners. In his memoir, he wrote about his friendship with Claudius C. Philippe, vice president and catering manager of the famed New York Waldorf Hotel. (He was also the second husband of food writer Poppy Cannon.) Hines noted that if ink ran through the veins of a printer, then wines and sauces ran through Philippe's veins. Furthermore, he wrote, "Philippe's philosophy regarding food and its enjoyment is closely akin to my own. We share the idea that dining is an almost-forgotten art in this country, and we have each tried to restore it."[10]

Other Reviewers

Many restaurant reviews did not consider themselves food experts. Mitchell Davis noted, "The lack of any expertise required to be a restaurant critic speaks in part to the lowly status reviewing food has held in the newspaper's hierarchy of culture beats."[11] Yet food was not part of the culture beats traditionally found in newspapers and instead has its roots in the women's pages. In terms of expertise, at least in the post–World War II era, many food critics did have backgrounds in home economics.

While Claiborne has been widely lauded, his predecessor at the newspaper, Jane Nickerson, also reviewed restaurants. Her dinner partners often included James Beard and Associated Press food editor Cecily Brownstone.[12] At that point, the reviewers ate for free at the restaurants. It was a practice that changed after the Charles Van Doren television scandal in the late 1950s—made famous by the 1994 movie *Quiz Show*. Van Doren confessed to cheating on the popular quiz program *Twenty-One*, and in the aftermath, many media outlets, including the

New York Times and the Associated Press, strengthened their ethics policies.

Clementine Paddleford was reviewing restaurants for the *New York Herald Tribune* and newspaper insert *This Week*. She visited local eateries and those in other cities by the 1950s. In the book, *Dining Out*, about restaurant reviewing, Gael Greene stated, "Clementine Paddleford was writing about restaurants before me. Food was considered women's work."[13] Paddleford wrote about the history of Waldorf Salad and Lindy's Cheesecake in her city. Often in her own plane, she flew to different cities to write about home cooks and restaurants. While in Milwaukee, she wrote about the city's famed Mader's restaurant, which had been serving German food since 1903. She described the history of the restaurant and included recipes for Sauerbraten, potato dumplings, and cheese torte.[14]

In 1964, the *New York Herald Tribune* published a collection of columns from its top writers, including Paddleford, who noted that "restaurants are my beat." Of the 18,000 eateries in the city, she detailed her hundred favorites. Rather than being negative about a restaurant's failings, she focused on what was best. In the French category, she recommended Café Argenteuil, writing, "My favorite appetizer there is Baked Clams done with garlic and herbs, with a dash of lemon and Pernod." She wrote that at Le Veau d'Or, 90 percent of the customers spoke French. She gave three stars to Italian Pavilion. Of Michael's Pub, she wrote, "When a pub becomes famous in New York City you can bet your buttons it's quite a place." Rather than being anonymous, she went into the kitchen to speak with the chef. At Karachi Restaurant, she described the chef bending over his curry pots.[15]

Some reviewers traveled the country to review restaurants in the style of Duncan Hines and later Clementine Paddleford. As Jeanne Voltz wrote, "Tasting around the country turns up, in Vermont, chicken pies as rich and creamy as Grandma's; in Maine, fish chowders and baked beans prepared as they were in Colonial times; in Massachusetts fishing villages, soup brewed to the rule of Portuguese settlers."[16] The food section normalized the otherwise exotic dishes, the growth of restaurants, and the increasing trend of eating out. The dishes were unique to the demographics of those who lived in the readership area versus national food-related magazines.

Voltz was reviewing restaurants for the *Los Angeles Times* in the 1960s. At the beginning of the decade, Voltz reviewed various local restaurants. Many of these restaurants introduced readers to food from different areas of the world, albeit often Americanized versions. For example, in February 1961, Voltz wrote, "A jaunt through Chinatown, then dinner at Gen. Lee Man Jen Low is a low-cost, if short, substitute for a trip to faraway lands."[17] The local analysis made a foreign-seeming dish sound less intimidating. Later that month, Voltz wrote, "Don't let the name Andre's of Beverly Hills mislead you. Andre's food and Chianti bottle décor is more Italian than French."[18] In April, she featured another European-themed restaurant, writing, "Diners who appreciate the warm spice of Spanish food will find it at Casa Madrid on La Cienega."[19] In July, she took on a new culture: "The nice, deftly seasoned foods of Old Russia are specialties of the Moskva Cliff on Ventura Blvd. in Studio City."[20]

One of the best-known female restaurant critics was Elaine Tait of the *Philadelphia Inquirer*. She had a background covering food news, including a recap of the Choate cereal controversy. She was best known for her restaurant criticism and ended up writing restaurant reviews for thirty-five years. Upon retirement, she said of the job, "I didn't realize how exhausting and invasive it was until I was out of it." She had a wheat allergy that prevented her from eating too much pasta or cake. She recalled, "You have to have a full battery of people to go out with you, and it has to be a convenient location and time for them. People tend to get very blasé about it after a few times."[21]

Tait wrote about the difficulties in learning about the new flavors of Asian and Indian dishes. She went to Asian markets in her city and bought ingredients like lime leaves and galangal so that she could recognize the flavors. A friend also taught her about the flavors of Indian dishes. Tait spent one summer cooking different kinds of fish in various ways. She said, "It helped me identify what freshness tasted like and what the textures were like."[22] This led to better descriptions in her restaurant reviews.

THE CHALLENGES OF REVIEWING

When eating out is expensive, trendy, or both, newspaper readers often seek out an expert opinion from the restaurant critic. It can be a contentious job. Former *Boston Globe* food critic Alison Arnett wrote a negative review that led the restaurant owner to call her editor and threaten to get a gun. She noted, "It's part of the job."[23] Another critic observed that when she writes a negative review, "it will be seen as a personal insult to everyone who likes it."[24]

Reviewing restaurants differs from typical journalism because as critics, these journalists can offer opinions. There is no specific training for being a restaurant critic, as many have written. According to a column in the *Chicago Tribune*, the skills needed for a critic include "knowing how to complete a sentence and articulate your gastronomic experience—good or bad." In addition, a critic "should possess keen reporting skills."[25] One reviewer noted the importance of checking restaurant inspection reports before a visit to the restaurant, for example.[26] Pete Wells, restaurant critic at the *New York Times*, wrote a column for the magazine *Food & Wine* before joining the newspaper. He wrote that he is satisfied that the only qualification needed for writing about food is an interest in the topic.[27]

The *Village Voice*'s restaurant critic Robert Sietsema said that being a journalist was the best preparation for the job. In his words, "We're reporters who happen to write about food." He added that his editor has forbidden certain terms and clichéd phrases like "food porn." *Washington Post* restaurant reviewer Tom Sietsema said that he received his training from his predecessor Phyllis Richman: "I learned what a good story was. I got to test the bulk of the recipes for the paper. I was making no money but I was eating very well." (The men with the same last name are often confused for one another; they are fifth cousins.[28]) Richman also said that journalism was central to her approach to restaurant reviewing. In an interview, she said, "I hardly ever use the first person in my reviews. Perhaps it's out of some traditional journalistic priggishness on my part. But I think it's appropriate that there be a distance and a sense of objectivity in that distance. I think that the review shouldn't be about me."[29]

Los Angeles Times and *New York Times* restaurant reviewer Ruth Reichl recommended working in restaurants as training for food critics, as she had done. She wrote that *New York Times* editor A. J. Liebling was wrong when he said that to write about food only requires an appetite. She wrote, "It's not enough. You need to have a lot of experience. You need to bite off as much of the world as you can."[30] None of the newspaper food editors seemed to have worked in restaurants, although Grace Barr and a friend owned a shop where they sold baked goods to help her family through the Great Depression. She went on to become the food editor of the *Orlando Sentinel* in the 1960s. The newspaper would not have a restaurant critic until the 1970s, when Disney World helped create a culinary community.

Other reviewers said that the primary role of a reviewer is to entertain. Reichl wrote, "Ultimately, I think my goal is to entertain people. If they're not entertained, they won't read you."[31] And, for that reason, at times, restaurant reviewing was not handled by the food section. Instead, it was covered by the entertainment sections.[32] In Los Angeles, newspaper food journalists said that there were few good restaurants in the city until the 1980s. *Times* food editor Rose Dosti said when she arrived at the newspaper in 1964, "There were a handful of very good restaurants that catered to celebrities for the most part." These restaurants were covered by the Entertainment or Calendar section but the food editors did write about the smaller ethnic restaurants that were developing in the city.[33] *New York Times* food critic Frank Bruni said that his reviews "are not about the menu and the food, though both are certainly present; rather, they are about the cultural phenomenon of restaurants."[34] A comparison of restaurant reviewing to other newspaper reviewers such as books or plays has been made.[35] But reviewing restaurants was not always accorded the same respect because it was associated with the women's pages.

Most of the major *New York Times* restaurant reviews have documented their lives through memoirs. Craig Claiborne became the food editor of the *Times* in 1957 and began using the star reviewing system in 1962. He wrote his memoir in 1982, and a biography of Claiborne was published in 2013.[36] Both documented his significance in reviewing. Ruth Reichl has published several memoirs. *Garlic and Sapphires* examined the challenges of reviewing in New York City and her later lack of enthusiasm for the role. She noted that, unlike the women's section community of the 1950s and the 1960s, there was a more individual structure under the new feature-based section: "The Style section was an odd little enclave. My colleagues tend to make themselves scarce."[37] Mimi Sheraton, who came after Claiborne, wrote a memoir about her years as a reviewer. She also documented that gender stood in the way of her initially being considered for the position. In *Eating My Words*, Sheraton wrote that when Claiborne (who took over from Jane Nickerson in 1957) left the newspaper in 1972, she and other female New York food writers were not considered as replacements: "Neither I nor any other female food writer I knew was given an interview for his job, no matter her credentials. (If any were interviewed, I still would like to hear about it.)"[38] Sheraton was eventually hired for the position, but it is telling that after so much time and so much that women in food journalism were accomplishing, gender could still stand in the way in 1972.

THE ETHICS OF RESTAURANT REVIEWING

To understand the importance of anonymity in reviewing, consider a relatively recent example. In December 2010, the *Los Angeles Times* published an article in its food section about the public outing of its food critic. This is the lead: "Well, that was interesting. A couple of days before Christmas, one of the owners of the new Beverly Hills restaurant Red Medicine created a firestorm by confronting *Times* restaurant critic S. Irene Virbila while she was waiting for a table, snapping her picture, kicking her and her party out of the restaurant and then posting the picture on the Internet for all to see." The writer noted that by the next morning, more than fifteen years of working to remain anonymous were destroyed.[39]

Like the reviewers of the future, Duncan Hines tried not to be recognized so that he did not get preferential treatment. For example, he used a photo that was two decades old on his book jacket. He did, however, ask to see the kitchen after his meal. He wrote, "Food is a matter of taste. Good food is fresh, carefully prepared under sanitary conditions."[40] Staying anonymous is a key to ethical reviewing for many critics. This practice is to ensure no special treatment by the restaurant management. The goal is to experience the restaurant the way an average customer would experience it. To demonstrate how different a dining experience can be when a critic is known, consider *New York Times* critic Ruth Reichl, who had two different experiences when she ate in disguise and later as herself; she wrote about both meals.

It is common for restaurants to keep a photo of the area newspaper critic in the kitchen.[41] In St. Petersburg, Florida, Ruth Gray wore hats and scarves and ducked inside the ladies' room to take notes and stay inconspicuous. The anonymity was needed, as some restaurants had her photo on the wall in the kitchen. When one server called her by name, saying the meal was on the house, she did not write the review. To keep her photo from being put in kitchens, one critic noted that she avoided "cameras like a vampire does the sun."[42] The need for anonymity is an American concept. French critics call ahead to let a restaurant know they are coming. In Britain, the photos of restaurant critics run next to their columns.[43]

The reviewers typically make reservations under false names and various phone numbers. They pay using cash or credit cards in other names. They often bring guests so that several dishes can be sampled. According to current *Los Angeles Times* food editor Russ Parsons, "This ensures that a restaurant has minimum warning that a critic is coming, on the theory that there is little that can be done once he or she is in the door. There is no way for a chef to dream up some super-elaborate dish or acquire higher-quality ingredients at the last minute."[44] However, when *New York Times* food critic Mimi Sheraton was asked what a chef could do on short notice to improve a meal, her answer was "Just about everything."[45]

Some of the restaurant critics wore disguises while dining. Mimi Sheraton worked hard to preserve her anonymity for as long as possible. She turned down all invitations to restaurant-related events, wore a wide-brimmed hat for press photos, and never appeared on television without a disguise.[46] Ruth Reichl not only ate in disguise but also created different characters, which she outlined in her memoir *Garlic and Sapphires*.[47] The concept of disguises may be a gendered one. Wells wrote that he does not wear a disguise, as the hair pieces for men tend to be of poor quality and draw attention to the person: "Anybody can spot those from across the street. The whole point of a disguise is to make you inconspicuous."[48]

The restaurant reviewer's job differs greatly from the typical work of a food journalist. "It's a lonely job," said Tait. "You're covering a beat, but of course, how can you cover a beat when you're hiding in the corner all the time?" Tait keeps her identity anonymous by dining in disguise, jotting down notes in the ladies' room, and calling later for menu prices.[49] She said that she tries to remain anonymous and makes reservations under fake names. She does not worry if someone knows it is her: "I've found when you are recognized, they sort of shoot themselves in the foot because they try too hard."[50] Over the years, Tait's been sold out (by a "friend" who worked for a public relations firm and tried to reveal Tait's identity to someone else in the business) and threatened anonymously (by a brick through her window).[51]

Washington Post restaurant critic Phyllis Richman was able to dine anonymously for the first five years in Washington, DC. She said her gender helped keep her identity a secret: "There were hardly any women reviewing restaurants in the 1970s, and restaurants did not recognize women." After *Washingtonian* magazine ran her photo, she was recognized at restaurants more often. She said that she did not think it impacted the meal, other than portions being larger and appearing with more garnish. Quality appeared to remain the same. She said in an interview, "It just astonishes me how much obviously bad food I get when I am recognized in restaurants."[52]

Most critics follow the recommendation that the restaurant be visited three to five times before a review was written. Claiborne initially dined at a restaurant twice before reviewing it. He later added a third visit.[53] Some newspapers will wait a certain amount of time after a restaurant opens before they review it. At the *Los Angeles Times*, the policy is to give a three-month grace period "to get the kinks worked out before reviewing."[54] Other critics feel that if a restaurant is open and charging full price for meals, it is fair to review it.[55]

The Association of Food Journalists (AFJ) created guidelines for restaurant critics. It built on the four-star system created by Craig Claiborne. He believed that the qualifications for a food critic were simply "the ability to write and converse with food."[56] The AFJ's ethical guidelines (listed on the organization's website) recommend that "Reviews should be conducted anonymously whenever possible. Critics should experience the restaurant just as ordinary patrons do." The organization also addressed ethical concerns about new restaurants: "To be fair to new restaurants, reviewers should wait at least one month after the restaurant starts serving before visiting. These few weeks give the fledgling enterprise some time to get organized."

SMALL-MARKET RESTAURANT CRITICS

Major foodie cities like New York, Chicago, and New Orleans provide their challenges as restaurant owners and chefs fight to uncover the identity of reviewers. In smaller cities, the challenge is to be honest and fair while not destroying a small restaurant's reputation. Consider, for example, an attempted 1975 review by the *Lakeland Ledger* food critic Jane Nickerson. The *Ledger* issued the following statement in an editorial:

> Food editor Jane Nickerson, who regularly does reviews of area restaurants, dined one evening last week at an old established eatery whose manager had changed. It was a motel restaurant which Jane had panned pretty badly a year ago. Wanting to do amends, Jane returned hoping to find new management serving better and more exciting dishes. But lo, what did Jane find? The usual fare, higher prices and poorly prepared food. Overly concerned that she would have to again give the restaurant a bad review, she talked it over with her editors. We agreed that we would forego the review at this time, try it again in six months to see if things get better.[57]

Ruth Gray was the food editor restaurant critic for the *St. Petersburg Times* in the 1970s. She became the food editor in 1963 and began reviewing restaurants in 1974. Gray got into food writing after earning a degree in home economics from Kansas State University. She regularly reviewed restaurants in her "The Realm of Dining Out" and her "A la Carte" columns. For example, between September 1974 and January 1977, she had reviewed 118 local restaurants. She would take her husband and two to four friends to eat at the restaurant. She rated the restaurants based on quality of food, atmosphere, service, and price. Only four restaurants earned excellent ratings in all areas that were evaluated. One unique element of her reviewing was a description of wheelchair accessibility for patrons in a South Florida community with an aging population—this was more than a decade before the national disability access law was passed.[58]

Gray's opinion also had power in the restaurant community. One restaurant named its crab sandwich after her.[59] Another restaurant fired its chef after a bad review by Gray.[60] And a 1975 editor's column clarified to readers that Gray remained anonymous when she reviewed restaurants and did not accept free meals. The clarification was needed because area residents were going into restaurants, claiming to be Gray and requesting free meals.[61] Mimi Sheraton noted that people falsely used her name to get hard-to-get reservations at New York restaurants.[62]

Gray's reviews typically featured a mix of accolades and criticism—a traditional journalistic approach. In one column, she noted that her party's goal was to enjoy a meal at a seafood restaurant while keeping to a budget of $5 per person. She wrote, "I liked the food, our service was quite good, although we were told we had just missed the big Sunday evening rush of customers." She went on to write that she would return to the restaurant even though the meals had been more expensive than $5 per person.[63] In another review, she wrote of a friend who said the lobster was very good: "She is from New England so we felt she knew what she was talking about." She also did some reporting for the piece. The waitress said all the seafood was fresh. Gray called the next day and learned that lobster was indeed flown in daily.[64] She was also willing to criticize an establishment. In one example, a return to a restaurant after new management came in, she described the atmosphere of the restaurant, writing, "The building is a small, one-story place and the restaurant is not elegant." She also didn't warm to the chicken cordon bleu: "It was a bit cool when served."[65]

One particular review led to a pile of letters in response, so many that an editor's column was devoted to the review and response. Gray's review had begun with an account of what she believed to be rude treatment by the staff. Gray and her husband arrived on a rainy evening and by the time they entered the restaurant, their clothes were soaked. Gray had removed her wet coat and was turned away by the hostess unless she had a coat on. She wrote that the embarrassment and indifference had impacted her meal. Readers wrote in to support the restaurant, arguing that the restaurant needed to have standards if it was to uphold its elegant reputation. Gray didn't back down from her assessment. "My assignment is to give a truthful account of my dining experience," Gray responded to her readers.[66]

RESTAURANTS AND EXCLUDING WOMEN

An early obstacle to female journalists reviewing restaurants was the practice of excluding women from restaurants during the lunch hour. This was a regular practice for the many places where men held lunch meetings. The theory was that men only had a limited time to eat lunch and women would gossip and eat slowly. In 1968, Miami feminist Roxcy Bolton met with the managers of local restaurants to explain why male-only eateries were problematic. In 1969, Burdine's Department Store had a restaurant called the Men's Grille. Bolton met with the store's management and complained about the exclusion of women, especially when they were the main shoppers. A vice president wrote a letter to Bolton: "We have made the decision to change the name, and the 'men only' concept, as expeditiously as possible. We have ordered the signs to be changed, and they are to state 'Executive Grille' with no references to restrictions as to male or female usage."[67] She did not have as much luck at the department store Jordan Marsh. The store had a restaurant called the Captain's Table that excluded women at the lunch hour. While the manager wrote that he believed in equality, there would be no immediate change. He went on to explain, "I am going to recommend that any changes in the present system not be affected for the next few months until we can discuss our ability to serve the working customer."[68]

A similar practice was being suggested in another Florida restaurant when *Ft. Lauderdale News'* women's page editor Edee Greene heard about it. A longtime advocate for women, she decided to take a stand. She and Virginia Shuman Young, the first female mayor of the city, fought against the proposed male-only policy for the Tower Club at the top of the Landmark Bank building. Greene said, "When we heard it was going to be a restaurant for men, we told the owner that if he tried it he'd have two grandmothers picketing on the sidewalk."[69] The male-only policy was changed.

The restaurant community has often excluded women—particularly if there was a bar involved. In August 1970, New York City establishment McSorley's Old Ale House was forced to admit women—for the first time in the bar's 116-year history. It happened after Mayor Lindsay signed a bill prohibiting discrimination in public places because of gender. A *New York Times* article with a female byline noted that the women initially "drank peaceably" after being admitted. Then Lucy Komisar, a vice president of the National Organization for Women, arrived. The bartender refused to accept her driver's license as proof that she was over age eighteen. He demanded her birth certificate instead. The two engaged in a short wrestling match before the manager allowed her in to a chorus of "boos" from regular patrons. Later, an angry man poured his stein of ale over her head.[70]

It was not only the practice of bars and restaurants to exclude women. In some places, laws restricted where and how women could dine and drink. It took until 1970 for women to be allowed to drink in restaurants. *Louisville Courier-Journal* editor Keith Runyon recalled the Board of Aldermen approving the ordinance and several of the women journalists, including women's page editor Carol Sutton, going to the famed Mazzoni's at noon that day: "Carol took pleasure in ordering me, the only male in the party, a martini and carrying it over to our table. She stood at the bar, I sat."[71]

PHYLLIS RICHMAN AND THE ROLE OF GENDER

Phyllis Richman was the longtime food critic at the *Washington Post*. She retired in 2000 and continued her work in her second career as a novelist. Her name was in the news in the summer of 2013 when she penned an editorial that went viral, as her message about gender, education, and familial roles still had relevance. Richman's column was a public response to a 1961 letter she had received from a Harvard professor when she was applying to graduate school as a young married woman. The letter asked Richman how she would balance a potential career in city planning with her "responsibilities" to her husband and possible future children. Fifty-two years later she responded as follows:

> I haven't encountered any women with "some feeling of waste about the time and effort spent in professional education." I've never regretted a single course. In all, I attended graduate school for a dozen years, though only part-time, since my "responsibilities to [my] husband," as you so perceptively put it, included supporting him financially through his own graduate studies, a 10-year project.

In 1970 the couple relocated to Washington and she worked on her master's degree long distance. She recalled that she focused on multitasking and raising three children. She was doing some freelance writing and needed some child care. She was not making enough to hire a babysitter, so she furnished the attic in her home and offered rent-free accommodations to a college student in exchange for babysitting. (She would later write a book about bartering.) She continued freelancing for magazines and newspapers and wrote, "If I concentrated on topics such as comparative ice cream shopping and home testing of microwave ovens, I could feed and entertain the kids while I gathered material."

She had coauthored the *Washingtonian* magazine's restaurant guidebook and was promised that she would replace the magazine's restaurant critic when he retired. She recalled, "Instead, the editor chose a man who had written nary a restaurant review." The next year, the *Washington Post* hired her as its restaurant critic. She was the first woman to hold that job at the newspaper, and "one of only a handful in newspapers and magazines around the country." She did it while raising her children. She adjusted her visits to restaurants based on their ages. She wrote, "The student tenants took care of dinner, often serving recipes they had tested for me. I went out to restaurants late when the kids were young, early when they were old enough to be awake when I returned."

Richman spent more than two decades writing about food and realized that gender was often part of that story: "Even in the field of food writing, I found a gender split. When food served home and family, it was considered the realm of women. When it involved sophistication and money, men were the writers. Women wrote about cooks; men wrote about chefs."[72]

7

THE DEATH OF THE WOMEN'S PAGES

A Changing Industry and the Legacy of
the Great Food Editors

The 1970s brought many changes to American society, not least the arrival of what is known as second-wave feminism. Feminists of this era wanted to see women included in the mainstream of society, and the societal changes that followed affected the newspaper business, career opportunities for women, home cooking, and ultimately the legacy of the food editors.

CHANGES TO THE NEWSPAPER BUSINESS: THE END OF THE WOMEN'S PAGES

The women's pages and their food sections continued to be strong throughout the mid-century and into the 1970s. But as the 1970s wore on, the women's pages began to disappear from major newspapers.[1] The loudest voices calling for the elimination of the women's sections were women's liberation movement leaders. They considered the pages a ghetto for women and an example of discrimination and segregation. The leaders called, instead, for women to be employed by all sections of the newspaper.

Newspaper editors and publishers responded by eliminating the sections. The sections were renamed—often Lifestyle or Style—and the content changed to become more entertainment-oriented at most newspapers.[2] As for women and women's news becoming more equitably distributed throughout the newspaper, men were often appointed editors of the new sections, and women did not make significant advances into other sections for several more decades. In fact, it can be argued women are still not well represented in several areas of a newspaper. Food sections, however, remained as stand-alone sections but were more often employing men.

The elimination of the women's pages has also been credited to the influence of the *Washington Post*. Time and again it has been repeated that editor Ben Bradlee's debut of the Style section in the *Post* revolutionized women's sections. In his autobiography, Bradlee wrote that his only fight with publisher Katharine Graham was over the introduction of the Style section and the elimination of the women's section.[3] Bradlee and his journalists had begun brainstorming about changing the women's section (then called "for and about Women") in 1969 because the content of the women's section made him "uncomfortable." He wrote of the section, "Women were treated exclusively as shoppers, party-goers, cooks, hostesses, and mothers, and men were ignored. We began thinking of a section that would deal with how men and women lived—together and apart—what they liked and were like."[4] Similar lifestyle sections soon popped up at the *Los Angeles Times* and the *St. Petersburg Times*. The truth is more complicated, as many women's pages had long been refining roles for women and setting the foundation for social change, as several oral histories[5] and recent scholarship have shown.[6]

The women's pages and food pages were never as superficial and insignificant as they are represented in the popular imagination. There was some fluff, and undoubtedly some of the material reinforced women's role in the private sphere. Yet there were also stories of career women and community development by clubwomen. In 1994, Joanne Meyerowitz reexamined the original source material, much of it from women's magazines, used to support Betty Friedan's thesis in *The Feminine Mystique* and came to a different conclusion. Rather than viewing women's magazines as offering only oppressive and traditional messages, a more complex discourse was present. "Mass culture is rife with contradictions, ambivalence, and competing voices," Meyerowitz wrote.[7]

CHANGES IN CAREER OPPORTUNITIES:
EQUITY FOR WOMEN JOURNALISTS

The same changes that led to the elimination of the women's pages brought new opportunities for women journalists. As women's public roles changed in the 1970s, they began to become members of organizations that had previously excluded them. The National Press Club was created in 1908 for journalists as a social outlet and a place for politicians to make speeches, but the club excluded women. In retaliation, women journalists began their own Women's National Press Club in 1919. They often sold cookbooks to raise funds, and in 1960 *Washington Post* food editor Elinor Lee was an officer in the organization. The group frequently fought the National Press Club for access to its speakers, and in 1959 it convinced Soviet prime minister Nikita Khrushchev not to speak at the NPC unless women were admitted. They were—for that one event. When the NPC finally voted to admit women in 1971, the women's club changed its name to the Washington Press Club and began admitting men. The groups merged in 1985.

Several of the women-only culinary organizations continue today. In 1959, food editor Dorothy Crandall covered the first meeting of the Boston chapter of Les Dames des Amis d'Escoffier and remained a member until her death. The group had been founded to counter the all-male Les Amis d'Escoffier, which brought together members of the culinary community for networking, friendship, and eventually professional development and education. Carol Brock, then Sunday food editor at the *New York Daily News*, was troubled by this inequality in the New York culinary community. She learned of the Boston women's group and wanted a similar society in New York to counter the men's organization. According to the history of the New York chapter of Les Dames des Amis d'Escoffier established by Brock, "In an industry rife with discrimination in hiring, pay and educational opportunities, the group's goal was to help open the world of food, wine and hospitality to women."[8] The organization continues to thrive today.

CHANGES IN FOOD: FEMINISM AND THE DEMISE OF HOME COOKING

Some critics have blamed feminism for the lack of home cooking and the increased reliance on convenience food. Perhaps the most vocal of these was Michael Pollan, who wrote in a 2009 essay in the *New York Times* that one of the reasons women do not cook is because women went to work. There is a glorification of stay-at-home mothers and their home-cooked meals; yet any parent of little children knows that finding the time to cook from scratch is quite difficult. In the essay, he also described Betty Friedan's 1963 *The Feminine Mystique* as "the book that taught millions of American women to regard housework, cooking included, as drudgery, indeed as a form of oppression."[9] The impact of the book was significant whether women actually read it or not, according to Stephanie Coontz's research about the book's influence.[10] Even before Friedan's missive, women were questioning their roles in the home. American housewives had already begun to receive messages aimed at the work of housekeeping from the likes of Erma Bombeck, who humorously mocked the work of a homemaker and mother in her newspaper columns and books, and author and newspaper columnist Peg Bracken, known as a "cookbook rebel" for her 1960 book *I Hate to Cook*.[11]

Pollan's writing led to various responses from the feminist community and the conversation has continued over the years. In 2013, Salon asked the question, "Is Michael Pollan a sexist pig?"[12] In the other corner, the Huffington Post posted "In Defense of Michael Pollan."[13] Regardless of the answer, it is just another example of feminism being blamed for people no longer cooking.

The truth about the relationship between food and feminism is more complicated, and Friedan's book is hardly at fault. It is more likely that the lack of knowledge about cooking can be traced back to taking home economics out of the schools. When Robin Morgan spoke to the national home economics convention in 1972, she was best remembered for referring to the home economists as the "enemy." Despite this inflammatory remark, her talk was remarkably nuanced: "Demand that if home economics is required for high school women, it should also be required for high school men," she requested. "We must break down the notion and that child care and homemaking are gender jobs."[14]

Similarly, in 1970, *Los Angeles Times* food editor Maggie Savoy wrote about how she explained women's liberation to men: "If he said—and some still do—'Women's place is in the home,' I brighten. 'It's so wonderful we want to share it. Here's my dishrag.'"[15] Feminists did not necessarily want to stop cooking; they just did not want to do *all* of the cooking.

Maybe the bigger concern is the following declaration from Pollan: "That learning to cook could lead an American woman to success of any kind would have seemed utterly implausible in 1949."[16] That is not quite true. Every metropolitan newspaper had a food editor—and many of them were good cooks. Furthermore, women created food-based careers in running food company test kitchens, writing advertising copy aimed at homemakers, and penning cookbooks of every kind. Consider food journalist and cookbook author Marian Tracy. By 1948, her classic *Casserole Cookery* was in its eighth printing. She would go on to write numerous other cookbooks.

Cooking and gender have long been intertwined. As previously noted, *New York Times* food critic Mimi Sheraton's wrote that when Craig Claiborne (who took over from Jane Nickerson in 1957) left the newspaper in 1972, she and other female New York food writers were not considered as replacements.[17] The female-dominated profession of newspaper food editor had shifted, and women were now being excluded. It was a time when even the fictional Betty Crocker was under attack. In 1972, the Minneapolis–St. Paul chapter of the National Organization of Women accused Betty Crocker of being a racist and sexist image. The chapter filed a class-action complaint against General Mills, which was later dropped, although the company did update the image that year.[18]

The female food editors of the 1950s and 1960s, aware of their designated but precarious positions in the newsroom, may not have been in a position to take the kind of stands that Robin Morgan wanted. For some women, feminism was simply a matter of demonstrating competence in the face of a condescending environment. For example, Helen Dollaghan started working at the *Denver Post* accepting classified ads over the phone. She then spent ten years as the assistant women's page editor before finally getting the job she really wanted: food editor. A colleague wrote of her, "The great part about Helen was that she had a brilliant wit and she didn't hesitate to use it to deflate the occasional boneheaded boss passing through during some of *The Post's* more tumultuous years. She only looked submissive. There was a sparkle in her eyes."[19]

Further, the female colleague who had started at the newspaper in the 1970s noted the importance of women journalists like Dollaghan: "I think of her every time I'm tempted to give up too easily, to be intimidated by somebody who doesn't deserve my respect or when I just might take it for granted that women finally make editorial decisions instead of just taking classified ads."[20]

FOOD EDITORS OVERSHADOWED

In 2006, Michael Pollan asked, "How did we ever get to the point where we need investigative journalists to tell us where our food comes from?"[21] The truth is that newspaper reporters have been investigating our food sources for more than a hundred years now. Much of the legislation that applies to our food safety is due to the muckraking journalists at newspapers and magazines in the early 1900s. According to journalism historian William David Sloan, "Muckrakers have been credited, at least in part, with producing an impressive array of legislative reforms."[22] Reformers who took on the food and drug industry include Upton Sinclair, with his unflinching examination of the meat packing industry in *The Jungle,* and Samuel Hopkins Adams, who investigated the fraudulent patent medicine industry for *Collier's Weekly*.

While the lives of these reformers have been well documented, there has been very little recognition of the role of the great food editors in the story of American food. Newspaper food editors such as Harriet Dakin MacMurphy at the *Omaha World-Herald* were also part of that crusade. As the paper's domestic sciences editor, MacMurphy wrote editorials about food safety that contributed to the passage of the Pure Food and Drug Act of 1906.[23] In 2005, the *New York Times* published a story about Clementine Paddleford and her papers at Kansas State University. In the article, R. W. Apple Jr. described her as the Nellie Bly (another famous muckraking journalist from the reform era) of culinary journalism, "a go-anywhere, taste-anything, ask-everything kind of reporter."[24]

Despite the incredible contributions of these talented journalists, their stories have largely been forgotten in the larger culture. A day after the *New York Times* story on Paddleford ran, the authors of her future biography signed a book contract with New York's Gotham Press. In that book, *Hometown Appetites*, written by Kelly Alexander and Cynthia Harris, the authors explore the reasons for her exclusion from history until 2005.[25] In part, she was overshadowed by the *New York Times*'s Craig Claiborne. Further, her newspaper, the *New York Herald Tribune*, went under in 1966, while the *Times* is still published today and widely considered the most prominent newspaper in North America, if not the world.

The cult of celebrity has exacerbated this neglect. James Beard and Craig Claiborne are well-known names today, but the food world was really dominated by women in the 1950s and 1960s—so much so that when culinary historian Laura Shapiro conducted an oral history with Associated Press food editor Cecily Brownstone, the question was raised about Beard's place in food circles: "Did he find anything peculiar about being a man in the woman's world of food?" Brownstone replied that he did not, which she credited to him being comfortable in his sexuality.[26]

WHAT HAPPENED TO THE FOOD EDITORS AFTER THE 1970s?

Most of the food editors from the 1940s to the 1970s have died. Clementine Paddleford died in 1967 and was largely forgotten until 2005. Peggy Daum retired from the *Milwaukee Journal* in 1988 and died two years later of a heart attack at age fifty-seven. Ruth Ellen Church was murdered in 1991 during a break-in at her Chicago home. She was eighty-eight years old. In her obituary, the *New York Times* reported that she was the country's first wine editor.[27] Rosa Tusa was the food editor at the *Milwaukee Sentinel* from 1961 to 1971 and the food editor at the *Palm Beach Post* in the 1970s and 1980s. In 1992, she died of a heart attack while speaking to a friend in England by phone. She was such a colorful character that her Milwaukee colleagues began a column of memories about her with the statement, "Rosa Tusa was her own best story."[28]

Jane Nickerson raised her four children in central Florida and did some freelance newspaper writing, while her replacement, Claiborne, went on to fame in New York and beyond. She and her husband, Alexander Steinberg, divorced in 1972. The following year, her book *Jane Nickerson's Florida Cookbook* was published by the University of Florida Press. Also that year, Nickerson became the food editor at the *Lakeland Ledger*, a *New York Times*–owned newspaper, and a syndicated columnist to ten Florida newspapers. She covered food news for the Taste section, using a similar approach to that which she used at the *New York Times*. Former *Lakeland Ledger* editor Skip Perez said of Nickerson, "Her graceful writing style and easy use of the language was envied by many of us in the newsroom, but Jane never forgot that her primary goal was to inform in a clear easy-to-understand way. She was a marvelous food teacher."[29] She retired from the *Lakeland Ledger* in 1987, and two years later she moved to Montana. She died in 2000 at age eighty-three after a long illness.

Upon Cecily Brownstone's retirement from the wire service in 1986, Nickerson wrote that "of the syndicated food writers, she's been the most widely read" and that the success was derived from "her sensitivity to readers' tastes and her insistence that recipes give high, appealing results."[30] During her retirement, she published *Classic Cakes and Other Great Cuisinart Desserts* along with Carl Sontheimer, the founder of the Cuisinart Company. In 2002, she donated her papers, cookbooks, and food pamphlets to the Fales Library at New York University. Library director Marvin Taylor wrote about a meeting he and Marion Nestle had with Brownstone: "Cecily was bedridden at the time, but we did get to meet and speak with her. She was a small woman with a sharp mind and quick wit."[31] Culinary historian Laura Shapiro also conducted a short oral history with Brownstone, available at the Fales Library. When Brownstone died in 2005, the Associated Press described her as a "cuisine maven."[32]

After more than a decade at the *Los Angeles Times* and authoring several cookbooks, Jeanne Voltz's work began to earn national attention. In 1973, Voltz became food editor of the magazine *Woman's Day* in New York, where she remained until 1986. She initially rejected the job offer from the magazine because she feared the close relationship the editorial side would have with advertisers. But after three months, the lure of a million and a half readers led her to take the job. Fellow magazine food editor Jean Anderson noted that it was unusual for a newspaper food editor to make the transition to the New York magazine community. "We were shocked that she was brought in with no magazine experience," Anderson said.[33] So when Voltz succeeded, regard for her abilities and leadership increased even more. In 1983, she stepped down as food editor but stayed at the magazine another three years working on several projects. Voltz also served as president of the New York chapter of Les Dames des Amis d'Escoffier from 1985 to 1987. Later, she moved to North Carolina and became active in the Society for the Preservation of Southern Food and was also a member of the Society of Woman Geographers. Voltz's application to the organization listed her specialization as food anthropology. She continued to write cookbooks, eventually writing a total of ten. Her final book, published in 1999, was *The Country Ham Book*. In her final years, she continued to judge barbecue contests.[34] She died in 2002 at age eighty-one. Upon her death, she was described as a "pioneering newspaper food editor."[35]

Some of the other food editors also were lauded in their obituaries. Dorothy Crandall retired in 1973 after twenty years as a food editor. After she retired, she taught high school culinary courses, worked with a chef's apprentice program, and remained on top of the latest food developments into her late nineties. According to her obituary, "Dorothy Crandall belongs to a generation of food writers that includes James Beard, Julia Child, Sam and Narcisse Chamberlain, Craig Claiborne, Pierre Franey, Marjorie Mills, Joyce Chen, and more. She knew them all. She was the kind of food writer who would go anywhere to get the heart of the story."[36] Atlanta food editor Grace Hartley also was extolled in her retirement and again when she died. "Miss Hartley, the legendary former food editor, has as zestful an appetite for life as several generations of Georgians have had for her recipes," said one writer.[37]

However, the significance of many of the other women was forgotten even in their obituaries. Barbara Clendinen was the food editor at the *Tampa Tribune* in the 1950s and was a friend of Paddleford. Her obituary began as follows: "Barbara Clendinen liked the news business, but she liked the thought of being a full-time mother better."[38] Her work as a journalist is barely mentioned. Yet in her son's memoir about a year at the Tampa nursing home where his mother lived, much more was revealed about the love she had for her career as a food editor, whether it was traveling to the food editors' conferences, interviewing numerous home cooks, or introducing new recipes.[39] The colorful Poppy Cannon seemed to have found a kindred spirit in *New York World-Telegram* food editor and cookbook author Marian Tracy. In 1967, Cannon wrote that Tracy's latest cookbook made her "want to clap and sing."[40] In 1970, Cannon credited Tracy for "catapulting a kind of revolution nearly 30 years ago."[41] Yet Tracy's four-paragraph obituary in 1992 notes none of the significant work during her career other than referring to her as a cookbook writer.[42] Similarly, Myra Waldo, who took over Paddleford's food column in *This Week* magazine (which ran in the *Baltimore Sun*), was also ignored. Her obituary in the *Los Angeles Times*, where she published a travel column, was only three paragraphs long, although she was described as "a prolific travel writer and cookbook author."[43]

THE LEGACY OF THE FOOD EDITORS

The role of women food editors at newspapers after the 1970s was not all diminished or ignored, however. Consider the career of Marian Burros. In the 1950s, she and her friend Lois Levine first wrote their own recipes. They put together a cookbook using a mimeograph machine and took copies to bookstores. The book, *Elegant but Easy*, was such a success that in 1960 Macmillan Publishing bought the rights and it went on to sell five hundred thousand copies nationwide. Burros started working as a part-time newspaper food writer. In an interview, she said, "I was a traditional housewife and mother back then."[44] In the 1960s, she was the food writer at the *Washington Star* where she spent time in many VIP kitchens including the White House. She had two big scoops in the *Star* regarding the wedding cake of first daughter Luci Johnson. Yet she did not always write about what she saw in the famous kitchens she visited. According to Burros, "The Marquise de Merry del Val was so nice I didn't write the story about the Spanish Embassy. They make the most glamorous dishes. I walked into the kitchen and saw all those things that had taken days to make and right beside them were cans and cans of Pillsbury refrigerated dough."[45]

A book about Washington, DC, reporters noted that Burros "will go down in history as the Paul Revere of modern times, riding through the countryside sounding the alarm about the food we eat—the harmful, the downright poisonous, or the merely nonfood food." The writers were referring to Burros uncovering the health risks of red dye no. 2 and her discovery about powdered wood pulp being added to one company's bread.[46] In 1981, Burros became a food writer at the *New York Times*; from 1983 to 1984, she was the newspaper's restaurant critic. She continued to write cookbooks. By 2010, she was covering First Lady Michelle Obama's obesity initiative for the website Rodale.com. Eleanor Ostman of the *St. Paul Pioneer Press* and Barb Ostmann of the *St. Louis Post-Dispatch* were well known in later decades, and food editor Elaine Tait earned national recognition as a restaurant reviewer in Philadelphia.

In 1998, Terry Ford, a food editor and a charter member of Julia Child's American Institute of Food and Wine, declared that Voltz had not been recognized for her significant contributions to culinary journalism. "She's an extraordinary person," he said. "Her career goes bicoastal. Her impact and her knowledge is vast. She is very gifted, very crafted. When you read something Jeanne Voltz writes, you can say it was 100 percent thoroughly researched."[47] Further, Jane Nickerson has been overlooked in almost all references to *New York Times* food history. It was Molly O'Neill who recognized the importance of Nickerson's work. In one of the best histories of food journalism, O'Neill wrote, "Interestingly, Nickerson was one of the first to apply news-side ethics to the food report."[48]

Too often, these female food journalists are overlooked. Their stories were not on the front pages, but they were serving an important role for their communities. These food journalists reached consumers and cooks. They held local grocers and the greater industry accountable, even at the risk of advertising losses. They documented problems, such as food safety, and promoted change in nutritional expectations. They covered the intersection of food and governmental regulation. They reviewed restaurants as they blossomed in cities across the country. These journalists did all of this, never forgetting that while food was important, it was also fun.

While advertising may have influenced the content of some food sections, many others were independently covering nutritional, cultural, and social news. In the case of many food journalists, their reporting included consumer news, food safety, and nutrition. Their stories foreshadowed issues that would make the front pages decades later—questions over truth in cereal labeling, the definition of organic food, and childhood obesity. The work of these women is important to recognize even if it was grounded in soft news.

More attention should be paid to the content of food sections and the careers of food editors. In a recent example of their continued marginalization, consider the 2011 edition of the *Associated Press Stylebook*—considered the most important source book for journalists.[49] The new edition included a section devoted to food. According to a press release, the reason for the new section was because of the media's supposedly newfound interest in reporting on food. The product manager stated, "With all the cooking shows, blogs and magazines focusing on food, as well as growing interest in organic and locally sourced foods, our new food section feels timely and on trend. With this new addition to the AP Stylebook, the Associated Press is proud to bring clarity to the writing that describes and informs the new food movement."[50] Unfortunately, this statement minimizes all of the important work done by women in food journalism in the decades of the twentieth century.

The women included in this book are not the only significant newspaper food editors of the era. There are likely many histories tucked away of forgotten food editors who were part of their communities' culinary conversations. Likewise, there were also likely some journalists with questionable ethics toward advertisers. Yet the women journalists described in this book were a formidable bunch of food experts and competent, professional journalists dedicated to their craft and their communities. Understanding these women and their food sections helps to better understand their place and influence on the history of home cooks, regional cookery, and gender roles.

APPENDIX
Editors List, 1945–1975

TOP FEMALE NEWSPAPER FOOD EDITORS, 1945–1975

Below are brief biographies of food editors based largely on personality profiles, retirement stories, and obituaries that ran in their newspapers. Cookbook dedication pages also provided information. The intent is to demonstrate the professional aspects of the editors' education and training, as well as their marital and familial roles. The editors were chosen based on being Vesta Award winners or being included in the 1952 *Coast to Coast* cookbook created by newspaper food editors. Two men are also profiled, as they were typically included in the annual food meetings and other food-editor events.

Grace Barr, *Orlando Sentinel*

Grace Warlow Barr worked as a baker during the Great Depression. The daughter of a judge, she first worked as a society editor and then became the food editor at the *Orlando Sentinel*, where she remained for twenty-seven years. She was known for her recipes that began with "start with a stick of butter." Her cookbook, *Cooking with Grace*, was published in 1970. She was divorced and raised two children.

Janet Beighle French, *Cleveland Plain-Dealer*

When Janet Beighle French began working at the *Cleveland Plain-Dealer* in 1963, she recalled that the women's page staff members were walled off from the city room by bookcases. She wrote small cookbooks for *Better Homes & Gardens* for six years, after earning a master's degree in agricultural journalism, which included home economics, from the University of Wisconsin. She oversaw a test kitchen, and several home economists were on staff. She helped produce color articles for the newspaper's Sunday magazine, cosponsored seminars with the extension service, and published a number of cooking booklets.

Julie Benell, *Dallas Morning News*

Julie Benell was a native of San Antonio and a concert pianist who later gave performances on radio and television. She eventually left her music career and became a reporter and editor on food who worked for twenty-five years at the *Dallas Morning News*. She was the author of several cookbooks, including the popular *Let's Eat at Home*. She had a daily television show about food and fashion while she was at the newspaper; it was her show that was interrupted when President Kennedy was assassinated in Dallas. She judged the 1962 great national Cookout Championship for Men Only in Hawaii, along with Clementine Paddleford. She donated her cookbook collection to Texas Woman's University.

Jane Benet, *San Francisco Chronicle*

Jane Gugel Benet started at the *San Francisco Chronicle* as a copygirl during World War II and worked in almost every part of the newspaper. She became the food editor in 1953 and often used the pen name "Jane Friendly." She judged numerous cooking competitions and wrote two cookbooks and three nationally syndicated columns. She retired in 1988. The Sonoma County Culinary Guild presents a scholarship each year in her name. She married James Walker Benet, a journalist and a veteran of the Abraham Lincoln Brigade in the Spanish Civil War.

Julie Bowes (Sue Baker), New Orleans *Times-Picayune*

Julie Duvac Bowes graduated from Louisiana State University in 1942 with a degree in home economics. She began her career of thirty years as the food editor of the *Times-Picayune* in 1949 under the pen name "Sue Baker." She tested on her family the recipes that she used in her twice-weekly column, published on Thursdays and in color on Sundays in the *Dixie Roto* magazine. She was married, raised five children, and was an accomplished golfer.

Carol Brock, *New York Daily News*

After several years covering food for women's magazines, Carol Brock began her reign as food reporter for the *New York Daily News* in 1971. She spent the next fifteen years producing the newspaper's weekly color food photography as well as developing recipes and writing food features. Brock received a charter from the New York chapter of Les Amis d'Escoffier Society for women in 1973.

Cecily Brownstone, Associated Press

Cecily Brownstone attended the University of Manitoba and came to New York City to pursue her studies and to work. She lived in Greenwich Village in a duplex apartment that included a test kitchen and a large cookbook collection. She was the Associated Press's food editor from 1947 to 1986. During that time she was the most widely published of syndicated food writers. Her work included five recipe columns and two food features each week. Earlier in her career, Brownstone was the food editor of *Parents* magazine, and the child care editor of *Family Circle* magazine. In 1972, she wrote *Cecily Brownstone's Associated Press Cookbook*. Brownstone was also a consultant to Carl Sontheimer, president of Cuisinart. With Sontheimer, Brownstone edited the magazine *Pleasures of Cooking* and wrote the 1994 *Classic Cakes and Other Great Cuisinart Desserts*. She donated her mass cookbook collection to New York University.

Marian Burros, *Washington Star* and *Washington Post*

Marian Burros earned an English degree from Wellesley and had two children. In the 1950s, she and her friend Lois Levine put together a cookbook using a mimeograph machine and took copies to bookstores. The book, *Elegant but Easy*, was such a success that in 1960, Macmillan Publishing bought the rights and it went on to sell 500,000 copies nationwide. Burros started working as a part-time newspaper food writer, though she said, "I was a traditional housewife and mother back then." In the 1960s, she was the food writer at the *Washington Star*, where she spent time in many VIP kitchens, including the White House. She scored major scoops in covering the White House when she learned that the cake for Luci Johnson's wedding was eight feet high and was carried to the White House by the Secret Service through the back roads of Washington. By 1981, Burros became a food writer at the *New York Times*, and from 1983 to 1984 she was the newspaper's restaurant critic. She continued to write cookbooks. By 2010, she was covering the First Lady's obesity initiative for the website Rodale.com.

Katie Carlson, *Daytona Beach News-Journal*

Katie Heg Carlson attended Seattle University and the University of Washington. During the 1960s she worked as a freelance writer for a variety of publications including *Sports Illustrated*. She worked briefly as a reporter at the *Daytona Beach News-Journal* before she became food editor in 1971 and then the women's page editor in 1977. A founding member of the Volusia County Women's Network, she wrote a cookbook about Christmas dishes based on recipes from local cooks. By the 1990s, she was the promotions director for the newspaper. She raised two children, and her daughter said of her mother, "She was Martha Stewart before there was a Martha Stewart."

Lowis Carlton, *Miami Herald*

Lowis Carlton had a bachelor's and master's degree in English from the University of Miami and a bachelor's degree in home economics from Florida International University. She was the food editor at the *Miami Herald* in the early 1960s and spent several years as the gourmet editor at *Palm Beach Life* magazine and as a columnist for the Florida Department of Agriculture. Like many of the top newspaper food editors of the 1950s and 1960s, she was a judge for the Pillsbury Bake-Off.

Helen Messenger Cass, *Denver Post*

Helen Messenger graduated from the University of Denver and initially worked for the Associated Press and KVOD-FM radio and taught high school journalism. In 1950 she became the women's page editor for the *Denver Post* and initiated food coverage. She wrote a popular food column that ran in the newspaper's Sunday publication, *Empire Magazine*, called "Munching Through Denver with Messenger." She left the newspaper in 1955 to raise her four children, but returned in 1973 and covered the entertainment beat. She retired in 1987.

Dorothy Chapman, *Orlando Sentinel*

Dorothy Chapman earned a degree from Arizona State University and moved to Orlando in 1959. She worked at a local weekly newspaper before she became the women's editor at the *Orlando Sentinel* in 1971, and she became the newspaper's first restaurant critic. She was a judge in the Pillsbury Bake-Off and testified about nutrition for a US Senate subcommittee. She was a member of the Florida Commission on the Status of Women and authored several cookbooks. She was divorced and raised three daughters. According to her daughter, "We were eating real guacamole and searching markets for radicchio long before they were Central Florida staples. Our friends thought we ate really strange."

Ruth Ellen Church (Mary Meade), *Chicago Tribune*

Ruth Ellen Church was a graduate of the home economics journalism program from Iowa State University. After a brief stint as society editor for a small Iowa newspaper, she joined the *Tribune* as cooking editor in 1936. She oversaw one of the first test kitchens at a newspaper. She published many cookbooks—several under the pen name "Mary Meade." Among her books were *The Indispensable Guide for the Mod-*

ern *Cook* (1955), *The Burger Cookbook* (1967), and *Entertaining with Wine* (1970). Her *Mary Meade's Country Cookbook* was named book of the month by the Cook Book Guild in October 1965. She remained the food editor until 1974 and became the nation's first newspaper wine editor in 1962. She was married and had two sons.

Rita Ciccone, Ft. Lauderdale News

Rita Ciccone was one of ten children and her mother was a school cook. After high school, she was a South Florida lounge singer at a restaurant where *Ft. Lauderdale News* reporters gathered, which is how she met her husband. He said, "People used to flock wherever she was. One of the reasons was because when they walked in the door, she would remember who they were and their favorite song." When the paper's society editor needed someone to cover north Broward County part time, her husband suggested his wife, noting that she was "the best gossip in town." Her lively writing style caught on with editors, and she was soon doing full-length features and profiles. She eventually became the food editor and wrote a column called "Rita's Kook Book." She left the *News* in 1972 to become managing editor of the local weekly *Deerfield (FL) Observer*. She raised two children.

Barbara Clendinen, Tampa Tribune

Barbara Clendinen was the food editor at the *Tampa Tribune* in the 1950s. She was a friend of Clementine Paddleford and she attended the annual food editors' meetings. She was married to an editor at the newspaper and the mother of two children. She was described as "a true steel magnolia, a charming honey-voiced Southern woman." She pushed to integrate the Tampa YMCA in the 1960s. Her recipes are included in the 1952 *Coast to Coast* cookbook.

Maude Coons, Omaha World-Herald

Maude Charron Coons graduated from the home economics program at Iowa State University after overcoming paralysis caused by polio. She started at the *Omaha World-Herald* as the household editor in 1936.

Initially, she wrote under the byline "Mary Cooks," but by the 1940s, she wrote under her own name. She wrote several food pamphlets and one cookbook. Known for her ability to answer any cooking question, she tracked down recipes for rattlesnake and black birds. She was married with one son and wrote about her adventures as a grandmother. She retired from the newspaper in 1973.

Dorothy Crandell, *Boston Globe*

Dorothy Crandall earned a home economics degree from the University of Vermont and a master's degree in education from the University of Vermont in 1952. After graduation, she did food and marketing commentaries for the US Department of Agriculture on Boston radio stations for five years and then joined the *Boston Globe* as food editor, where she served from 1953 to 1973. She was the editor for Julia Child's recipe column in the *Globe*. While writing food features for the *Sunday Globe*, she took classes at Boston University in food photography and journalism.

Ann Criswell, *Houston Chronicle*

Ann Criswell was the longtime food editor of the *Houston Chronicle*—from 1966 to 2000. She started the column "Looking for Cooking" her first year. She described it as a "backyard type of discussion about cooking." She reviewed restaurants, wrote several cookbooks, and judged the Pillsbury Bake-Off. During her tenure she sampled chocolate-covered ants, fried parsley, raw tuna, quail eggs, black rice, rattlesnake, armadillo, and everything that "tastes like chicken." She raised two children.

Anne Cutcher, *Washington Star* and *Washington Daily News*

Anne Cutcher was a graduate of Syracuse University and then became a diplomat's wife and mother of four. During her husband's assignment to Paris, she took classes at Cordon Bleu. When her husband died in 1962, she became the food editor at the *Washington Star* and *Washington Daily News*. She helped to establish the Washington, DC, chapter of Les Dames des Amis d'Escoffier, which supports women in the culinary world. Later, the chapter gave out a scholarship in her name. She went on to be an editorial page writer for the *Washington Times*.

Peggy Daum, *Milwaukee Journal*

Peggy Daum Judge earned an undergraduate degree in journalism and a minor in home economics from the University of Arizona. She earned a master's degree in journalism from Marquette University and her thesis was a study of the women's pages. She began working in the women's pages in the 1950s and was the food editor at the *Milwaukee Journal* from 1968 to 1988. She edited two cookbooks for the *Milwaukee Journal* with recipes from home cooks. She is listed as a food consultant for the popular children's book *Eating the Alphabet*, written by Lois Ehlert. Daum initiated the creation of what is now known as the Association of Food Journalists and was its first president. She married late in life and died two years after her retirement.

Naomi Doebel, *Cedar Rapids Gazette*

Naomi Doebel had a varied career in the newspaper business. Early in her career she worked in Omaha, where she tracked the mob underground for stories. A colleague said of Doebel, "She knew gangsters and carried a gun. I looked up to her." Later she was the real estate and travel editor at the *Gazette* in Cedar Rapids, Iowa, and in the 1950s she became the food editor. Doebel is included in the 1952 *Coast to Coast* cookbook.

Helen Dollaghan, *Denver Post*

Helen Dollaghan Vogel earned a journalism degree from the University of Denver. After graduation, she worked at the *Denver Post* taking classified advertising. She became the food editor in 1958 and remained at that post until 1993. She tested recipes in her own kitchen and was known for breaking ground with on-site food photography, such as having photographs taken at the local Squaw Pass. She was also known for the recipe Apricot Brandy Chicken: when some readers improvised by adding extra brandy, which was then covered in foil, they essentially constructed a tiny bomb that caused oven doors to be blown off. She was considered one of the nation's experts on high-altitude cooking. She wrote one cookbook and judged the Pillsbury Bake-Off. She was married to Cecil Vogel.

Rose Dosti, *Los Angeles Times*

Rose Dosti was a writer in the *Los Angeles Times* food section from 1964 to 1992. She wrote many cookbooks and continued to write the column "Culinary S.O.S." for another nine years after leaving the *Times*. She described the 1960s and 1970s as the golden era of newspaper food journalism when she spoke at a 2010 meeting of the Culinary Historians of Southern California.

Violet Faulkner, *Washington Star*

Violet Faulkner graduated from the University of Wisconsin and taught home economics in Minnesota high schools in the 1920s. She wrote a weekly column for the *St. Paul Dispatch* and taught in cooking schools before moving to Washington in 1935. There she taught home economics before joining the *Washington Star*. She was the food editor of the *Washington Star* from 1946 until she retired in 1967. She was a judge in the Pillsbury Bake-Off and was married.

Cecil Fleming, *Detroit Times*, *Detroit Free Press*, and *Los Angeles Times*

Cecil Fleming graduated from the University of Washington and joined the *Detroit Free Press* as the home economist, testing recipes and answering readers' phone calls. While at the newspaper, she was one of several women in the Hearst chain who used the byline "Prudence Penny" at the *Detroit Times*. She joined the *Detroit Free Press* and served as the home economist, testing recipes and answering readers' phone calls. Food editor Kay Savage said of Fleming, "She knows why the jelly doesn't jell and why the meringue weeps." She joined the *Los Angeles Times* in 1965 and wrote many food stories, including consumer and nutrition stories through the 1970s. She was married to Quentin Fleming.

Eudora Garrison, *Charlotte Observer*

Eudora Blackeney Garrison was hired as the secretary to the editor of the *Charlotte Observer* in 1932. She became the newspaper's food editor in 1953. She authored a cookbook based on her recipe column, *It's Not Gourmet—It's Better*, and several recipe booklets. She was married to a sports reporter at the newspaper and raised a daughter. She stepped down as food editor in 1966 but continued to write a column until 1980. Garrison was known for her collection of brimmed hats.

Josephine Gibson, *Pittsburgh Press*

Josephine Gibson earned a degree in home economics from Carnegie Institute of Technology in 1924. In 1927, she directed the new home economics department at the H. J. Heinz Company. At a model kitchen arranged on a stage in the Heinz plant auditorium, she lectured while demonstrating how to cook specific dishes. She developed recipes using Heinz products and gave demonstrations to more than 80,000 people a year who toured the company's plant. She had a radio show, "Hostess Talk to Women," which aired three times a week on the NBC network. She joined the *Pittsburgh Press* in 1937, where she had a twenty-four-year career as food editor. In that capacity she answered thousands of letters in a column called "Recipe Exchange." She tested many of her recipes at home in the evening. She was married to attorney William H. Eckert and had two daughters.

Ruth Gorrell Gray, *Detroit Times* and *St. Petersburg Times*

Ruth Gorrell earned a bachelor's degree in home economics from Kansas State University. After graduation, she became the food editor at the *Detroit Times* in the early 1950s. Her recipes were included in the 1952 *Coast to Coast* cookbook, and she attended the annual food editors meetings. She became the food editor in 1963 of the *St. Petersburg Times* and began reviewing restaurants in 1974. She married while in

Florida and began writing as Ruth Gray. She was included in the *Coast to Coast* cookbook. She married and had a daughter.

Cissy Gregg, *Louisville Courier-Journal*

Mary "Cissy" Peterson graduated from the University of Kentucky with a degree in agriculture and home economics in 1924. She married Edd R. Gregg in 1930 and became the food editor at the *Louisville Courier-Journal* in April 1942. She oversaw a test kitchen at the newspaper and wrote a popular cookbook. She collected more than 700 cookbooks and tied her interest in cooking to her collection of world maps. She retired in 1963 and died in 1966. Her recipes are still found on the newspaper's blog.

Marion Ferriss Guinn (Dorothy Neighbors), *Seattle Times*

Marion Prior Ferriss Guinn graduated from the University of Washington in 1929 with degrees in journalism and home economics. After graduation, she was hired by the *Seattle Times* as a reporter and later became their food editor, writing under the pen name "Dorothy Neighbors." During World War II, when events were held in Victory Square, Guinn presented a number of "Housewives Go to War" programs advising women of ways to help the war effort. Her recipes were included in the 1952 cookbook *Coast to Coast*. She was married and raised a daughter.

Carol Haddix, *Detroit Free Press* and *Chicago Tribune*

Carol Haddix graduated from Michigan State University with a degree in home economics and communication arts. She started out covering fashion and food at the *Detroit Free Press* before moving on to the food section of the *Chicago Tribune*, where she spent thirty-four years. She was a founding member of the Culinary Historians of Chicago. She retired in 2011.

Bertha Cochran Hahn, *Miami News*

Bertha Cochran Hahn earned a home economics degree from Purdue University and worked as a home demonstration agent. During World War II, she became a second lieutenant in the Army Medical Corps and was stationed in Air Force hospitals. After the war, she earned a journalism degree from the University of Miami. She became the food editor at the *Miami News* in 1953 and remained in the position through the 1960s. She was married.

Ann Hamman, *Evansville (IN) Courier*

Annie Hamman earned degrees from Oklahoma State University and the University of Chicago before enrolling in the military during World War II. She served two years in North Africa and Italy as part of the Women Army Auxiliary Corps. She married and had a son before divorcing. Using the GI Bill, she earned a master's degree in home economics from Purdue University. She then worked as a home economist and an extension agent. She came to the *Evansville Courier* as the food editor in 1967. She retired in 1973 to join the Peace Corps.

Mary Acton Hammond, *Philadelphia Bulletin*

Mary Acton Hammond was hired as the *Philadelphia Bulletin*'s first food editor in 1929. She worked out of her own kitchen, where she tested her recipes for fifty-three years. In 1941, she traveled to England interviewing British women about how they prepared food during the war. It led to a series of columns that First Lady Eleanor Roosevelt mentioned in her "My Day" column. Her trip was eventually published in the book *Mrs. England Goes on Living*. She wrote under the byline "Frances Blackwood," which was her grandmother's name. She had two sons.

Carol McCready Hartley, *Phoenix Gazette*

Carol McCready Hartley graduated from Iowa State University with a bachelor's degree in home economics. Initially she staged fashion shows in Chicago for Carson Pirie Scott, the city's second largest department store. She married and had a daughter. After a divorce, she relocated to Arizona. She became the first food editor at the *Phoenix Gazette* in 1961. Her section was one of the largest in the country at the time. She was a judge in the Pillsbury Bake-Off. She remarried in 1975 and left the newspaper. She died in 2011.

Grace Hartley, *Atlanta Journal*

Grace Hartley earned a home economics degree from the Georgia College for Women in Milledgeville (now Georgia College). Her first job was with a social service agency, where, in the depths of the Great Depression, she taught social workers how to plan meals for families and instructed people in food preparation. In 1936, she became the food editor at the *Atlanta Journal*, where she served for more than four decades and continued to write for the newspaper's weekly magazine for another decade. She worked for the War Production Board during World War II and wrote a well-respected cookbook about Southern food. She had one of the first electric ranges in Atlanta, and likely the first microwave, a massive piece of equipment that stood five feet tall, with a conventional oven underneath. She was one of three judges in the 1964 Miss America Pageant. When she wed her husband, Judson G. Germon, they had to get married during her lunch hour because she was on a deadline.

Virginia Heffington, *Miami Herald* and *Long Beach (CA) Independent Press-Telegram*

Virginia Newman Heffington earned a home economics degree from Iowa State University in 1954. She worked in the food department of women's magazines before becoming the food editor at the *Miami Herald* in the 1960s. While there she wrote a cookbook about Florida food. By 1971, she became the food editor at the *Long Beach (CA) Independent Press-Telegram*. She was once kicked out of Liberace's kitchen while covering a story. She said to the singer, "I think we should forget the story because you're a better piano player than you are a cook. Your beef stroganoff tastes more like canned beef stew." She authored a cookbook for the *Miami Herald* and another cookbook about tropical foods. By 1980, she was writing about food for the Knight-Ridder newspaper chain.

Marj Heyduck, *Dayton Journal Herald*

Marj Heyduck graduated from Ohio State University and began working as a columnist at the *Dayton Journal Herald* in 1944. Five years later she became the women's page editor. She also covered food including contributing to the food editors' 1952 *Coast to Coast* cookbook. She had a popular column, "Third and Main," that was published in several books. She was editor of the women's department for sixteen years until becoming the assistant to the editor of the newspaper in 1966.

Elinor Lee, *Washington Post*

Elinor Lee was a graduate of Beaver College. She was a teacher of dietetics at a hospital and a home economist before taking a Washington radio job in 1937. When she left radio, her morning program, "At Home with Elinor Lee," was the top-rated radio show in the 9:15 time slot, and her 12:15 p.m. show, "Home Edition," was one of the top ten daytime shows in the nation's capital. Lee joined the staff of the *Washington Post* in 1953, but she continued to do her food and homemaking program on the radio. She resigned from the radio show in 1955 to work full time at the *Post's* food section. Under Lee's direction, the paper's food and homemaking coverage grew from a single page to a full-color section, which appeared on Thursdays. She wrote that she collected recipes the way others collect stamps or coins. Lee retired in 1970. She married and had one daughter.

Jane Nickerson, *New York Times* and *Lakeland Ledger*

In 1938, Jane Nickerson graduated from the all-female Radcliffe College. The following year, she began her journalism career as an editorial assistant for the *Ladies' Home Journal*. She moved on to the *Saturday Evening Post* before moving to New York City in 1942 to work at the *New York Times* as the newspaper's first food editor. She wrote news and feature stories about food, as well as reviewed restaurants. She left the newspaper in 1957 and moved to Florida with her husband, Alexander Steinberg. The couple divorced in 1972. After raising four children, she wrote a cookbook and became the food editor in 1973 at *the Lakeland Ledger* in Florida.

Eleanor Ostman, *St. Paul Pioneer Press*

Eleanor Ostman graduated from Macalester College's journalism program and wrote about home furnishings before covering food at the *St. Paul Pioneer Press*. At the time, she was a young wife without much cooking experience, but she wrote about her family's love of a dish or a disaster that she had in the kitchen. She initiated a recipe column, "This Sunday," that ran for more than twenty-five years. She is known for having lunch with Paul Newman after winning his recipe contest. She was often confused with her counterpart at the *St. Louis Post-Dispatch*, Barb Ostmann. She was married to Ron Aune and had a son.

Barb Ostmann, *St. Louis Post-Dispatch*

Barb Ostmann earned a journalism degree from the University of Missouri. She traveled the world, including China, Switzerland, and Cuba, and learned about international cuisine. During her travels, she ate fried scorpions in China, horse kidneys in Italy, and emu carpaccio in Australia. She was the food editor at the *St. Louis Post-Dispatch* from 1975 to 1990. She then became a food writer for the New York Times Company's Regional Newspaper Group, which included twenty-five newspapers in ten states, from 1993 to 2005. She wrote and edited many cookbooks. She is married.

Clementine Paddleford, *New York Herald Tribune*

Clementine Paddleford earned a journalism degree from Kansas State University in 1921 and began writing for the *New York Herald Tribune* and *This Week* magazine beginning in the 1920s. In 1932, doctors removed a malignant growth from her larynx and vocal cords, which left her with a husky voice. For the rest of her life, she breathed through a tube in her throat, concealed by a black ribbon. She had a popular recipe feature, "How America Eats," that was turned into a cookbook. She worked for the *New York Herald Tribune* until the newspaper went under in 1966. She was briefly married and later raised the daughter of a friend who had died.

Polly Paffilas, *Akron Beacon Journal*

Polly Paffilas broke into the newspaper business as a temporary hire at the *Akron Beacon Journal*, called in to assist short staff in the newsroom during World War II. She was hired at $23.50 a week as a clerk in the reference library, but she tried to learn every job at the paper even learning how to operate the manual elevator. Paffilas became a cub reporter on the city desk, later moving to the women's pages, where she became food editor. Her career at the *Akron Beacon Journal* covered more than forty-five years before she retired in 1987. When she learned she had diabetes in 1971, she shared it with her readers, as well as her eighty-pound weight loss.

Dorothy Parnell, *Milwaukee Sentinel*

Dorothy Parnell was the daughter of a state senator who started work at the *Milwaukee Sentinel* in 1919. She worked until 1926 when she resigned to get married. After having a daughter, she returned to the newspaper in 1937. She became women's page editor in 1942 and covered fashion and food. She was known for being a dogged reporter; she sprained an ankle in 1952 racing to the phone to get the first interview with Pat Nixon when it was announced that her husband would be the Republican presidential nominee. Her recipes were included in the 1952 *Coast to Coast* cookbook. She retired in 1962.

Dorothee Polson, *Arizona Republic*

Dorothee Polson earned a journalism degree from the University of Minnesota. She followed her husband to Kansas and then to Arizona. She oversaw the first stand-alone food section at the *Arizona Republic*. In an oral history, she said, "I think it helped me that there had not been a food section, because there were no rules and regulations to follow. I could just do whatever I wanted to. And I did. I would do interviews with interesting people that had nothing to do with food and just bring in their favorite recipes, because everyone eats. Most people cook a little bit, and most people have a favorite recipe, whether it's theirs or somebody else's. No matter what I wrote about, I could bring in a food angle." She had a food column that eventually resulted in the 1971 cookbook, *Pot au Feu*. She was a judge in the Pillsbury Bake-Off and the mother of two children.

Diana Rowell, *St. Petersburg Times*

Diana Rowell attended Michigan State Normal College before relocating to South Florida. She became the society editor at the *St. Petersburg Times* in 1931 and helped establish the annual Debutante Ball in 1937. In 1948, she became the newspaper's food editor. She oversaw a cooking contest in the 1950s and retired from the newspaper in 1956. She was married and the mother of three children.

Clarice Rowlands, *Milwaukee Journal*

Clarice Rowlands was a 1936 graduate of the University of Wisconsin. After graduation, she was a society reporter at a Green Bay newspaper from 1937 until 1943 and then joined the *Milwaukee Journal* as food editor (an interest she developed as a member of the 4-H Club in high school). She occasionally wrote under the pen name "Alice Richards." She was married to fellow *Journal* employee Charles Nevada. She died of a heart attack in 1968.

Kay Savage, *Detroit Free Press*

Kay Savage was the food editor at the *Detroit Free Press* from 1945 through the 1960s. She answered readers' questions through her column "Tower Kitchen Recipe Box" and her "Recipes from the Tower Kitchen" pamphlet. She had a test kitchen and one assistant. She was named to the Detroit reporters' hall of fame. In 1955, she married

Howard Kennedy. She wrote the 1962 cookbook *Secrets of Michigan Cooks* and a pamphlet about cooking with flowers.

Dorothy Sinz, *Dallas Times Herald*

Dorothy Sinz graduated from Southern Methodist University in Dallas in 1931 and was the food editor of the *Dallas Times Herald* from the 1940s through 1969. She was a judge in the Miss America pageant in 1964 and 1966 and was also a judge for the Pillsbury Bake-Off. She wrote a recipe book for the newspaper in 1964.

Nell Snead, *Kansas City Star*

After earning a college degree and teaching English in Nebraska, Nell Snead applied for a job at the *Kansas City Star* while in the city on vacation in the 1930s. She started on the city desk but soon took on the job of women's page editor after being promised that she could go to New York to learn about fashion. She also covered food, and her recipes were included in the 1952 *Coast to Coast* cookbook. There were four women on the staff when she was hired and she encouraged the hiring of more women. She trained sixteen of them, who became known as "Nell's chicks." She survived a 1957 plane crash in France. According to the executive editor of the newspaper, "No label fits Nell Snead. She is a free spirit, and you will never know another like her." She worked for the women's pages for more than four decades.

Mary Sorensen (Mary Hart), *Minneapolis Tribune*

Mary Engelhart graduated from the University of Minneapolis and was hired by the *Minneapolis Tribune* in 1945. The newspaper shortened her name to "Mary Hart," which they put under copyright to use with the "Ask Mary" taste column; they had planned to allow other women to use the name after she left the newspaper. Yet Engelhart, who married and used the name Sorensen, remained at the *Tribune* for forty-four years. Her column was so popular that a 1978 tabulation of mail received by *Tribune* columnists listed advice columnist Ann Landers with

763 letters, while "Mary Hart" racked up 1,056. She was married to Franklin L. Sorensen Jr., who helped invent instant cream of wheat.

Elaine Tait, *Philadelphia Bulletin* and *Philadelphia Inquirer*

Elaine Tait initially wrote food stories for women's page editor Marjorie Paxson at the *Philadelphia Bulletin* as early as the 1970s and then became a well-known restaurant reviewer at the *Philadelphia Inquirer*. She had a thirty-five-year career as a Philadelphia food writer and authored several cookbooks.

Phyllis Tamor, *Cincinnati Enquirer*

Phyllis Tamor was a home economics graduate of Pennsylvania State University. She worked as a home economist for a Chicago meat company in the 1950s, which involved a great deal of travel and daily taste-testing of steak when she was in town. She sometimes made presentations under the name of "Martha Logan." She went on to become the food editor for the *Cincinnati Enquirer*. She judged several cooking contests, including a 1964 meat-roasting contest that was also covered by a *Sports Illustrated* reporter. She did graduate work in nutrition, and then left the journalism field and went into public relations when she developed multiple sclerosis at age forty-six. This caused her to write a cookbook for those cooking from a wheelchair and led to the publication of several of her recipes in newspapers in the 1980s.

Marian Tracy, *New York World-Telegram* and *The Sun*

Marian Coward Tracy attended Miami University of Ohio and Randolph-Macon Women's College. She was the food editor for *New York World-Telegram* and *The Sun*. She wrote many cookbooks—including several with her husband, Nino, who died in 1942. The most popular was *Casserole Cookery*, which was reissued more than ten times. In one version, there was an introduction written by Pulitzer Prize–winning poet and social critic Phyllis McGinley. She described the cookbook author as "the prophet of a new gospel—immensely stylish." Tracy was the editor of the 1952 cookbook *Coast to Coast*, which featured the work of many food editors.

Rosa Tusa, *Milwaukee Sentinel* and *Palm Beach Post*

Rosa Tusa learned to cook from her Italian father and was hired by the *Milwaukee Sentinel*'s women's pages in 1953. She became the *Sentinel* food editor in 1962. After meeting and interviewing Russian painter Kyril Vassilev for a story, she married him five years later. The couple lived in a castle and raised many Great Danes—up to a dozen at a time. She was a good friend of Poppy Cannon and judged the 1970 Pillsbury Bake-Off. In 1971, she and her husband moved to Florida and she became the food editor of the *Palm Beach Post*. She retired in 1987. During her career, she attempted to cook a moose nose and fought a bull in Spain. She also wrote a cookbook about grits.

Jo Ann Vachule, *Fort Worth Star-Telegram*

Jo Ann Eidom Vachule already had newspaper journalism experience before she earned a journalism degree from the University of Texas and married a classmate. The couple went to work at the *Austin American-Statesman*. In 1950, she became a reporter on the news side and was later promoted to assistant city editor. Despite her position, she still experienced bias in assignments; for example, when Adlai Stevenson came to town, she was assigned to interview his sister rather than the politician. She left the newspaper in 1953 to raise her two children, but returned in 1963 when the newspaper needed a food editor. She worked part of the week from home because there was no test kitchen. Under the alias "Jacqueline Jones," she penned the *Star-Telegram*'s culinary Q&A column, "C.U.P.S." (Cooking Up a Storm). She judged many cooking contests, including the Pillsbury Bake-Off. Wolfgang Puck, Paul Prudhomme, and Martha Stewart visited her home while she was food editor.

Ann Valder, *Las Vegas Review-Journal* and *Valley Times*

Ann Valder moved to Las Vegas from the Midwest in 1957. In 1958, as "Kathy Keno," she handled promotional activities for Radio KENO. She joined the *Las Vegas Review-Journal* newspaper as a columnist in 1964, followed by an appointment as assistant women's editor and food editor. She judged the Pillsbury Bake-Off and other cooking competitions. After nine years she moved to the *Valley Times* as women's editor. In 1977, she returned to the *Review-Journal* as assistant society editor, a position she held until her retirement in 1983. She was married and had two children.

Veronica Volpe, *Pittsburgh Press*

Veronica Volpe earned a degree in home economics from Carnegie Institute of Technology (now Carnegie Mellon University) in 1934. During World War II, she served in the US Navy WAVES (Women Accepted for Volunteer Emergency Service). She worked briefly as food editor of the *Pittsburgh Post-Gazette* in the 1950s, resigning to direct publicity and advertising for the Penn-Sheraton Hotel. She returned to journalism in 1961 as food editor at the *Pittsburgh Press*, a job from which she retired in 1977. She was known as a woman of style who signed her name "V-squared" and was an advocate for Pittsburgh's historic preservation. She edited the 1958 fundraising cookbook *Cooking with the Groundhog* (which did indeed include a recipe for cooking a groundhog) to benefit the Punxsutawney Women's Press Club. It was positively reviewed in the *New York Times*.

Jeanne Voltz, *Miami Herald* and *Los Angeles Times*

Jeanne Appleton Voltz earned a journalism degree from what is now the University of Montevallo. She worked the news beat during World War II and married a fellow journalist. She then became the food editor at the *Miami Herald* in the 1950s and at the *Los Angeles Times* in the 1960s through the early 1970s. She later became the food editor at *Woman's Day* magazine. She wrote many cookbooks and was considered an expert on barbecue and Southern cooking. She was married for most of her career and raised two children.

Charlotte Walker, *News & Courier* and *Evening Post*

Charlotte Walker came to the United States from Newfoundland after working there as a newspaper editor. She joined Charleston's *Evening Post* in 1950 and became the women's page editor a year later. She became the food editor of both the *Evening Post* and the *News & Courier* in 1961. She wrote a popular recipe request column, "Loved & Lost . . . ," that resulted in a 1970 cookbook. She was on the organizing committee for what later became the Association of Food Journalists. She retired in 1974 but continued to write a recipe column. She was married to Henry Frost Pinckney Walker.

Erma Young, *Kansas City Star*

Erma Young graduated from the University of Missouri. She started on the city desk of the *Kansas City Star* in 1944 after a few years at another Missouri newspaper. She joined the women's pages at the *Star* in 1954. She started the food column "Come into My Kitchen" the following year, which highlighted home cooks. The column would continue to run for more than fifty years. She retired in 1969.

MALE FOOD EDITORS

Ben G. Cooper, *Mobile Register*

Ben Cooper was an assistant news editor and the food editor at the *Mobile Register* from 1948 to 1955. He had a syndicated food column. He was the only man included in the 1952 cookbook *Coast to Coast* and also wrote cookbooks on his own.

Gaynor and Dorothy Maddox, NEA, wire service

Gaynor Maddox wrote several cookbooks and attended some of the annual food editor meetings, as well as judged several of the cooking competitions. Dorothy Maddox also wrote occasional food columns, as "Mrs. Gaynor Maddox." Together, they recorded the album *How to*

Plan the Perfect Dinner Party, which centered on a steak meal. The audio is available online.

NOTES

PREFACE

1. Gaynor Maddox, "Food Pages No More a Woman's Domain," *Rome (GA) News-Tribune*, February 19, 1975.

2. Polly Paffilas, "Comments from the Food Section," *Matrix* (Winter 1971–1972), 15.

3. Polly Paffilas Collection, Akron Library, Akron, OH, http://sc.akronlibrary.org/files/2011/03/Polly-Paffilas-Collection.pdf.

4. Janet Beighle French Collection, Cleveland State Library, Cleveland, OH, http://ead.ohiolink.edu/xtf-ead/view?docId=ead/OClU0048.xml;query=;brand=default.

5. Jayne E. Simms, "Public Relations Information and Practices as Viewed by Women's Newspaper Editors" (master's thesis, University of Wisconsin, 1973).

6. Laura Shapiro, *Something from the Oven* (New York: North Point Press, 1986), xxii.

7. Dorothy Crandall, "Women Drivers Cook under Hood," *Owosso (MI) Argus-Press*, October 27, 1965, http://news.google.com/newspapers?nid=1978&dat=19651027&id=Q0wiAAAAIBAJ&sjid=k6sFAAAAIBAJ&pg=5821,6140949.

8. Laura Shapiro, "American Originals: Rethinking the Pillsbury Bake-Off," speech at the Culinary Historians of Southern California, November 10, 2012, Downtown Los Angeles Public Library.

9. Column with a Heart, "Real Working Mother's the One at Home," *Miami Herald*, October 5, 1966; Column with a Heart, "This 'Working Mom' Wishes Job at Home Had Paid Off," *Miami Herald*, October 16, 1966.

10. Garrett D. Byrnes, *Food in Newspapers*, Handbook for Editors No. 1 (New York: American Press Institute, Columbia University, 1951), 2.

11. "Mildred Davis: A Woman of Faith and Music" (obituary), December 10, 2010, http://www.hunterallenmyhand.com/obituaries/Mildred-Miller-Davis2871449907/#!/Obituary.

12. David Kamp, *The United States of Arugula: How We Became a Gourmet Nation* (New York: Broadway Books, 2006), 75.

13. Cecily Brownstone, oral history interview by Laura Shapiro, Cecily Brownstone Papers, Fales Library and Special Collections, New York University, 15.

14. Kathleen Purvis, "She Always Had a New Idea Cooking," *Charlotte Observer*, January 23, 2002.

15. Nora Ephron, "The Food Establishment," in *Wallflower at the Orgy* (New York: Bantam Books, 2007), 1–19.

16. Ephron, "Food Establishment," 17.

17. "Sherried Chicken Salad Sandwich," *Oprah Magazine*, http://www.oprah.com/food/Sherried-Chicken-Salad-Sandwiches.

18. Jeanne Voltz, *Barbecued Ribs, Smoked Butts and Other Great Feeds* (New York: Knopf, 1990).

19. "Jeanne Voltz, 81; Past Editor of the *Times'* Food Section" (obituary) *Los Angeles Times*, January 16, 2002.

20. Maddox, "Food Pages No More a Woman's Domain."

1. THE ORIGINS OF FOOD JOURNALISM IN US NEWSPAPERS

1. Amy Bentley, "Booming Baby Food: Infant Foods and Feeding in Post-World War II America," *Michigan Historical Review* 32, no. 2 (2006): 63–87. Aaron Bobrow-Strain, *White Bread: A Social History of the Store-Bought Loaf* (Boston: Beacon Press, 2012). Susan Yager, *The Hundred Year Diet* (New York: Rodale, 2010).

2. Sylvia Lovegren, *Fashionable Food: Seven Decades of Food Fads* (New York: Simon & Schuster, 1995). Joanne Lamb Hayes, *Grandma's Wartime Kitchen: World War II and the Way We Cooked* (New York: St. Martin's Press, 2000).

3. Jessica Weiss, "She Also Cooks," in Sherrie A. Inness, ed., *Kitchen Culture in America* (Philadelphia: University of Pennsylvania Press, 2001), 216.

4. David Kamp, *The United States of Arugula* (New York: Broadway Books, 2006), 10.

5. Kamp, *United States of Arugula*, 10.

6. Betsy Balsley, Donna Deane, Rose Dosti, and Barbara Hansen, "*L.A. Times* Food Gals," discussion at the Culinary Historians of Southern California, Los Angeles Public Library, Downtown Central Library, April 10, 2010. Video available at http://chscsite.org/food-section-gals/.

7. Kamp, *United States of Arugula*, 3.

8. Jeanne Voltz, "Dynamic Influence: Californians Bow to Chinese Cookery, Californians Bow to Chinese Cuisine," *Los Angeles Times*, June 26, 1969.

9. Jeanne Voltz, *The California Cookbook* (New York: Bobbs-Merrill, 1970), xii.

10. Diane Eicher, "Food Writer Dollaghan Dies at 70," *Denver Post*, August 4, 1998.

11. Garrett D. Byrnes, *Food in Newspapers*, Handbook for Editors No. 1 (New York: American Press Institute, Columbia University, 1951), 2.

12. Maurine Beasley and Sheila Gibbons, eds., *Taking Their Place: A Documentary History of Women and Journalism* (Washington, DC: American University Press, 1993).

13. For example, the *Evansville (IN) Courier* women's page editor Ann Hamman had a master's degree in home economics from Purdue University.

14. Laura Shapiro, *Something from the Oven: Reinventing Dinner in 1950s America* (New York: Viking, 2004), 95.

15. Richard Kluger, *The Paper* (New York: Knopf, 1986).

16. Lloyd Wendt, Chicago Tribune: *The Rise of a Great American Newspaper* (Chicago: Rand McNally, 1979).

17. Frank Angelo, *On Guard: A History of the* Detroit Free Press (Detroit: Detroit Free Press, 1981), 198.

18. Jack Claiborne, Charlotte Observer: *Its Time and Place* (Chapel Hill: University of North Carolina Press, 1986).

19. Nixon Smiley, *Knights of the Fourth Estate: The Story of the* Miami Herald (Miami: Banyan, 1984).

20. Kathleen Purvis, "Words to Eat By," *Charlotte Observer*, February 18, 1998.

21. Richard Karp, "Newspaper Food Pages: Credibility for Sale," *Columbia Journalism Review* (November/December 1971): 36–44.

22. "Elizabeth Howkins, Editor, Dies; Headed *Times*'s Women's News," *New York Times*, January 12, 1972.

23. Ann Criswell, "Thanks for the Memories," *Houston Chronicle*, September 27, 2000.

24. Ruth Ellen Lovrien Church, "Bobbs-Merrill Biographical Questionnaire," Fall 1955, Bobbs-Merrill Mss, Box 32, Lilly Library, Indiana University, Bloomington.

25. Byrnes, *Food in Newspapers*, 13.

26. Marian Tracy, ed., *Coast to Coast Cookery* (Bloomington: Indiana University Press, 1952), 62.

27. Ruth Reichl, "Magazine Editing Then and Now," in *The Art of Making Magazines*, ed. Victor S. Navasky and Evan Cornog (New York: Columbia University Press, 2012), 29-46.

28. Dorothy Jurney, "Detroit Free Press," Food Editors Seminar, University of Houston, February 25, 1972, 2, Marjorie B. Paxson Papers, National Women and Media Collection, State Historical Society of Missouri.

29. Norman Isaacs, speech at Food Editors Seminar, University of Houston, February 25, 1972, 7, Marjorie B. Paxson Papers.

30. Church, "Bobbs-Merrill Biographical Questionnaire."

31. Molly O'Neill, "Food Porn," *Columbia Journalism Review* (September/October 2003): 38–45.

32. Evan Jones, *Epicurean Delight* (New York: Touchstone, 1992), 170.

33. James Beard, letter to Helen Evans Brown, September 16, 1957, in John Ferrone, ed., *Love and Kisses and a Halo of Truffles* (New York: Arcade Publishing, 1994), 192.

34. James Beard, letter to Helen Evans Brown, September 1957, in *Love and Kisses and a Halo of Truffles*, ed. John Ferrone (New York: Arcade Publishing, 1994), 190.

35. Thomas McNamee, The *Man Who Changed the Way We Eat* (New York: Simon & Schuster, 2013), 65.

36. Craig Claiborne, "Elegance of Cuisine on Wane in the U.S.," *New York Times*, April 13, 1959.

37. Craig Claiborne, *A Feast Made for Laughter* (New York: Doubleday, 1982), 141.

38. Elizabeth Penrose Howkins, memo to Mr. Sulzberger, April 24, 1959, New York Times Company Records, Arthur Hays Sulzberger Papers, Box 169, Food News folder, Manuscript and Archives Division, New York Public Library.

39. Nan Robertson, *The Girls in the Balcony: Women, Men, and the* New York Times (New York: Random House, 1992).

40. Mitchell Davis, "A Taste for New York," doctoral diss., New York University, 2009, 47.

41. "Food Columnist Reveals Recipes for Exciting Career," *Ocala (FL) Star-Banner*, April 28, 1974.

42. Claiborne, *A Feast Made*, 122.

43. Claiborne, *A Feast Made*, 122–23.

44. Ivan Veit, memo to Mr. Sulzberger, May 29, 1957, Arthur Hays Sulzberger Papers, Box 169, Food News folder.

45. Claiborne, *A Feast Made*, 122.

46. Kamp, *United States of Arugula*, 65.

47. Betty Fussell, *Masters of American Cookery* (Lincoln: University of Nebraska Press, 2006), 42.

48. Jane Nickerson, "News of Food: Graduate of Swiss Hotel School Tells of Study of French Cooking," *New York Times*, May 10, 1954.

49. Nickerson, "News of Food: Graduate of Swiss Hotel."

50. Jane Nickerson, "News of Food: Sturdy New Packages for Frozen Food," *New York Times*, June 13, 1946.

51. Claiborne, *A Feast Made*, 125.

52. Marion Marzlof, *Up from the Footnote: A History of Women Journalists* (New York: Hasting House, 1977), 207. Agnes Hooper Gottlieb, "Women's Pages," in *The Encyclopedia of American Journalism* (New York: Routledge, 2008), 601–2.

53. Nancy Stohs, "A Place at Your Table," *Milwaukee Journal*, March 29, 1995.

54. Kristin Eddy, "Serving Food News for 150 Years," *Chicago Tribune*, July 16, 1997.

55. John Kleber, "Cissy Gregg," in *Louisville Encyclopedia* (Lexington: University Press of Kentucky, 1992), 392.

56. "1915: The *Picayune*'s Creole Cook Book Was Wildly Popular," *Times-Picayune* (New Orleans), October 19, 2011.

57. "1915: The Picayune's Creole Cook Book Was Wildly Popular," *Times-Picayune* (New Orleans), October 19, 2011, http://www.nola.com/175years/index.ssf/2011/10/1915_the_picayunes_creole_cook.html.

58. Kay Powell, "Grace Hartley Germon," *Atlanta Journal-Constitution*, September 16, 2000.

59. Byrnes, *Food in Newspapers*, 4.

60. Jane Nickerson, "War Brides, Beware!" *New York Times Magazine*, June 17, 1945.

61. Shapiro, *Something from the Oven.*

62. Mitchell Davis, "Power Meal," *Gastronomica* (Summer 2004): 60–72.

63. Ray Irwin, "Newspapers Find Food Profitable News Subject," *Editor & Publisher*, July 15, 1950.

64. "Elinor Lee, 83, Former *Post* Food Editor, Dies," *Washington Post*, December 23, 1988.

65. Dorothee Polson, email interview with the author, June 5, 2011.

66. Dorothee S. Polson, oral history, July 29, 1994. Shema Arizona: The Arizona Jewish Historical Society Oral History Project, Arizona Jewish Historical Society, Arizona State University Libraries, Phoenix.

67. Kristen Browning-Blas, "Stirring Up the Past," *Denver Post*, August 16, 2006.

68. Cecily Brownstone Papers, Fales Library and Special Collections, New York University, http://dlib.nyu.edu/findingaids/html/fales/brownstone/.

69. Darren Barbee, "Ex-*Star-Telegram* Food Editor Became Expert on Cuisine," *Fort Worth Star-Telegram*, September 4, 2009.

70. Gregg Jones, "Tasting Her Way around the World," *Missourian*, May 1, 2012.

71. Janet Beighle French, email interview with the author, May 5, 2013.

72. Cecily Brownstone, oral history conducted by Laura Shapiro, 13, Cecily Brownstone Papers.

73. "Services Set for Daum, Led *Journal* Food Section," *Milwaukee Journal*, October 22, 1990.

74. Tim McNulty, "Tales from the Test Kitchen," *Chicago Tribune*, December 21, 2007.

75. Julia Ferrante, "Jane Steinberg, 83, Food Editor," *Lakeland Ledger*, March 2, 2000.

76. Jane Nickerson, "Countless Read Her," obituary of Cicely Brownstone, *Lakeland Ledger*, June 12, 1994.

77. "Top Honors for Women's Pages," *Milwaukee Journal*, September 15, 1961.

78. Kelly Alexander and Cynthia Harris, *Hometown Appetites: The Sory of Clementine Paddleford, the Forgotten Food Writer Who Chronicled How America Ate* (New York: Gotham Press, 2008).

79. Sarah Stage, "Home Economics: What's in a Name?" In *Rethinking Home Economics* (Ithaca, NY: Cornell University Press, 1997), 1.

80. Carolyn M. Goldstein, *Creating Consumers: Home Economics in Twentieth-Century America* (Chapel Hill: University of North Carolina Press, 2012).

81. Alexander and Harris, *Hometown Appetites*, 92.

82. Diane Carman, "Helen Wrote the Recipe for Success," *Denver Post*, August 8, 1998.

83. Eleanor Ostman, *Always on Sunday* (St. Paul, MN: Sexton Printing, 1998), 111.

84. Criswell, "Thanks for the Memories."

85. Wm. David Sloan, *The Media in America: A History* (Northport, AL: Vision Press, 2011), 294.

86. Beverly Stephen Koch, "The History and Evolution of Women's Pages in American Newspapers" (master's thesis, University of California, 1974), 17.

87. Jenn Garbee, "Marian Manners, Prudence Penny, the First Celebrity Chefs," *Los Angeles Times*, April 22, 2009.

88. "Hyman Goldberg, 'Prudence Penny,' Dies," *Norwalk (CT) Hour*, September 21, 1970.

89. Kay Savage, *Secrets of Michigan Cooks* (Detroit: Foods Arts, 1962).

90. Catherine C. Laughton, *Mary Cullen's Northwest Cook Book* (Portland, OR: Journal Publishing Company, 1946).

91. "Beverly Robison Poling," *(Portland) Oregon Journal*, April 15, 2007.

92. Raeanne S. Sarazen, "Q. We Recently Came across a Booklet," *Chicago Tribune*, October 3, 2001.

93. "Fleeta Louise Hoke, 94; Retired *Times* Food Editor," *Los Angeles Times*, April 13, 1995.

94. "Margot McConnell, Editor, Food Writer," *New York Times*, July 8, 1976.

95. Dorothee S. Polson, *Pot au Feu Cookbook* (Phoenix: Arizona Republic, 1971), 6.

96. Purvis, "Words to Eat By."

97. Dean Johnson, "Dorothy Chapman Plans to Savor Her Retirement," *Orlando Sentinel*, April 25, 1986.

98. Dorothy Chapman, "Memories Are Made of Christmas Joys, Santa's Helper," *Orlando Sentinel*, December 21, 1985.

99. Ruth Gorrell, "Conference Food with a Flair," *St. Petersburg Times*, October 11, 1957.

100. Balsley et al., "*L.A. Times* Food Gals."

101. "Services Set for Daum."

102. Janet Beighle French, email interview with the author, May 5, 2013.

103. Johnson, "Dorothy Chapman Plans to Savor Her Retirement."

104. Kristen Browning-Blas, "Keeping Helen D., in Mind," *Denver Post*, November 28, 2001.

105. "The Press: The Kitchen Department," *Time*, October 19, 1953.

106. Alexander and Harris, *Hometown Appetites*, 91.

107. Ruth D'Arcy, "Detroit News," Food Editors Seminar, University of Houston, February 25, 1972, 3, Marjorie B. Paxson Papers.

108. Laura Crooks, "Our Very Own Kitchen Queen," *Spokesman Review* (Spokane, WA), October 19, 2005.

109. John Ferrone, ed., *Love and Kisses and a Halo of Truffles* (New York: Arcade Publishing, 1994), 27.

110. "1969 Conference on Food, Nutrition and Health: Final Report," National Nutrition Summit 2000, http://www.nns.nih.gov/1969/conference.htm.

111. Peggy Daum, "Conference Delegates Hope to Spread Awareness of Hunger," *Milwaukee Journal*, December 10, 1969.

112. Peggy Daum, "A Retrospective," *Milwaukee Journal*, February 17, 1988.

113. Jeanne Voltz, "Malnutrition Detection Urged," *Los Angeles Times*, September 12, 1969.

114. Jeanne Voltz, "FDA Readying First Guidelines on Nutrition," *Los Angeles Times*, April 8, 1971.

115. Jeanne Voltz, "Labeling System Proposed by FDA," *Los Angeles Times*, March 2, 1972.

116. Jeanne Voltz, "Cheers and Jeers for New Nutrient Labeling Regulations," *Los Angeles Times*, January 25, 1973.

117. Jeanne Voltz, "Grain Enrichment Law—1970's Gift to Californians," *Los Angeles Times*, December 27, 1971.

118. Dorothy Crandall, "Canned Foods in the Future to List Vitamins, Minerals," *Boston Globe*, May 26, 1972.

119. Jeanne Voltz, "Hungry—A Lot of Talk about It, But What's Being Done?" *Los Angeles Times*, September 28, 1972.

120. Jeanne Voltz, speech at Food Editors Seminar, University of Houston, February 25, 1972, 4, Marjorie B. Paxson Papers.

121. Jeanne Voltz, "Malnutrition Blamed on Eating Habits," *Los Angeles Times*, February 15, 1973.

122. Jeanne Voltz, "Little Water Goes a Long Way," *Los Angeles Times*, February 15, 1973.

123. Jeanne Voltz, "For Gourmets on a Budget," *Los Angeles Times*, January 30, 1972.

124. Lois Decker O'Neill, ed., *The Women's Book of World Records and Achievements* (New York: Doubleday, 1979), 468.

125. D'Arcy, "Detroit News," 3.

126. D'Arcy, "Detroit News," 4.

127. Maude Coons, "Omaha on High Side of the List," *Omaha World-Herald*, August 4, 1972.

128. Jeanne Voltz, *An Apple a Day* (New York: Irena Chalmers Cookbooks, 1983), 6.

129. Jeanne Voltz, "You Can Thank Mad Dogs and Englishmen for Indian Curry," *Los Angeles Times*, June 4, 1972.

130. Jane Nickerson, "The Legendary Cakes of Vienna," *New York Times*, September 16, 1956.

131. Jane Nickerson, "The Fine Flavors of Lakeland Half a Century Ago," *Lakeland Ledger*, August 22, 1973.

132. Dorothy Crandall, "Priscilla Alden Would Be Amazed by 1957 Thanksgiving," *Boston Globe*, November 24, 1957.

2. FOOD AND FOOD JOURNALISM
DURING AND AFTER WORLD WAR II

1. Amy Bentley, *Eating for Victory* (Urbana-Champagne: University of Illinois Press, 1998), 35.

2. Joanne Lamb Hayes, *Grandma's Wartime Kitchen: World War II and the Way We Cooked* (New York: St. Martin's Press, 2000).

3. Bentley, *Eating for Victory*, 35.

4. Bentley, *Eating for Victory*, 27–29.

5. Jane Nickerson, "War Brides, Beware!" *New York Times Magazine*, June 17, 1945.

6. Bentley, *Eating for Victory*, 39.

7. Bentley, *Eating for Victory*, 25.

8. Bentley, *Eating for Victory*, 117.

9. "More Victory Gardens Needed," *St. Petersburg Times*, January 30, 1943.

10. Steven Gdula, *The Warmest Room in the House* (New York: Bloomsbury, 2007), 67.

11. Darren Barbee, "Ex-Star-Telegram Food Editor Became Expert on Cuisine," *Fort Worth Star-Telegram*, September 4, 2009.

12. Ann Criswell, "Thanks for the Memories," *Houston Chronicle*, September 27, 2000.

13. Kelly Alexander and Cynthia Harris, *Hometown Appetites: The Story of Clementine Paddleford, the Forgotten Food Writer Who Chronicled How America Ate* (New York: Gotham Press, 2008), 108.

14. Frances Blackwood, *Mrs. England Goes On Living* (New York: Creative Age Press, 1943).

15. Frances Blackwood, "Mrs. England Goes On Living," *Philadelphia Bulletin*, July 2–4, 1942.

16. Margot Murphy, *Wartime Meals* (New York: Greenberg, 1942).

17. Bentley, *Eating for Victory*, 40.

18. Alexander and Harris, *Hometown Appetites*, 111.

19. Nancy Stohs, "A Place at Your Table," *Milwaukee Journal Sentinel*, March 29, 1995.

20. Jane Nickerson, "Emergency Potatoes," *New York Times*, April 14, 1946.

21. "Meatless Days Draws Blank," *Milwaukee Journal*, October 8, 1947.

22. "Food Supplies Reported Adequate," *Milwaukee Journal*, January 31, 1947.

23. Jane Nickerson, "News of Food: Cutting Food Costs 10% Suggested," *New York Times*, May 15, 1946.

24. Jane Nickerson, "News of Food: New Packages Made Up by CARE Replaces Army Ten-in-One," *New York Times*, February 12, 1947.

25. David Davies, *The Postwar Decline of American Newspapers, 1945–1965* (Westport, CT: Praeger, 2006), 4.

26. Purvis, "Words to Eat By," *Charlotte Observer*, February 18, 1998.

27. Andrea Preston, "Former Food Guru and Editor Dies," *Evansville (IN) Courier*, June 17, 2003.

28. Diana Nelson Jones, "Veronica Volpe: Food Editor at *Post-Gazette, Press* for Many Years," *Pittsburgh Press*, February 10, 2005, http://www.post-gazette.com/stories/local/obituaries/obituary-veronica-volpe-food-editor-at-post-gazette-press-for-many-years-569552/.

29. "Bertha Hahn Receives Coveted Vesta Award," *Miami News*, October 3, 1960.

30. Jane Nickerson, "Making the Most of Oranges and Grapefruit," *New York Times*, January 13, 1946.

31. Jane Nickerson, "News of Food: New Merchandizing Feature in Chain Store Pleases Customers," *New York Times*, October 31, 1946.

32. Marian Tracy and Nino Tracy, *Casserole Cookery: One Dish Meals for the Busy Gourmet* (New York: Viking Press, 1948).

33. Cecily Brownstone, "Casserole Dishes 'Naturals' for Lent, Is Author's Claim," *Lewiston (ID) Morning Tribune*, March 14, 1952.

34. Andrew F. Smith, *Eating History: 30 Turning Points in the Making of American Cuisine* (New York: Columbia University Press, 2009), 71–72.

35. Mary Meade, "New Canned Foods Give Variety to Menus," *Chicago Tribune*, July 9, 1955.

36. Mary Meade, "Canned Foods Are Easy on Budget," *Chicago Tribune*, November 15, 1963.

37. Ann Vileisis, *Kitchen Literacy* (New York: Island Press, 2010), 8.

38. Joanne Lamb Hayes, *Grandma's Wartime Kitchen: World War II and the Way We Cooked* (New York: St. Martin's Press, 2000), 103, 67.

39. Pia Sarkar, "Scrambling for Customers," *San Francisco Chronicle*, August 4, 2005, http://www.sfgate.com/business/article/Scrambling-for-customers-The-supermarket-was-2618709.php.

40. Jane Nickerson, "News of Food: New Merchandising Feature in Chain Store," *New York Times*, October 31, 1946.

41. Clementine Paddleford, "Grandmother Shopped Here," *Los Angeles Times*, August 18, 1946.

42. Clarice Rowlands, "Supermarket Managers Get Customers' Views," *Milwaukee Journal*, January 24, 1957.

43. Dorothy Crandall, "Markets Welcome Consumer Advice," *Boston Globe*, June 25, 1968.

44. Janet Beighle French, email interview with the author, July 4, 2013.

45. Joshua Gitelson, "Populox: The Suburban Cuisine of the 1950s," *Journal of American Culture* 15, no. 3 (Fall 1992): 73.

46. Gitelson, "Populox," 76.

47. Nora Ephron, "Food Establishment," in *Wallflower at the Orgy* (New York: Bantam Books, 2007), 5–6.

48. David Kamp, *The United States of Arugula: How We Became a Gourmet Nation* (New York: Broadway Books, 2006), 69.

49. Cecily Brownstone, oral history conducted by Laura Shapiro, 17, Cecily Brownstone Papers.

50. Associated Press, "Food Writer Cecily Brownstone," *Washington Post*, September 5, 2005.

51. Molly O'Neill, "Long Ago Smitten, She Remains True to the Country Captain," *New York Times*, April 17, 1991.

52. O'Neill, "Long Ago Smitten."

53. Kamp, *United States of Arugula*, 57.

54. Jane Nickerson, "Countless Read Her," *Lakeland Ledger*, June 12, 1994.

55. Jane Nickerson, "News of Food: Oriental Dishes Available to Americans in 'Far Eastern Cookery,'" *New York Times*, September 16, 1947.

56. Jane Nickerson, "Meatless Dishes, Italian Style," *New York Times*, March 6, 1949.

57. Jane Nickerson, "Famous Classic of French Kitchen at Last Makes Its Debut in English," *New York Times*, May 7, 1949.

58. Jane Nickerson, "Creole Tradition Offers Jambalaya to Grace Era of the Buffet Supper," *New York Times*, January 23, 1953.

59. Elinor Lee, "Chinese Are Fine Cooks," *Miami News*, September 17, 1953.

60. Elinor Lee, "Chilean Casserole Is a Most Elegant Dish," *Miami News*, October 1, 1953.

61. Evan Jones, *Epicurean Delight* (New York: Touchstone, 1992), 300.

62. Julia Child, *My Life in France* (New York: Anchor Press, 2007), 235.

63. Smith, *Eating History*, 237.

64. Nan Ickeringill, "Food: Ways with Fish," *New York Times*, October 14, 1964.

65. Julia Child, "A French Cook," *Boston Globe*, June 21, 1965.

66. Julia Child, "A French Cook," *Boston Globe*, July 5, 1965.

67. Julia Child, "A French Cook," *Boston Globe*, November 8, 1965.

68. Katie Carlson, "Paul and Julia Child Take an Unrestful Year Off," *Daytona Beach Morning News*, October 23, 1976.

69. Dorothy Crandall, "Julia and Jim Cook a Deux," *Boston Globe*, October 19, 1968.

70. David Strauss, *Setting the Table for Julia Child* (Baltimore: Johns Hopkins University Press, 2011), 191.

71. Jeanne Voltz, "Roar of Approval for Curry, as Exotic as Sikhs and Saris," *Los Angeles Times*, January 28, 1973.

72. Jeanne Voltz, "Sushi a Great Snack from Japan," *Los Angeles Times*, February 7, 1971.

73. Jeanne Voltz, "Lexicon with a Latin Accent for California Cooking," *Los Angeles Times*, August 5, 1971.

74. Jeanne Voltz, "A Mexican Party Buffet by the Pool," *Los Angeles Times*, April 27, 1969.

75. Jeanne Voltz, "Tamales," *Los Angeles Times*, June 1, 1972.

76. Jeanne Voltz, "Enchiladas: They're Easy on the Budget and Hard to Resist," *Los Angeles Times*, March 15, 1973.

77. Jeanne Voltz, "Almendrado," *Los Angeles Times*, January 24, 1971.

78. Virginia Heffington, "A Taste of Old New Orleans," *Miami Herald*, October 24, 1968.

79. Virginia Heffington, "Fall with a Foreign Accent," *Miami Herald*, October 31, 1968.

80. Jane Nickerson, "News of Food: Cheeseburgers for Supper," *New York Times*, May 3, 1947.

81. Gdula, *The Warmest Room*, 98.

82. Gdula, *The Warmest Room*, 100.

83. Kim Gutierrez (daughter of Rita Ciccone), email interview with the author, July 2013.

84. Barbee, "Ex-*Star-Telegram* Food Editor."

85. Criswell, "Thanks for the Memories."

86. Jeanne Voltz, "Expert Hits Myths on Male Taste," *Los Angeles Times*, February 6, 1963.

87. Purvis, "Words to Eat By."

88. Eleanor Ostman, *Always on Sunday* (St. Paul, MN: Sexton Printing, 1998), 250–51.

89. Associated Press, "Liberace, Food Editor Have Argument," *The Day* (New London, CT), May 1, 1971.

90. "Grace Rescues Food Editors," *Baltimore Sun*, September 27, 1962.

91. Mary Meade, "Nation's Food Editors Meet Here Next Week," *Chicago Tribune*, September 2, 1949.

92. Jane Nickerson, "News of Food: Nation's Newspaper Food Editors Arrive on Seventh Annual Epicurean Pilgrimage," *New York Times*, October 9, 1950.

93. Jane Nickerson, "News of Food: Food Editors Hear Actor and Chemist," *New York Times*, October 14, 1950.

94. Dorothy Parnell, "New York Chit Chat," *Milwaukee Sentinel*, October 22, 1950.

95. Clarice Rowlands, "Editors' Fare," *Milwaukee Journal*, October 30, 1952.

96. Maude Coons, "Price Control Is Attacked," *Evening World-Herald* (Omaha), October 14, 1952.

97. Maude Coons, "Weight Control Problem Great," *Evening World-Herald* (Omaha), October 19, 1952.

98. Veronica Volpe, "Florida, Pakistan Represented with Citrus and Saucy Recipes," *Pittsburgh Post-Gazette*, October 3, 1955.

99. Mary Meade, "Fiesta of Food Ideas," *Chicago Tribune*, September 25, 1956.

100. Clarice Rowlands, "Food Conference Has International Theme," *Milwaukee Journal*, September 23, 1956.

101. Veronica Volpe, "Dry Soup Flavoring, Smoked Bear Hams," *Pittsburgh Post-Gazette*, September 28, 1956.

102. Bertha Cochran Hahn, "A Reunion in Chicago," *Miami News*, September 30, 1957.

103. Bertha C. Hahn, "Diets Are Overlooked," *Miami News*, October 2, 1957.

104. Clarice Rowlands, "Manhattan Merry Go Round," *Milwaukee Journal*, September 25, 1958.

105. Maude Coons, "Statistics Prove Americans Like Canned, Frozen Food," *Evening World-Herald* (Omaha), October 5, 1959.

106. Mary Meade, "Newspaper Food Editors Eat, Eat, and Eat," *Chicago Tribune*, October 6, 1960.

107. "Editors to Hear Florida Citrus Story from Hooks," *Lakeland Ledger*, October 2, 1960.

108. Lowis Carlton, "Editors Look into Food Future," *St. Petersburg Times*, September 15, 1961.

109. Dorothy Crandall, "Americans Eat Better, Cheaper Than Anyone," *Boston Globe*, October 6, 1964.

110. Crandall, "Americans Eat Better."

111. Charlotte Walker, "Food Editors Find Shoppers Sharper Now!" *Charleston News & Courier*, October 5, 1964.

112. Dorothy Crandall, "Self-Basting Turkeys and Odorless Onions," *Boston Globe*, September 27, 1966.

113. Charlotte Walker, "Pilgrim's Special Is Today's Instant Snack," *Charleston News & Courier*, September 26, 1966.

114. Virginia Heffington, "The Best Tasters Testing," *Miami Herald*, November 7, 1968.

115. Janet Beighle French, email interview with the author, July 3, 2013.

116. Ruth Ellen Church, "Serious Message Behind Fluff at Food Meetings," *Chicago Tribune*, October 2, 1968.

3. FOOD JOURNALISM AND THE RISE OF CONSUMER ACTIVISM

1. Bernice Rothman Hasin, *Consumers, Commissions, and Congress* (New Brunswick, NJ: Transaction Books, 1987), 5.

2. Frances Pollack, "Consumer Reporting: Underdeveloped Region," *Columbia Journalism Review* (May/June 1971): 38.

3. Jeanne Voltz, "How to Protect Consumer," *Los Angeles Times*, October 16, 1970.

4. Pollack, "Consumer Reporting," 41.

5. Lois Decker O'Neill, ed., *The Women's Book of World Records and Achievements* (New York: Doubleday, 1979), 468.

6. Jeanne Voltz, "Food Shopping Rapped by Housewives," *Los Angeles Times*, November 4, 1971.

7. Jayne E. Simms, "Public Relations Information and Practices as Viewed by Women's Newspaper Editors" (master's thesis, University of Wisconsin, 1973), 5–6.

8. Rose Dosti, *Dear S.O.S.: Thirty Years of Recipe Requests to the* Los Angeles Times (Los Angeles: Los Angeles Times Syndicate Books, 1994), 6.

9. Linda Ambrose, "Food Page Puffery," *Houston Journalism Review* (August 1972): 22.

10. Ambrose, "Food Page Puffery," 24.

11. Ruth Reichl, "Magazine Editing Then and Now," in *The Art of Making Magazines*, ed. Victor S. Navasky and Evan Cornog (New York: Columbia University Press, 2012), 29–46.

12. Frances Cawthon, "A Main Ingredient in the Recipes for Southern Tradition," *Atlanta Journal*, March 9, 1986, 23.

13. Beverly Stephen Koch, "The History and Evolution of Women's Pages in American Newspapers" (master's thesis, University of California, Berkeley, 1974), 34.

14. Eleanor Clark French, memo to Arthur Hays Sulzberger, September 16, 1952, Box 169, Food News folder, New York Times Company Records. Arthur Hays Sulzberger Papers, Manuscripts and Archives Division, New York Public Library.

15. Arthur Hays Sulzberger, memo to Mr. Catledge, September 6, 1956, Box 169, Food News folder, Arthur Hays Sulzberger Papers.

16. Charlotte Walker, "Loved, Lost . . ." *Charleston News & Courier*, February 18, 1968.

17. "Senator Moss, Posing as Ragged Patient, Sees Medicaid Abuse in New York City," *New York Times*, August 30, 1976.

18. Frank Moss, "Business, the Consumer and You," speech presented at the National Food Editors' Conference, Chicago, October 7, 1971, 1. Frank E. Moss Papers, J. Willard Marriott Library, University of Utah, Salt Lake City.

19. Moss, "Business," 24.

20. Carol DeMasters, email interview with the author, February 26, 2013.

21. Moss, "Business," 25.

22. "Breakfast Cereal," *Consumer Reports*, May 1961, 239–40.

23. Thomas Green, "Tricksters and the Marketing of Breakfast Cereals," *Journal of Popular Culture* 40, no. 1 (2007): 49–66.

24. Richard Halloran, "F.C.C. Study Urged of TV Cereal Ads," *New York Times*, August 6, 1970.

25. Moss, "Business," 26.

26. "Senator Explodes Bomb as Food Editors Seethe," *Editor & Publisher*, October 16, 1971, 14–15.

27. Jeanne Voltz, speech at Food Editors Seminar, University of Houston, February 25, 1972, Marjorie Paxson Papers, National Women and Media Collection, State Historical Society of Missouri.

28. Peggy Daum, "Editors Criticized by Senator, Feminist," *Milwaukee Journal*, October 8, 1971.

29. Daum, "Editors Criticized."

30. Daum, "Editors Criticized."

31. Jack Anderson, "Moss to Probe Newsmen," *Tuscaloosa (AL) News*, January 9, 1972.

32. Richard Karp, "Newspaper Food Pages: Credibility for Sale," *Columbia Journalism Review* (November/December 1971): 36.

33. Peggy Daum, "Stare Defends His Ethics, Stand," *Milwaukee Journal*, September 22, 1970.

34. Jeanne Voltz, "Experts Defend Cereals," *Los Angeles Times*, August 5, 1970.

35. Simms, "Public Relations," 5.

36. Simms, "Public Relations," 37.

37. Garrett D. Byrnes, *Food in Newspapers*, Handbook for Editors No. 1 (New York: American Press Institute, Columbia University, 1951), 3.

38. Byrnes, *Food in Newspapers*, 13.

39. Marjorie Paxson, speech at Food Editors Seminar, University of Houston, February 25, 1972, 2, Marjorie Paxson Papers.

40. Melinda Blanchard and Robert Blanchard, *At Blanchard's Table* (New York: Clarkson Potter, 2003), 28.

41. Dorothy Chapman, *A Taste of Florida: The Best of "Thought You'd Never Ask"* (Orlando: Sentinel Communications, 1990), 9.

42. Darrell Christian, Sally Jacobsen, and David Minthorn, eds., *The Associated Press Stylebook* (New York: Associated Press, 2013), 36.

43. Ann Hamman, letter to the editor, *Columbia Journalism Review* (May/June 1972): 61.

44. Polly Paffilas, "Comments from the Food Section," *Matrix* (Winter 1971–1972): 15.

45. Voltz, speech at Food Editors Seminar, 1.

46. Voltz, speech at Food Editors Seminar, 2.

47. "Feedback from Food Editors," *Matrix* (Winter 1971–1972): 14.

48. Hamman, letter to the editor, 61.

49. Carol Demasters, email interview with the author, June 4, 2010.

50. Simms, "Public Relations," 101–2.

51. Dorothee Polson, email interview with the author, June 5, 2011.

52. Betsy Balsley, Donna Deane, Rose Dosti, and Barbara Hansen, "*L.A. Times* Food Gals," discussion at the Culinary Historians of Southern California, Los Angeles Public Library, Downtown Central Library, April 10, 2010. Video available at http://chscsite.org/food-section-gals/.

53. Balsley et al., "*L.A. Times* Food Gals."

54. Hamman, letter to the editor, 61.

55. Ambrose, "Food Page Puffery," 20–22.

56. Ambrose, "Food Page Puffery," 21.

57. Louise Oettinger, "Food Editors Are Criticized at Seminar," *Tuscaloosa News*, March 8, 1972.

58. Louise Oettinger, "News Editors—More Concerned about Consumer Coverage," *Tuscaloosa News (AL)*, March 8, 1972.

59. Ruth D'Arcy, "Detroit News," speech at Food Editors Seminar, University of Houston, February 25, 1972, 3, Marjorie B. Paxson Papers.

60. Dorothy Jurney, "Detroit Free Press," speech at Food Editors Seminar, University of Houston, February 25, 1972, 2, Marjorie Paxson Papers.

61. Christian et al., *The Associated Press Stylebook*, 36.

62. Marjorie Paxson, speech at Food Editors Seminar, 2.

63. Norman E. Isaacs, speech at Food Editors Seminar, University of Houston, February 25, 1972, 7, Marjorie B. Paxson Papers.

64. Simms, "Public Relations," 97.

65. Simms, "Public Relations," 103.

66. Simms, "Public Relations," 76.
67. Simms, "Public Relations," 77.
68. Simms, "Public Relations," 77.
69. Simms, "Public Relations," 105.
70. Pollock, "Consumer Reporting," 39.
71. Pollock, "Consumer Reporting," 41.
72. Simms, "Public Relations," 90.
73. Simms, "Public Relations," 96.
74. Claiborne, *A Feast Made*, 128.
75. Bynes, *Food in Newspapers*, 12.
76. Voltz, speech at Food Editors Seminar, 4.
77. Dorothee Polson, email interview with the author, June 5, 2011.
78. Cecily Brownstone, oral history conducted by Laura Shapiro, 17, Cecily Brownstone Papers, Fales Library and Special Collections, New York University.
79. Ruth Ellen Church, "Ruth Ellen Church Reports What's Cooking in Europe," *Chicago Tribune*, April 23, 1967.
80. Eleanor Ostman, *Always on Sunday* (St. Paul, MN: Sexton Printing, 1998), 99.
81. Gregg Jones, "Tasting Her Way around the World," *Missourian*, May 1, 2012.
82. Ann Criswell, "Thanks for the Memories," *Houston Chronicle*, September 27, 2000.

4. COOKBOOKS, EXCHANGING RECIPES, AND COMPETITIVE COOKING

1. Kennan Ferguson, "Intensifying Taste, Intensifying Identity: Collectively through Community Cookbooks," *Signs* 37, no. 3 (Spring 2012): 696.
2. Jan Longone, "Feeding America: The Historic American Cookbook Project," Digital and Multimedia Center, Michigan State University, http://digital.lib.msu.edu/projects/cookbooks/.
3. Carol Fisher, *The American Cookbook: A History* (Jefferson, NC: McFarland, 2006), 1.
4. Robert Roberts, *The House Servant's Directory* (Boston, 1827).
5. Fisher, *The American Cookbook*, 5.
6. Jessamyn Neuhaus, *Manly Meals and Mom's Cooking* (Baltimore: Johns Hopkins University Press, 2012), 1.
7. Ruth Ellen Lovrien, "Good Cook Book Basic Necessity in Every Home," *Chicago Daily Tribune*, January 3, 1941.

8. Neuhaus, *Manly Meals*, 164.

9. Neuhaus, *Manly Meals*, 166.

10. Jane Nickerson, "News of Food: Oriental Dishes Available to Americans in 'Far Eastern Cookery,'" *New York Times*, September 16, 1947.

11. *Rocky Mountain News Recipe Book* (Denver: Rocky Mountain News, 1964).

12. Charlotte Turgeon, "Including Hush Puppies," *New York Times*, October 19, 1952.

13. Marian Tracy, ed., *Coast to Coast Cookery* (Bloomington: Indiana University Press, 1952), ix.

14. Tracy, *Coast to Coast Cookery*, 39.

15. Tracy, *Coast to Coast Cookery*, 112–13.

16. Tracy, *Coast to Coast Cookery*, 80–81.

17. Tracy, *Coast to Coast Cookery*, 50.

18. Jane Nickerson, *Jane Nickerson's Florida Cookbook* (Gainesville: University of Florida Press, 1973), 158.

19. *Rocky Mountain News Recipe Book*.

20. Peggy Daum, ed., *The Best Cook on the Block Cookbook* (Milwaukee: Milwaukee Journal, 1979).

21. Virginia Heffington, *Food with a Florida Flair* (Miami: Miami Herald, 1968), 3.

22. Julie Benell, "Reader's Recipe Takes the Cake," *Dallas Morning News*, June 5, 1957.

23. Ruth Ellen Church, "Fiesta of Food Ideas Presented at Parley," *Chicago Tribune*, September 25, 1958.

24. Jessamyn Neuhaus, "The Way to a Man's Heart: Gender Roles, Domestic Ideology, and Cookbooks in the 1950s," *Journal of Social History* (Spring 1999): 537.

25. John Harriman, "Men-in-the-Kitchen Era Horrifies Columnist," *Boston Globe*, October 15, 1956.

26. James Beard, *The Fireside Cookbook* (New York: Simon & Schuster, 1949).

27. Jeanne Voltz, *Barbecued Ribs, Smoked Butts and Other Great Feeds* (New York: Knopf, 1990), x.

28. Voltz, *Barbecued Ribs*.

29. Morrison Wood, "For Men Only," *Chicago Tribune*, September 20, 1947.

30. Morrison Wood, "For Men Only," *Chicago Tribune*, August 27, 1954.

31. Evan Jones, *Epicurean Delight* (New York: Touchstone, 1992), 173.

32. Julie Benell, *Let's Eat at Home* (New York: Thomas Y. Crowell, 1961), ix.

33. Marvin J. Taylor and Clark Wolf, eds., *101 Classic Cookbooks: 501 Classic Recipes* (New York: Rizzoli, 2012), 658.

34. Marian Fox Burros and Lois Levine, *Freeze with Ease* (New York: Macmillan, 1965), ix.

35. Ann Hamman, "Cookbooks for Every Taste and Purse," *Evansville (IN) Courier*, May 5, 1972.

36. Jeanne Voltz, *Natural Foods Cookbook* (New York: Putnam's, 1973), 7.

37. Peggy Daum, "A Rachel Carson for Food?" *Milwaukee Journal*, October 3, 1973.

38. Gaynor Maddox, "Food Fad Flourishing," *Sumter (SC) Daily Items*, September 20, 1971.

39. Morrison Wood, "Amateur Chef Recommends Food Editors Book," *Chicago Tribune*, November 5, 1952.

40. Ruth Ellen Church, *Mary Meade's Magic Recipes* (New York: Bobbs-Merrill, 1965).

41. Anne Mendelson, *Stand Facing the Stove: The Story of the Women Who Gave America the Joy of Cooking* (New York: Scribner, 2003), 175.

42. Bonnie S. Benwick, "Irma Rombauer and Marion Rombauer Becker," in *Icons of American Cooking*, ed. Victor W. Geraci and Elizabeth Demers (Santa Barbara, CA: Greenwood, 2011), 234.

43. Cecily Brownstone, *Cecily Brownstone's Associated Press Cookbook* (New York: David McKay, 1972), x.

44. Mendelson, *Stand Facing the Stove*, 160.

45. Jane Nickerson, "They Wanted to Cook Like Mother," *New York Times Book Review*, August 12, 1951.

46. Kim Severson, "Does the World Need Another Joy? Do You?" *New York Times*, November 1, 2001.

47. Taylor and Wolf, *101 Classic Cookbooks*, 306.

48. Irma S. Rombauer, "Introduction," in *Joy of Cooking* (Indianapolis: Bobbs-Merrill, 1953)

49. Nickerson, "They Wanted to Cook."

50. Mendelson, *Stand Facing the Stove*, 221.

51. "Cook Book Offers 1,000 Photographs," *New York Times*, September 7, 1950.

52. Morrison Wood, "How to Cook the Way Mother Used To," *Chicago Tribune*, September 10, 1950.

53. Joan Reardon, ed., *As Always, Julia: The Letters of Julia Child and Avis DeVoto* (New York: Houghton Mifflin, 2010), 161.

54. Poppy Cannon, *The New New Can-Opener Cookbook* (New York: Thomas Y. Crowell, 1968), 1.

55. Jane Nickerson, "Delicious and Out of the Can," *New York Times*, October 19, 1952.

56. Robert Misch, "No Pernod in Bouillabaisse?" *New York Times*, June 11, 1961.

57. Poppy Cannon, *A Gentle Giant* (New York: Popular Library, 1956).

58. Poppy Cannon, *Bride's Cookbook* (New York: Holt, 1954).

59. Laura Shapiro, "In the Mix," *Gourmet*, August 2002, http://www.gourmet.com/magazine/2000s/2002/08/in_the_mix.

60. Poppy Cannon, "'Food's High Fashion to the Young,' Says Poet," *Hartford (CT) Courant*, January 18, 1970.

61. Poppy Cannon, "Soup Is the Result of Refined Tradition," *Hartford (CT) Courant*, July 30, 1967.

62. Cannon, "'Food's High Fashion.'"

63. Joanne Will, "Lifelong Love Affair with 'Real' Food," *Chicago Tribune*, March 9, 1978.

64. Pat Robison, "Humorous Recipes Taste Good, Too," *St. Petersburg Times*, March 6, 1962.

65. Peg Bracken, foreword, in *I Hate to Cook Book* (New York: Grand Central Publishing, 2010), xi.

66. Bracken, *I Hate to Cook Book*, 1.

67. Bracken, *I Hate to Cook Book*, 77.

68. Arleen Abrahams, "Witty Approach to Homemaking Spells Success for Humorist Wife," *Southern Missourian*, December 11, 1969.

69. "Peg Bracken Series Will Begin Sunday," *Los Angeles Times*, June 12, 1964.

70. Ruth Ellen Church, "Myra Waldo Is Lovely—and Can She Cook!" *Chicago Daily Tribune*, October 31, 1953.

71. "Myra Waldo's Barbecue Book," *Baltimore Sun*, August 29, 1963.

72. Nora Ephron, *Wallflower at the Orgy* (New York: Bantam Books, 2007), 17.

73. Theodora Illenberger and Avonne Eyre Keller, *The Cartoonist Cookbook* (New York: Gramercy, 1966), xii.

74. Fisher, *The American Cookbook*, 83–84.

75. Karola Saekel, "We've Come a Long Way since 1902," *San Francisco Chronicle*, April 4, 2001.

76. Dorothy Sinz, *Dallas Times Herald Recipe Book*, insert in the *Dallas Times Herald*, October 5, 1964.

77. Dorothee Polson, *Pot au Feu Cookbook* (Phoenix: Arizona Republic, 1971), 3.

78. Polson, *Pot au Feu*.

79. Daum, *The Best Cook*, 2.

80. Daum, *The Best Cook*, 66.
81. Daum, *The Best Cook*, 67.
82. Daum, *The Best Cook*, 2.
83. Eudora Garrison, *It's Not Gourmet—It's Better* (Charlotte, NC: Washburn, 1978).
84. Garrison, *It's Not Gourmet*, v.
85. Heffington, *Food with a Florida Flair*.
86. Phyllis Richman, foreword, in *The* Washington Post *Cookbook*, ed. Bonnie S. Benwick (Washington, DC: Washington Post, 2013), 7.
87. Bonnie S. Benwick, ed., *The* Washington Post *Cookbook* (Washington, DC: Washington Post, 2013), 8.
88. Women's National Press Club, *Who Says We Can't Cook!* (Washington, DC: McIver, 1955), 38.
89. Women's National Press Club, *Second Helping* (Washington, DC: McIver, 1962), 5.
90. Women's National Press Club, *Who Says*, 18.
91. Nan Robertson, *The Girls in the Balcony: Women, Men, and the* New York Times (New York: Random House, 1992), 101.
92. Women's National Press Club, *Second Helping*, 16.
93. Frances Lewine, "Press Cookbook Simmers Before Done," *Eugene (OR) Register-Guard*, October 17, 1962.
94. Eudora Garrison, *Eudora's Cookbook* (Charlotte, NC: Charlotte Observer, 1960), 3.
95. Eudora Garrison, *Eudora's Holiday Cook Book* (Charlotte, NC: Charlotte Observer, 1967).
96. Kay Savage, *Secrets of Michigan Cooks* (Detroit: Foods Arts, 1962).
97. Grace Hartley, *Grace Hartley's Southern Cookbook* (New York: Doubleday, 1976).
98. Frances Cawthon, "A Main Ingredient in the Recipe for Southern Tradition," *Atlanta Journal*, March 9, 1986, 24.
99. Cissy Gregg, *Cissy Gregg's Cookbook* (Louisville, KY: Louisville Courier-Journal, 1953).
100. Alexander Bainbridge, "Books in Brief," Florida Magazine, *Orlando Sentinel*, 26-F, n.d., available in "Grace Warlow Barr" file, Orange County Regional History Center, Orlando, FL.
101. Helen Dollaghan, *Best Main Dishes* (New York: McGraw-Hill, 1980).
102. Cecily Brownstone, *Cecily Brownstone's Associated Press Cookbook* (New York: David McKay, 1972).
103. Taylor and Wolf, *101 Classic Cookbooks*, 158–59.
104. Nickerson, *Jane Nickerson's Florida Cookbook*, vii.
105. Nickerson, *Jane Nickerson's Florida Cookbook*, 8–9.

106. Cecily Brownstone, "What's Cooking in Florida?" *Los Angeles Times*, August 22, 1974.

107. Rosa Tusa, *True Grits* (New York: Bantam Books, 1977).

108. Ruth Ellen Lovrien Church, "Bobbs-Merrill Biographical Questionnaire," Fall 1955, Bobbs-Merrill Mss, Box 32, Lilly Library, Indiana University, Bloomington.

109. Clementine Paddleford, *How America Eats* (New York: Scribner, 1960), vi.

110. Pat Willard, *America Eats!* (New York: Macmillan, 2008).

111. Amanda Hesser, "Recipe Redux: The Community Cookbook," *New York Times*, October 5, 2010.

112. Mary Meade, "Mary Meade's Gift to Readers: A Pledge of Continued Service," *Chicago Daily Tribune*, December 25, 1950.

113. Carol Haddix, email interview with the author, December 6, 2012.

114. "Maude Won't Stay Out of the Kitchen," *Omaha World-Herald*, April 29, 1973.

115. Tracy, *Coast to Coast Cookery*, 130.

116. Savage, *Secrets of Michigan Cooks*, 142.

117. Charlotte Walker, "Loved, Lost . . ." *Charleston News & Courier*, May 12, 1968.

118. Ann Criswell, "Thanks for the Memories," *Houston Chronicle*, September 27, 2000.

119. Eleanor Ostman, *Always on Sunday* (St. Paul, MN: Sexton Printing, 1998), 1

120. Rose Dosti, *Dear S.O.S.: Thirty Years of Recipe Requests to the* Los Angeles Times (Los Angeles: Los Angeles Times Syndicate Books, 1995).

121. Gail Borelli, "Come into My Kitchen Turns 50," *Kansas City Star*, January 19, 2005.

122. "Mary A. Hammond, Food Editor," *Philadelphia Inquirer*, January 21, 1983.

123. Mary Meade, "Follow Rules When Entering Recipe Contest," *Chicago Tribune*, March 21, 1942.

124. Carol Haddix, "A Food Editor's Memories," speech to the Culinary Historians of Chicago, Chicago, August 13, 2011.

125. Ann Criswell, *Houston Gourmet: Cooks and Caterers* (Houston: Fran Fauntleroy, 1990), 10.

126. Ostman, *Always on Sunday*, 52.

127. John Raven, "The History of Chili Cook-Offs," *Texas Cooking*, March 2007, http://www.texascooking.com/features/march2007_chili_cookoffs.htm.

128. Betty Wason, *Cooks, Gluttons and Gourmets* (New York: Doubleday, 1962).

129. Wason, *Cooks, Gluttons and Gourmets*, 324.
130. "All about Mushrooms," *Sunday Star* (Wilmington, DE), November 4, 1951.
131. Jane Nickerson, "News of Food: $50,000 Recipe Award Goes to Housewife," *New York Times*, December 14, 1949.
132. Savage, *Secrets of Michigan*, 112.
133. Ostman, *Always on Sunday*, 56.
134. Ostman, *Always on Sunday*, 54.
135. Steven Gdula, *The Warmest Room in the House* (New York: Bloomsbury, 2007), 106.
136. Ellie Mathews, *The Ungarnished Truth* (New York: Berkley Books, 2008), 216–17.
137. Pillsbury Company, "Press Guests, 19th Bake-Off," San Antonio, October 1967, A Guide to the San Antonio Fair, Inc., Records, 1962–1995 (bulk 1964–1968), Series 7: Public Relations Department, University of Texas San Antonio Libraries Special Collections.
138. "Carol McCready Hartley," *Honolulu Star-Advertiser*, March 16, 2011, http://obits.staradvertiser.com/2011/03/16/carol-mccready-hartley/.
139. Laura Shapiro, "American Originals: Rethinking the Pillsbury Bake-Off," speech to the Culinary Historians of Southern California, November 10, 2012, Downtown Los Angeles Public Library.
140. Joyce Kay Nelson, "Questionnaire for Betty Crocker Search for the American Homemaker of Tomorrow," April 3, 1970, Ann Valder Collection, MS 90-60, Special Collections, UNLV Libraries, University of Nevada, Las Vegas.

5. HOME ECONOMICS

1. Laura Shapiro, *Perfection Salad* (New York: North Point Press, 1988), 9.
2. Sarah Stage and Virginia B. Vincenti, "Introduction: Home Economics, What's in a Name?" in *Rethinking Home Economics: Women and the History of a Profession*, ed. Sarah Stage and Virginia B. Vincenti (Ithaca, NY: Cornell University Press, 1997), 1.
3. Carolyn M. Goldstein, *Creating Consumers: Home Economists in Twentieth-Century America* (Chapel Hill: University of North Carolina Press, 2012).
4. "Was Home Economics a Profession?" Online supplement to exhibition "From Domesticity to Modernity: What Was Home Economics?" 2001, Division of Rare and Manuscript Collections, Carl A. Kroch Library, Cornell University, http://rmc.library.cornell.edu/homeEc/masterlabel.html.
5. Goldstein, *Creating Consumers*, 1.

6. Amy Sue Bix, "Equipped for Life: Gendered Technical Training and Consumerism in Home Economics, 1920–1980," *Technology and Culture* 43, no. 4 (October 2002): 731.

7. "Was Home Economics a Profession?"

8. Shapiro, *Perfection Salad*, 9.

9. Goldstein, *Creating Consumers*, 4.

10. Lisa Mae Robinson, "Safeguarded by Your Refrigerator," in *Rethinking Home Economics: Women and the History of a Profession*, ed. Sarah Stage and Virginia B. Vincent (Ithaca, NY: Cornell University Press, 1997), 259.

11. Eloise Davison, "Stove Efficiency Tests" (master's thesis, Iowa State College, 1923).

12. Harriet B. Breckenridge and Louise J. Peet, "Combination Dry and Steam Flatirons Tested," *Journal of Home Economics* 40 (March 1948): 137–39.

13. Bix, "Equipped for Life," 731.

14. May E. Foley, "Awakening in Home Economics Journalism," *Journal of Home Economics* (August 1923): 417–18.

15. Elizabeth Sweeney Herbert, "When the Homemaker Goes to Work," *Journal of Home Economics* (April 1952): 258.

16. Annie Longley Hamman, "The Cost per Hour of Time Saved by the Use of Selected Pieces of Household Equipment" (master's thesis, Purdue University, 1952).

17. Andrea Preston, "Former Food Guru and Editor Dies," *Evansville (IN) Courier*, June 17, 2003.

18. Jane Nickerson, "Powered by Water from the Kitchen Faucet," *New York Times*, September 28, 1946.

19. Eleanor Ostman, "Tested at 25," *St. Paul Pioneer Press*, August 22, 1993.

20. Eleanor Ostman, *Always on Sunday* (St. Paul, MN: Sexton Printing, 1998), 275.

21. Ruth Ellen Church, *Mary Meade's Magic Recipes* (Indianapolis: Bobbs-Merrill, 1965), 1.

22. Dorothy Crandall, "Cooking for the Camping Family Can Be Easy," *Boston Globe*, June 21, 1964.

23. Dennis Getto, "Daum Retiring as Food Editor," *Milwaukee Journal*, February 17, 1988.

24. Barbara Gibbs Ostmann and Jane Baker, eds., *Food Editors' Hometown Favorites Cookbook: American Regional and Local Specialties* (New York: Dial, 1984), 32.

25. Janet Beighle French, email interview with the author, July 2013.

26. Ann Criswell, "Thanks for the Memories," *Houston Chronicle*, September 27, 2000.

27. Ostman, *Always on Sunday*, 9.

28. Dick Kreck, "Helen Dollaghan More Than Sum of Exploding-Chicken Parts," *Denver Post*, July 7, 1993.

29. Lou Richardson and Genevieve Callahan, *How to Write for Homemakers* (Ames: Iowa State College Press, 1949), ix.

30. Jayne E. Simms, "Public Relations Information and Practices as Viewed by Women's Newspaper Editors" (master's thesis, University of Wisconsin, 1973), 83.

31. Goldstein, *Creating Consumers*, 205.

32. Nancy Stohs, "A Place at Your Table," *Milwaukee Journal*, March 29, 1995.

33. Nancy Stohs, "Newspaper Institute Raised the Bar for Homemaking," *Milwaukee Journal Sentinel*, April 18, 2001.

34. Kelly Alexander and Cynthia Harris, *Hometown Appetites: The Story of Clementine Paddleford, the Forgotten Food Writer Who Chronicled How America Ate* (New York: Gotham Press, 2008), 88–91.

35. Alexander and Harris, *Hometown Appetites*, 110.

36. Home Institute of the *New York Herald Tribune*, *America's Cook Book* (New York: Scribner, 1937), xiii.

37. Betsy Balsley, Donna Deane, Rose Dosti, and Barbara Hansen, "*L.A. Times* Food Gals," discussion at the Culinary Historians of Southern California, Los Angeles Public Library, Downtown Central Library, April 10, 2010. Video available at http://chscsite.org/food-section-gals/.

38. Janet Beighle [French], *The* Plain-Dealer's *Cleveland Meat Cook Book* (Cleveland: Plain-Dealer, 1968).

39. Garrett D. Byrnes, *Food in Newspapers*, Handbook for Editors No. 1 (New York: American Press Institute, Columbia University, 1951), 13.

40. Irene Powers, "Woman of Distinction: Mary Meade," *Chicago Daily Tribune*, November 19, 1959.

41. "A Picture Recipe: Mary Meade Makes Creamy Chocolate Fudge," *Chicago Daily Tribune*, October 19, 1956.

42. Tim McNulty, "Tales from the Test Kitchen," *Chicago Tribune*, December 21, 2007.

43. Nancy Stohs, "Food Team Aims to Help Readers Do Recipes Right," *Milwaukee Journal Sentinel*, January 31, 2012.

44. Carol Haddix, "A Food Editor's Memories," speech to the Culinary Historians of Chicago, Chicago, August 13, 2011.

45. Jeanne Voltz and Burke Hamner, *The L.A. Gourmet* (New York: Doubleday, 1971), 3.

46. Heather McPherson, "Dorothy Chapman, 1921–2004," *Orlando Sentinel*, December 14, 2004.

47. Peggy Daum, "Preparation Is Family Project," *Milwaukee Journal*, December 21, 1956.

48. Peggy Daum, "Tourist's Eye View of Milwaukee," *Milwaukee Journal*, July 7, 1957.

49. Peggy Daum, "Club Keeps Gay 'First Footing' Custom," *Milwaukee Journal*, December 28, 1958.

50. "Price of Milk Boosted Again," *Milwaukee Journal*, January 11, 1954.

51. Peggy Daum, "Bread Rich in Nutrition Introduced," *Milwaukee Journal*, February 16, 1956.

52. Heffington likely meant *Agnello e annellini.*

53. Virginia Heffington, "Fall with a Foreign Accent," *Miami Herald*, October 31, 1968.

54. Virginia Heffington, "Chicken Hawaiian," *Miami Herald*, January 23, 1969.

55. Elinor Lee, "Chicken Has Long and Noble Heritage," *Los Angeles Times*, March 26, 1970.

56. Teri Lyn Fisher and Jenny Park, *Tiny Food Party* (Philadelphia: Quirk Books, 2012).

57. Virginia Heffington, "Mini-Bites," *Miami Herald*, September 19, 1968.

58. Jane Nickerson, "Steak Worthy of the Name," *New York Times*, January 25, 1953.

59. Jane Nickerson, "Easy-to-Make 'Jambalaya' Produces Festive Party," *New York Times*, January 23, 1953.

60. Jane Nickerson, "'From the Sea around Us," *New York Times*, January 4, 1953.

61. Todd Coleman, "The Queen's Beans," *Saveur*, October 2, 2007.

62. Bernice Gross and Kay Young Mackley, "Should the Homemaker Use Ready-Made Mixes?" *Journal of Home Economics* (June 1950): 451.

63. "The History of Mixes," *Practical Home Economics* (September 1958): 76.

64. Rose Dosti, "L.A. and Carrot Cake," *Los Angeles Times*, August 22, 1974.

65. Winzola McLendon and Scottie Smith, *Don't Quote Me! Washington Newswomen and the Power Society* (New York: Dutton, 1970), 178.

66. Associated Press, "The Wedding Cake: White House Chef Explains Mrs. Nixon's Recipe," *New York Times*, June 2, 1971.

67. Cecily Brownstone, oral history conducted by Laura Shapiro, 18, Cecily Brownstone Papers, Fales Library and Special Collections, New York University.

68. Ostman, *Always on Sunday*, 301.

69. Women's National Press Club, *Second Helping* (Washington, DC: McIver, 1962), 83.

70. Clementine Paddleford, "To a Man's Heart Frozen Blintzes," *New York Sun*, May 20, 1949.

71. Ruth Ellen Church, *Pancakes Aplenty* (Chicago: Rand McNally, 1962), 7.

72. Dorothy Crandall, "Pancake Cooks Will Flip Today," *Boston Globe*, March 2, 1965.

73. Jane Nickerson, "News of Food: Vitamins, Minerals Added to Ice Cream," *New York Times*, January 29, 1946.

74. Jane Nickerson, "'Making the Most of Oranges and Grapefruit," *New York Times*, January 13, 1946.

75. Jeanne Voltz, "FDA Readying First Guidelines on Nutrition," *Los Angeles Times*, April 8, 1971.

76. Jeanne Voltz, "Labeling System Proposed by FDA," *Los Angeles Times*, March 2, 1972.

77. Jeanne Voltz, "Cheers and Jeers for New Nutrient Labeling Regulations," *Los Angeles Times*, January 25, 1973.

78. Jeanne Voltz, "Grain Enrichment Law—1970's Gift to Californians," *Los Angeles Times*, December 27, 1971.

79. Jeanne Voltz, "Are Americans Programmed to Overconsumption of Sugar?" *Los Angeles Times*, April 19, 1973.

80. Jeanne Voltz, "Malnutrition Blamed on Eating Habits," *Los Angeles Times*, February 15, 1973.

81. Ruth Ellen Lovrien, "Mary Meade's 99 Bread Recipes in Booklet Form," *Chicago Tribune*, November 17, 1939.

82. Aaron Bobrow-Strain, *White Bread: A Social History of the Store-Bought Loaf* (Boston: Beacon Press, 2012), 118.

83. Jane Nickerson, "Bread from Whole Grains," *New York Times*, February 9, 1947.

84. Jane Nickerson, "News of Food: Adding Vitamin D to White Bread Follows Nutritional Trend," *New York Times*, March 12, 1953.

85. Daum, "Bread Rich in Nutrition Introduced."

86. Janet Beighle French, *Plain-Dealer* Food/Home Economics Scrapbook Index, Part 3, Janet Beighle French Collection, Michael Schwartz Library, Cleveland State University.

87. Jeanne Voltz, "Home Made Bread," *Los Angeles Times*, August 9, 1970.

88. Peggy Daum, "Tom Farley: The Man Behind School Lunch," *Milwaukee Journal*, May 27, 1970.

89. James Beard, *Beard on Food* (New York: Knopf, 1974), 199.

90. Jane Nickerson, "News of Food: Sturdy New Packages for Frozen Food," *New York Times*, June 13, 1946.

91. "What's the Average Cost of a Thanksgiving Meal?" *USA Today*, November 19, 2012.

92. Jane Nickerson, "Food: Cost of Thanksgiving Dinner," *New York Times*, November 18, 1955.

93. Ostman, *Always on Sunday*, 8.

94. Jeanne Voltz, "Round the World on a Meatball Budget," *Los Angeles Times*, March 4, 1973.

95. Ann Hamman, "Thrifty Buying Important as Food Prices Continue High," *Evansville (IN) Courier*, January 7, 1972.

96. Ann Hamman, "Period of Change in Supply, Quality, Price of Fresh Produce," *Evansville (IN) Courier*, May 26, 1972.

97. Ann Hamman, "Sometimes Larger Sizes Really Are Thriftier," *Evansville (IN) Courier*, February 25, 1972.

98. Ann Hamman, "Prices May Be Partly Due to Packaging," *Evansville (IN) Courier*, March 3, 1972.

99. Ann Valder, "Cooking with Commodities," *Las Vegas Review-Journal*, June 27, 1971.

100. "1969 Conference on Food, Nutrition and Health: Final Report," National Nutrition Summit 2000, http://www.nns.nih.gov/1969/conference.htm.

101. Dorothy Crandall, "The All-American Lunch," *Boston Globe*, October 15, 1969.

102. Jeanne Voltz, "Nutritionists Back School Lunch Bill," *Los Angeles Times*, December 22, 1972.

103. Marjorie Paxson, speech at Food Editors Seminar, 4, University of Houston, February 25, 1972, 2, Marjorie Paxson Papers.

104. Jeanne Voltz, "Hungry—A Lot of Talk about It, But What's Being Done?" *Los Angeles Times*, September 28, 1972.

105. Jeanne Voltz, "Malnutrition in the City," *Los Angeles Times*, September 7, 1972.

106. Jeanne Voltz, "Overcoming Food Stamp Reservations," *Los Angeles Times*, December 21, 1972.

107. Jeanne Voltz, "Markets Listening to Shoppers," *Los Angeles Times*, October 4, 1971.

108. Jeanne Voltz, "Standards on Organic Food Questioned," *Los Angeles Times*, November 11, 1971.

109. Jeanne Voltz, "Panel Rakes Grocers over the Coals," *Los Angeles Times*, June 29, 1972.

110. Voltz, "Panel Rakes Grocers."

111. Jeanne Voltz, "Looking into Health Food Movement," *Los Angeles Times*, June 22, 1972.
112. Jeanne Voltz, *The* Los Angeles Times *Natural Foods Cookbook* (New York: Putnam's, 1973), 7.
113. Voltz, Los Angeles Times *Natural Foods Cookbook*, 9.
114. Sherrie A. Inness, *Secret Ingredients: Race, Gender and Class at the Dinner Table* (New York: Palgrave Macmillan, 2006), 89, 101.
115. Goldstein, *Creating Consumers*, 295.
116. Jacqui Michot Ceballos, letter to Robin Morgan, February 23, 1971, Robin Morgan Papers, David M. Rubenstein Rare Book & Manuscript Library, Duke University.
117. "What Robin Morgan Said in Denver," *Journal of Home Economics* (January 1973): 13.
118. Joan Osgood Rainey, letter to Robin Morgan, July 16, 1972, Robin Morgan Papers.

6. THE RESTAURANT REVIEWER
AS JOURNALIST

1. Ann Criswell, *Houston Gourmet: Cooks and Caterers* (Houston: Fran Fauntleroy, 1990), 1.
2. Marian Tracy, ed., *Coast to Coast Cookery* (Bloomington: Indiana University Press, 1952), 143.
3. Tracy, *Coast to Coast Cookery*, 190.
4. Phyllis Richman, foreword, in *The* Washington Post *Cookbook: Readers' Favorite Recipes*, ed. Bonnie Benwick (Washington, DC: Washington Post Company, 2013), 7.
5. Jane Nickerson, "News of Food: Head of the Baltimore & Ohio Railroad," *New York Times*, June 28, 1951.
6. Jane Nickerson, "Food: Vive la France," *New York Times*, February 20, 1957.
7. Heather McPherson, "Dorothy Chapman, 1921–2004," *Orlando Sentinel*, December 14, 2004.
8. Doris Reynolds, "Let's Talk Food: Duncan Hines Much More Than Cake Mixes," *Naples (FL) News*, August 8, 2012.
9. Reynolds, "Let's Talk Food."
10. Duncan Hines, *Duncan Hines' Food Odyssey* (New York: Thomas Y. Crowell, 1955), 39.
11. Mitchell Davis, "A Taste for New York" (doctoral diss., New York University, 2009), 104.

12. Cecily Brownstone, oral history conducted by Laura Shapiro, Cecily Brownstone Papers, Fales Library and Special Collections, New York University.

13. Andrew Dornenburg and Karen Page, *Dining Out* (New York: Wiley), 8.

14. Clementine Paddleford, *How America Eats* (New York: Scribner, 1960), 346–47.

15. Clementine Paddleford, "Gourmets' Choice," in *New York, New York* (New York: Delta Books, 1964), 147–88.

16. Paddleford, "Gourmet's Choice."

17. Jeanne Voltz, "Dining Out," *Los Angeles Times*, February 5, 1961.

18. Jeanne Voltz, "Dining Out," *Los Angeles Times*, February 12, 1961.

19. Jeanne Voltz, "Dining Out," *Los Angeles Times*, April 30, 1961.

20. Jeanne Voltz, "Dining Out," *Los Angeles Times*, July 2, 1961.

21. Elisa Ludwig, "Will Work for Food," *Philadelphia Weekly*, January 31, 2001.

22. Dornenburg and Page, *Dining Out*, 65.

23. Susan Donaldson James, "Food Critics Swallow Pounds and Punishment," abcnews.go.com, May 18, 2009, http://abcnews.go.com/Business/story?id=7598761&page=1.

24. Amy Pataki, "Five Not-So-Easy Tips to Being a Restaurant Critic," thestar.com, January 4, 2013, http://www.thestar.com/life/2013/01/04/five_notsoeasy_tips_to_being_a_restaurant_critic.html.

25. "Restaurant Critic," *Chicago Tribune*, June 4, 2010.

26. Pataki, "Five Not-So-Easy Tips."

27. "Pete Wells, Restaurant Critic, Answers Readers' Questions," *New York Times*, December 3, 2012.

28. Hanna Raskin, "Critics Are Just Reporters Who Write about Food," *Association of Food Journalists' Newsletter* (October 2012): 1–2.

29. Dornenburg and Page, *Dining Out*, 165.

30. Ludwig, "Will Work for Food."

31. Dornenburg and Page, *Dining Out*, 164.

32. Betsy Balsley, Donna Deane, Rose Dosti, and Barbara Hansen, "*L.A. Times* Food Gals," discussion at the Culinary Historians of Southern California, Los Angeles Public Library, Downtown Central Library, April 10, 2010. Video available at http://chscsite.org/food-section-gals/.

33. Balsley et al., "*L.A. Times* Food Section Gals."

34. Davis, "A Taste for New York," 155.

35. Davis, "A Taste for New York."

36. Craig Claiborne, *A Feast Made for Laughter* (New York: Doubleday, 1982); Thomas McNamee, *The Man Who Changed the Way We Eat* (New York: Simon & Schuster, 2013).

37. Ruth Reichl, *Garlic and Sapphires* (New York: Penguin, 2005), 93.

38. Mimi Sheraton, *Eating My Words* (New York: HarperCollins, 2004).

39. Christopher Reynolds and Rene Lynch, "Food Critic Outed and Ousted by Restaurant," *Los Angeles Times*, December 23, 2010.

40. Hines, *Duncan Hines' Food Odyssey*, 30.

41. Sheraton, *Eating My Words*, 119.

42. Pataki, "Five Not-So-Easy Tips."

43. Russ Parsons, "The Outing of a Restaurant Critic," *Los Angeles Times*, December 30, 2010.

44. Parsons, "Outing of a Restaurant Critic."

45. Sheraton, *Eating My Words*, 104.

46. Sheraton, *Eating My Words*, 115.

47. Reichl, *Garlic and Sapphires.*

48. "Pete Wells, Restaurant Critic, Answers Readers' Questions."

49. Ludwig, "Will Work for Food."

50. Dornenburg and Page, *Dining Out*, 44.

51. Ludwig, "Will Work for Food."

52. Dornenburg and Page, *Dining Out*, 44.

53. Pete Wells, "When He Dined, the Stars Came Out," *New York Times*, May 8, 2012.

54. Parsons, "Outing of a Restaurant Critic."

55. Signe Rousseau, *Food and Social Media: You Are What You Tweet* (Lanham, MD: Rowman & Littlefield, 2012), 55.

56. Claiborne, *A Feast Made for Laughter*, 146.

57. "A Six Months' Reprieve," *Lakeland Ledger*, December 20, 1975.

58. Stan Witwer, "Column Points Readers to Good Restaurants," *St. Petersburg Times*, January 26, 1977.

59. "Being Critical Did Not Come Naturally to Food Critic," *St. Petersburg Times*, May 31, 2008.

60. Stan Witwer, "Column Points Readers to Good Restaurants," *St. Petersburg Times*, January 26, 1977.

61. Stan Witwer, "*Times* Computer Gets An Assist," *St. Petersburg Times*, April 19, 1975.

62. Sheraton, *Eating My Words*, 112.

63. Ruth Gray, "The Realm of Dining Out," *St. Petersburg Times*, January 2, 1975.

64. Ruth Gray, "Carol's Pleases Both Palate, Eye," *St. Petersburg Times*, October 15, 1976.

65. Ruth Gray, "La Cote Basque Is Out of the Ordinary Dining Experience," *St. Petersburg*, April 15, 1977.

66. Anne Goldman, "Restaurant Reviews Serve Readers First," *St. Petersburg Times*, October 9, 1978.

67. S. M. McColloch, letter to Roxcy Bolton, October 13, 1969, "Roxcy Bolton: A Force for Equality," Florida Memory Project, http://www. floridamemory.com/photographiccollection/photo_exhibits/roxcy/rights.php.

68. William S. Ruben, letter to Roxcy Bolton, September 24, 1969, "Roxcy Bolton: A Force for Equality," Florida Memory Project, http://www. floridamemory.com/photographiccollection/photo_exhibits/roxcy/rights.php.

69. Susan Gillis, *Fort Lauderdale: The Venice of America* (Charleston, SC: Arcadia Publishing, 2004), 135.

70. Grace Lichtenstein, "McSorley's Admits Women under a New City Law," *New York Times*, August 11, 1970.

71. Keith L. Runyon, "Mazzoni's Last Rolled Oyster," *Louisville Courier-Journal*, December 3, 2008.

72. Phyllis Richman, "Answering Harvard's Question about My Personal Life, 52 Years Later," *Washington Post*, June 6, 2013.

7. THE DEATH OF THE WOMEN'S PAGES

1. Marion Marzlof, *Up from the Footnote: A History of Women Journalists* (New York: Hasting House, 1977); Maurine Beasley and Sheila Gibbons, eds., *Taking Their Place: A Documentary History of Women and Journalism* (Washington, DC: American University Press, 1993).

2. Susan Miller, "Changes in Women's/Lifestyle Section," *Journalism and Mass Communication Quarterly* 53 (1976): 641–47.

3. Ben Bradlee, *A Good Life* (New York: Simon & Schuster, 1996), 300–301.

4. Bradlee, *A Good Life*, 298.

5. All four of the women's page editors interviewed for the "Women in Journalism" oral histories described changing the content of their sections starting in the late 1950s or early 1960s: Marie Anderson, Vivian Castleberry, Dorothy Jurney, and Marjorie Paxson. Washington Press Club Foundation, http://wpcf.org/women-in-journalism/.

6. Kimberly Wilmot Voss, "Anne Rowe Goldman: Refashioning Women's News in St. Petersburg, Florida," *FCH Annals: Journal of the Florida Conference of Historians* (March 2011): 104–11; Voss, "Forgotten Feminist: Women's Page Editor Maggie Savoy and the Growth of Women's Liberation Awareness in Los Angeles," *California History* (Spring 2009): 48–64; Voss, "Florence

Burge: Representing Reno's Women in a Changing Time," *Nevada Historical Quarterly* (Winter 2006): 294–307; Voss, "Colleen 'Koky' Dishon: A Journalism Legend," *Timeline* (Summer 2010).

7. Joanne Meyerowitz, ed., *Not June Cleaver: Women and Gender in Postwar America, 1945–1960* (Philadelphia: Temple University Press, 1994), 231.

8. Katherine Newell Smith, "Les Dames d'Escoffier International: A History," www.ldei.org/history.asp.

9. Michael Pollan, "Out of the Kitchen, Onto the Couch," *New York Times*, August 2, 2009.

10. Stephanie Coontz, *A Strange Stirring* (New York: Basic Books, 2011).

11. "Peg Bracken, Cookbook Rebel, Dead at 89," CBS News, February 11, 2009, http://www.cbsnews.com/2100–511_162–3389846.html.

12. Emily Matchar, "Is Michael Pollan a Sexist Pig?" *Salon*, April 27, 2013.

13. Michelle Konstantinovsky, "In Defense of Michael Pollan," *Huffington Post*, May 1, 2013, http://www.huffingtonpost.com/michelle-konstantinovsky/in-defense-of-michael-pol_1_b_3189419.html.

14. "What Robin Morgan Said in Denver," *Journal of Home Economics* 65 (January 1973): 13.

15. Maggie Savoy, "Man's Primer to Womlib," *Los Angeles Times*, November 29, 1970.

16. Pollan, "Out of the Kitchen."

17. Mimi Sheraton, *Eating My Words* (New York: HarperCollins, 2004).

18. JoAnn E. Castagna, "Betty Crocker," in *Icons of American Cooking*, ed. Victor W. Geraci and Elizabeth S. Demers (Santa Barbara, CA: Greenwood, 2011), 85.

19. Diane Carman, "Helen Wrote the Recipe for Respect," *Denver Post*, August 8, 1998.

20. Carman, "Helen Wrote the Recipe for Respect."

21. Carol Ness, "Michael Pollan: Down to a Science," *San Francisco Chronicle*, March 15, 2006.

22. Wm. David Sloan, *The Media in America: A History* (Northport, AL: Vision Press, 2011), 321.

23. Eileen E. Wirth, *From Society Page to Front Page: Nebraska Women in Journalism* (Lincoln: University of Nebraska Press, 2013).

24. R. W. Apple Jr., "A Life on the Culinary Front Lines," *New York Times*, November 30, 2005.

25. Kelly Alexander and Cynthia Harris, *Hometown Appetites: The Story of Clementine Paddleford, the Forgotten Food Writer Who Chronicled How America Ate* (New York: Gotham Press, 2008).

26. Cecily Brownstone, oral history conducted by Laura Shapiro, 18, Cecily Brownstone Papers, Fales Library and Special Collections, New York University, 31.

27. "Ruth Ellen Church, 81, Food Critic and Author," *New York Times*, August 23, 1991.

28. William Janz, "Rosa Tusa Was Colorful, Funny and She Could Cook Up a Storm," *Milwaukee Sentinel*, December 2, 1992.

29. Julia Ferrante, "Jane Steinberg, 83, Food Editor," *Lakeland Ledger*, March 2, 2000.

30. Jane Nickerson, "Countless Read Her," *Lakeland Ledger*, June 12, 1994.

31. Marvin J. Taylor and Clark Wolf, eds., *101 Classic Cookbooks: 501 Classic Recipes* (New York: Rizzoli, 2012), 13.

32. Associated Press, "Food Writer Cecily Brownstone," *Washington Post*, September 5, 2005.

33. Jean Anderson, interview with the author, June 30, 2010.

34. Kathleen Purvis, interview with the author, June 24, 2010.

35. "Jeanne Voltz, 81; Past Editor of the *Times*' Food Section," *Los Angeles Times*, January 16, 2002.

36. Gloria Negri, "Dorothy Crandall: Acclaimed Food Writer," *Boston Globe*, February 12, 2007.

37. Frances Cawthon, "A Main Ingredient in the Recipes for Southern Tradition," *Atlanta Journal*, March 9, 1986.

38. Jim Tunstall, "Barbara Clendinen 'Loved Being a Character' in Life," *Tampa Tribune*, January 19, 2007.

39. Dudley Clendinen, *A Place Called Canterbury: Tales of the New Old Age in America* (New York: Penguin Books, 2009).

40. Poppy Cannon, "Soup Is the Result of Refined Tradition," *Hartford (CT) Courant*, July 30, 1967.

41. Poppy Cannon, "'Food's High Fashion to the Young,' Says Poet," *Hartford (CT) Courant*, January 18, 1970.

42. Associated Press, "Lee Salk, Child Psychologist, Author of Parenting Book, Dies," *Washington Post*, May 5, 1992.

43. "Myra Schwartz, 88," *Los Angeles Times*, July 29, 2004.

44. Rose DeWolf, "Oldies Are Still Goodies: Marian Burros and Lois Levine Update Their '50s Recipes," *Philadelphia Inquirer*, April 29, 1998.

45. Winzola McLendon and Scottie Smith, *Don't Quote Me! Washington Newswomen and the Power Society* (New York: Dutton, 1970), 179.

46. Ken Hoyt and Frances Spatz Leighton, *Drunk Before Noon* (Englewood Cliffs, NJ: Prentice Hall, 1979), 152–53.

47. Kathleen Purvis, "Words to Eat By," *Charlotte Observer*, February 18, 1998.

48. Molly O'Neill, "Food Porn," *Columbia Journalism Review* (September/October 2003): 38–45.

49. Darrell Christian, Sally Jacobsen, and David Minthorn, eds., *The Associated Press Stylebook 2011* (New York: Associated Press, 2011).

50. "Food Is a Focus in 2011 A.P. Stylebook," Associated Press, May 16, 2011, http://www.poynter.org/latest-news/mediawire/132481/ap-stylebook-has-new-food-guidelines-section/.

SELECTED BIBLIOGRAPHY

"1915: The *Picayune*'s Creole Cook Book Was Wildly Popular." *Times-Picayune* (New Orleans), October 19, 2011.

"1969 Conference on Food, Nutrition and Health: Final Report." National Nutrition Summit 2000. http://www.nns.nih.gov/1969/conference.htm.

Alexander, Kelly, and Cynthia Harris. *Hometown Appetites: The Story of Clementine Paddleford, the Forgotten Food Writer Who Chronicled How America Ate.* New York: Gotham Press, 2008.

Alford, Henry. "Tribute: James Beard Uncensored." *Food & Wine*, November 2003. http://www.foodandwine.com/articles/tribute-james-beard-uncensored.

"All about Mushrooms." *Sunday Star* (Wilmington, DE), November 4, 1951.

Ambrose, Linda. "Food Page Puffery." *Houston Journalism Review* (August 1972): 21.

Anderson, Jack. "Moss to Probe Newsmen." *Tuscaloosa (AL) News*, January 9, 1972.

Angelo, Frank. *On Guard: A History of the* Detroit Free Press. Detroit: Detroit Free Press, 1981.

Associated Press. "Food Is a Focus in 2011 A. P. Stylebook." May 16, 2011. http://www.poynter.org/latest-news/mediawire/132481/ap-stylebook-hasnew-food-guidelines-section/.

———. "Food Writer Cecily Brownstone." *Washington Post*, September 5, 2005.

———. "Lee Salk, Child Psychologist, Author of Parenting Book, Dies." *Washington Post*, May 5, 1992.

———. "Liberace, Food Editor Have Argument." *The Day* (New London, CT), May 1, 1971.

———. "The Wedding Cake: White House Chef Explains Mrs. Nixon's Recipe." *New York Times*, June 2, 1971.

Balsley, Betsy, Donna Deane, Rose Dosti, and Barbara Hansen. "*L.A. Times* Food Gals." Discussion at the Culinary Historians of Southern California, Los Angeles Public Library, Downtown Central Library, April 10, 2010. Video available at http://chscsite.org/food-section-gals/.

Barbee, Darren. "Ex-*Star-Telegram* Food Editor Became Expert on Cuisine." *Fort Worth Star-Telegram*, September 4, 2009.

Beard, James. *Beard on Food*. New York: Knopf, 1974.

———. *The Fireside Cookbook*. New York: Simon & Schuster, 1949.

Beasley, Maurine, and Sheila Gibbons, eds. *Taking Their Place: A Documentary History of Women and Journalism.* Washington, DC: American University Press, 1993.

Beighle French, Janet. *Plain-Dealer*/Home Economics Scrapbook Index. 1966–1967. Janet Beighle French Collection, Michael Schwartz Library, Cleveland State University.

Beighle [French], Janet. *The* Plain-Dealer's *Cleveland Meat Cook Book*. Cleveland: Plain Dealer, 1968.

"Being Critical Did Not Come Naturally to Food Critic." *St. Petersburg Times*, May 31, 2008.

Benell, Julie. *Let's Eat at Home*. New York: Thomas Y. Crowell, 1961.

———. "Reader's Recipe Takes the Cake." *Dallas Morning News*, June 5, 1957.

Bentley, Amy. *Eating for Victory*. Urbana-Champagne: University of Illinois Press, 1998.

———. "Booming Baby Food: Infant Foods and Feeding in Post–World War II America." *Michigan Historical Review* 32, no. 2 (2006): 63–87.

Benwick, Bonnie S. "Irma Rombauer and Marion Rombauer Becker." In *Icons of American Cooking*, ed. Victor W. Geraci and Elizabeth Demers. Santa Barbara: CA: Greenwood, 2011.

———, ed. *The* Washington Post *Cookbook*. Washington, DC: Washington Post Company, 2013.

"Bertha Hahn Receives Coveted Vesta Award." *Miami News*, October 3, 1960.

Bix, Amy Sue. "Equipped for Life: Gendered Technical Training and Consumerism in Home Economics, 1920–1980. *Technology and Culture* 43, no. 4 (October 2002): 731.

Blackwood, Frances. "Mrs. England Goes On Living." *Philadelphia Bulletin*, July 2–4, 1942.

———. *Mrs. England Goes On Living*. New York: Creative Age Press, 1943.

Bobrow-Strain, Aaron. *White Bread: A Social History of the Store-Bought Loaf*. Boston: Beacon Press, 2012.

Borelli, Gail. "Come into My Kitchen Turns 50." *Kansas City Star*, January 19, 2005.

Bower, Anna. "Romanced by Cookbooks." *Gastronomica: The Journal of Food and Culture* 4, no. 2 (2004): 35–42.

Bracken, Peg. *I Hate to Cook Book*. New York: Grand Central Publishing, 2010.

"Breakfast Cereal." *Consumer Reports*, May 1961, 239–40.

Breckenridge, Harriet B., and Louise J. Peet. "Combination Dry and Steam Flatirons Tested." *Journal of Home Economics* 40 (March 1948).

Browning-Blas, Kristen. "Keeping Helen D., in Mind." *Denver Post*, November 28, 2001.

———. "Stirring Up the Past." *Denver Post*, August 16, 2006.

Brownstone, Cecily. "Casserole Dishes 'Naturals' for Lent, Is Author's Claim." *Lewiston (IN) Morning Tribune*, March 14, 1952.

———. *Cecily Brownstone's Associated Press Cookbook*. New York: David McKay, 1972.

———. Oral history conducted by Laura Shapiro. Cecily Brownstone Papers, Fales Library and Special Collections, New York University.

———. "What's Cooking in Florida?" *Los Angeles Times*, August 22, 1974.

Burros, Marian Fox, and Lois Levine, *Freeze with Ease*. New York: Macmillan, 1965.

Byrnes, Garrett D. *Food in Newspapers*. Handbook for Editors No. 1. New York: American Press Institute, Columbia University, 1951.

Cannon, Poppy. *Bride's Cookbook*. New York: Holt, 1954.

———. "'Food's High Fashion to the Young,' Says Poet." *Hartford (CT) Courant*, January 18, 1970.

———. *A Gentle Giant*. New York: Popular Library, 1956.

———. *The New New Can-Opener Cookbook*. New York: Thomas Y. Crowell, 1968.

———. "Soup Is the Result of Refined Tradition." *Hartford (CT) Courant*, July 30, 1967.

Carlson, Katie. "Paul and Julia Child Take an Unrestful Year Off." *Daytona Beach Morning News*, October 23, 1976.

Carlton, Lowis. "Editors Look into Food Future." *St. Petersburg Times*, September 15, 1961.

Carman, Diane. "Helen Wrote the Recipe for Respect." *Denver Post*, August 8, 1998.

"Carol McCready Hartley." *Honolulu Star-Advertiser*, March 16, 2011. http://obits.staradvertiser.com/2011/03/16/carol-mccready-hartley/.

Chapman, Dorothy. "Memories Are Made of Christmas Joys, Santa's Helper." *Orlando Sentinel*, December 21, 1985.

———. *A Taste of Florida: The Best of "Thought You'd Never Ask."* Orlando: Sentinel Communications, 1990.

Child, Julia. "A French Cook." *Boston Globe*, June 21, 1965.

————. "A French Cook." *Boston Globe*, July 5, 1965.

————. "A French Cook." *Boston Globe*, November 8, 1965.

————. *My Life in France*. New York: Anchor Press, 2007.

Christian, Darrell, Sally Jacobsen, and David Minthorn, eds. *The Associated Press Stylebook*. New York: Associated Press, 2013.

Church, Ruth Ellen Lovrien. "Bobbs-Merrill Biographical Questionnaire." Fall 1955. Bobbs-Merrill Mss, Box 32, Lilly Library, Indiana University, Bloomington.

————. "Fiesta of Food Ideas Presented at Parley." *Chicago Tribune*, September 25, 1958.

————. *Mary Meade's Magic Recipes*. Indianapolis: Bobbs-Merrill, 1965.

————. "Myra Waldo Is Lovely—And Can She Cook!" *Chicago Daily Tribune*, October 31, 1953.

————. *Pancakes Aplenty*. Chicago: Rand McNally, 1962.

————. "Ruth Ellen Church Reports What's Cooking in Europe." *Chicago Tribune*, April 23, 1967.

————. "Serious Message Behind Fluff at Food Meetings." *Chicago Tribune*, October 2, 1968.

Claiborne, Craig. "Elegance of Cuisine on Wane in the U.S." *New York Times*, April 13, 1959.

————. *A Feast Made for Laughter*. New York: Doubleday, 1982.

Claiborne, Jack. *Charlotte Observer: Its Time and Place*. Chapel Hill: University of North Carolina Press, 1986.

Coleman, Todd. "The Queen's Beans." *Saveur*, October 2, 2007.

"Cook Book Offers 1,000 Photographs." *New York Times*, September 7, 1950.

Coons, Maude. "145 Editors at Meeting." *Evening World-Herald* (Omaha), October 14, 1952.

————. "Cowboy Stars at Conference." *Evening World-Herald* (Omaha), October 17, 1952.

————. "For Busy Women, Topovers a Boon." *Evening World-Herald* (Omaha), October 7, 1964.

————. "Omaha on High Side of the List." *Omaha World-Herald*, August 4, 1972.

————. "Price Control Is Attacked." *Evening World-Herald* (Omaha), October 14, 1952.

————. "Statistics Prove Americans Like Canned, Frozen Food." *Evening World-Herald* (Omaha), October 5, 1959.

————. "Weight Control Problem Great." *Evening World-Herald* (Omaha), October 19, 1952.

Crandall, Dorothy. "The All-American Lunch." *Boston Globe*, October 15, 1969.

————. "Americans Eat Better, Cheaper Than Anyone." *Boston Globe*, October 6, 1964.

————. "Canned Foods in the Future to List Vitamins, Minerals." *Boston Globe*, May 26, 1972.

————. "Cooking for the Camping Family Can Be Easy." *Boston Globe*, June 21, 1964.

————. "Eat Less, Walk More, Nutritionist Prescribes." *Boston Globe*, October 7, 1964.

————. "Julia and Jim Cook a Deux." *Boston Globe*, October 19, 1968.

————. "Markets Welcome Consumer Advice." *Boston Globe*, June 25, 1968.

————. "Packers Urge Meat Breakfasts for Needed Protein." *Boston Globe*, October 7, 1955.

————. "Pancake Cooks Will Flip Today." *Boston Globe*, March 2, 1965.

————. "Priscilla Alden Would Be Amazed by 1957 Thanksgiving." *Boston Globe*, November 24, 1957.

————. "Self-Basting Turkeys and Odorless Onions." *Boston Globe*, September 27, 1966.

————. "Women Drivers Cook under Hood." *Owosso (MI) Argus-Press*, October 27, 1965.

Criswell, Ann. *Houston Gourmet: Cooks and Caterers*. Houston: Fran Fauntleroy, 1990.

————. "Thanks for the Memories." *Houston Chronicle*, September 27, 2000.

D'Arcy, Ruth. "Detroit News." Speech at Food Editors Seminar, University of Houston, February 25, 1972. Marjorie B. Paxson Papers, National Women & Media Collection, State Historical Society of Missouri.

Daum, Peggy. *The Best Cook on the Block Cookbook*. Milwaukee: Milwaukee Journal, 1979.

————. "Bread Rich in Nutrition Introduced." *Milwaukee Journal*, February 16, 1956.

———. "Club Keeps Gay 'First Footing' Custom." *Milwaukee Journal*, December 28, 1958.

———. "Conference Delegates Hope to Spread Awareness of Hunger." *Milwaukee Journal*, December 10, 1969.

———. "Editors Criticized by Senator, Feminist." *Milwaukee Journal*, October 8, 1971.

———. "Imitation Food Issue Put to Editors." *Milwaukee Journal*, September 24, 1970.

———. "Preparation Is Family Project." *Milwaukee Journal*, December 21, 1956.

———. "A Rachel Carson for Food?" *Milwaukee Journal*, October 3, 1973.

———. "A Retrospective." *Milwaukee Journal*, February 17, 1988.

———. "Stare Defends His Ethics, Stand." *Milwaukee Journal*, September 22, 1970.

———. "Tom Farley: The Man Behind School Lunch." *Milwaukee Journal*, May 27, 1970.

———. "Tourist's Eye View of Milwaukee." *Milwaukee Journal*, July 7, 1957.

Davis, Mitchell. "Power Meal." *Gastronomica* (Summer 2004): 60–72.

———. "A Taste for New York." Doctoral diss., New York University, 2009, 155.

Dollaghan, Helen. *Best Main Dishes*. New York: McGraw-Hill, 1980.

Dornenburg, Andrew, and Karen Page. *Dining Out*. New York: Wiley, 1998.

Dosti, Rose. *Dear S.O.S.: Thirty Years of Recipe Requests to the* Los Angeles Times. Los Angeles: Los Angeles Times Syndicate Books, 1994.

———. "L.A. and Carrot Cake." *Los Angeles Times*, August 22, 1974.

Eaton, Elizabeth Bragdon. "News about Books and Authors." January 16, 1956. Bobbs-Merrill Mss, Ruth Ellen Church Folder, Lilly Library, Indiana University, Bloomington.

Eddy, Kristin. "Serving Food News for 150 Years." *Chicago Tribune*, July 16, 1997.

"Editors to Hear Florida Citrus Story from Hooks." *Lakeland Ledger*, October 2, 1960.

Eicher, Diane. "Food Writer Dollaghan Dies at 70." *Denver Post*, August 4, 1998.

"Elinor Lee, 83, Former *Post* Food Editor, Dies." *Washington Post*, December 23, 1988.

"Elizabeth Howkins, Editor, Dies; Headed *Times*'s Women's News." *New York Times*, January 12, 1972.

Ephron, Nora. "Food Establishment." In *Wallflower at the Orgy*, 1–19. New York: Bantam Books, 2007.

"Feedback from Food Editors." *Matrix* (Winter 1971–1972): 14.

Ferguson, Keenan. "Intensifying Taste, Intensifying Identity: Collectively through Community Cookbooks." *Signs* 37, no. 3 (Spring 2012): 696.

Ferrante, Julia. "Jane Steinberg, 83, Food Editor." *Lakeland Ledger*, March 2, 2000.

Ferrone, John, ed. *Love and Kisses and a Halo of Truffles*. New York: Arcade Publishing, 1994.

Fisher, Carol. *The American Cookbook: A History*. Jefferson, NC: McFarland, 2006.

Fisher, Teri Lyn, and Jenny Park. *Tiny Food Party*. Philadelphia: Quirk Books, 2012.

"Fleeta Louise Hoke, 94; Retired *Times* Food Editor." *Los Angeles Times*, April 13, 1995.

Foley, May E. "Awakening in Home Economics Journalism." *Journal of Home Economics* (August 1923): 417–18.

"Food Supplies Reported Adequate." *Milwaukee Journal*, January 31, 1947.

Fussell, Betty. *Masters of American Cookery*. Lincoln: University of Nebraska Press, 2006.

Garbee, Jenn. "Marian Manners, Prudence Penny, the First Celebrity Chefs." *Los Angeles Times*, April 22, 2009.

Garrison, Eudora. *Eudora's Cookbook*. Charlotte, NC: Charlotte Observer, 1960.

———. *Eudora's Holiday Cook Book*. Charlotte, NC: Charlotte Observer, 1967.

———. *It's Not Gourmet—It's Better*. Charlotte, NC: Washburn, 1978.

Gdula, Steven. *The Warmest Room in the House*. New York: Bloomsbury, 2007.

Getto, Dennis. "Daum Retiring as Food Editor." *Milwaukee Journal*, February 17, 1988.

Gibson, Josephine. "New and Delicious Foods Intrigue Writers." *Pittsburgh Press*, October 10, 1951.

Gillis, Susan. *Fort Lauderdale: The Venice of America*. Charleston, SC: Arcadia Publishing, 2004.

Gitelson, Joshua. "Populux: The Suburban Cuisine of the 1950s." *Journal of American Culture* 15, no. 3 (Fall 1992): 73.

Goldman, Anne. "Restaurant Reviews Serve Readers First." *St. Petersburg Times*, October 9, 1978.

Goldstein, Carolyn M. *Creating Consumers: Home Economists in Twentieth-Century America*. Chapel Hill: University of North Carolina Press, 2012.

Gorrell, Ruth. "Conference Food with a Flair." *St. Petersburg Times*, October 11, 1957.

Gottlieb, Agnes Hooper. "Women's Pages." In *The Encyclopedia of American Journalism*, 601–2. New York: Routledge, 2008.

"Grace Rescues Food Editors." *Baltimore Sun*, September 27, 1962.

Gray, Ruth. "Carol's Pleases Both Palate, Eye." *St. Petersburg Times*, October 15, 1976.

———. "La Cote Basque Is Out of the Ordinary Dining Experience." *St. Petersburg Times*, April 15, 1977.

———. "The Realm of Dining Out." *St. Petersburg Times*, January 2, 1975.

Green, Thomas. "Tricksters and the Marketing of Breakfast Cereals." *Journal of Popular Culture* 40, no. 1 (2007): 49–66.

Gregg, Cissy. *Cissy Gregg's Cookbook*. Louisville, KY: Louisville Courier-Journal, 1953.

Gross, Bernice, and Kay Young Mackley. "Should the Homemaker Use Ready-Made Mixes?" *Journal of Home Economics* (June 1950): 451.

Haddix, Carol. "A Food Editor's Memories." Speech to the Culinary Historians of Chicago, Chicago, August 13, 2011.

Hahn, Bertha C. "Diets Are Overlooked." *Miami News*, October 2, 1957.

———. "A Reunion in Chicago." *Miami News*, September 30, 1957.

Halloran, Richard. "F.C.C. Study Urged of TV Cereal Ads." *New York Times*, August 6, 1970.

Hamman, Ann. "Cookbooks for Every Taste and Purse." *Evansville (IN) Courier*, May 5, 1972.

———. Letter to the Editor. *Columbia Journalism Review* (May/June 1972): 61.

———. "Period of Change in Supply, Quality, Price of Fresh Produce." *Evansville (IN) Courier*, May 26, 1972.

———. "Prices May Be Partly Due to Packaging." *Evansville (IN) Courier*, March 3, 1972.

———. "Sometimes Larger Sizes Really Are Thriftier." *Evansville (IN) Courier*, February 25, 1972.

———. "Thrifty Buying Important as Food Prices Continue High." *Evansville (IN) Courier*, January 7, 1972.

Harriman, John. "Men-in-the-Kitchen Era Horrifies Columnist." *Boston Globe*, October 15, 1956.

Hartley, Grace. *Grace Hartley's Southern Cookbook*. New York: Doubleday, 1976.

Hayes, Joanne Lamb. *Grandma's Wartime Kitchen: World War II and the Way We Cooked*. New York: St. Martin's Press, 2000.

Heffington, Virginia. "The Best Tasters Testing." *Miami Herald*, November 7, 1968.

———. "Chicken Hawaiian." *Miami Herald*, January 23, 1969.

———. "Fall with a Foreign Accent." *Miami Herald*, October 31, 1968.

———. *Food with a Florida Flair*. Miami: Miami Herald, 1968.

———. "Mini-Bites." *Miami Herald*, September 19, 1968.

———. "A Taste of Old New Orleans." *Miami Herald*, October 24, 1968.

Herbert, Elizabeth Sweeney. "When the Homemaker Goes to Work." *Journal of Home Economics* (April 1952): 258.

Hesser, Amanda. "Recipe Redux: The Community Cookbook." *New York Times*, October 5, 2010.

Hines, Duncan. *Duncan Hines' Food Odyssey*. New York: Thomas Y. Crowell, 1955.

"The History of Mixes." *Practical Home Economics* (September 1958): 76.

"Hyman Goldberg, 'Prudence Penny,' Dies." *Norwalk (CT) Hour*, September 21, 1970.

Ickeringill, Nan. "Food: Ways with Fish." *New York Times*, October 14, 1964.

Illenberger, Theodora, and Avonne Eyre Keller. *The Cartoonist Cookbook*. New York: Gramercy, 1966.

Inness, Sherrie A. *Secret Ingredients: Race, Gender and Class at the Dinner Table*. New York: Palgrave Macmillan, 2006.

Irwin, Ray. "Newspapers Find Food Profitable News Subject." *Editor & Publisher*, July 15, 1950.

Isaacs, Norman E. Speech at Food Editors Seminar, Houston, Texas, February 25, 1972, 7. Marjorie B. Paxson Papers, National Women & Media Collection, State Historical Society of Missouri.

Johnson, Dean. "Dorothy Chapman Plans to Savor Her Retirement." *Orlando Sentinel*, April 25, 1986.

Jones, Diana Nelson. "Veronica Volpe: Food Editor at *Post-Gazette, Press* for Many Years." *Pittsburgh Press*, February 10, 2005. http://www.post-gazette.com/stories/local/obituaries/ obituary-veronica-volpe-food-editor-at-post-gazette-press-for-many-years-569552/.

Jones, Evan. *Epicurean Delight*. New York: Touchstone, 1992.

Jones, Gregg. "Tasting Her Way around the World." *Missourian*, May 1, 2012.

Jurney, Dorothy. "Detroit Free Press." Speech at Food Editors Seminar, Houston, Texas, February 25, 1972, 2. Marjorie B. Paxson Papers, National Women & Media Collection, State Historical Society of Missouri.

Kamp, David. *The United States of Arugula: How We Became a Gourmet Nation*. New York: Broadway Books, 2006.

Karp, Richard. "Newspaper Food Pages: Credibility for Sale." *Columbia Journalism Review* (November/December 1971): 36–44.

Kitchen Treasures: A Recipe Book of Prize Winners in the Kitchen Treasure Hunt. Milwaukee: Milwaukee Journal, 1930.

Kleber, John. "Cissy Gregg." In *Louisville Encyclopedia*, 392. Lexington: University Press of Kentucky, 1992.

Kluger, Richard. *The Paper*. New York: Knopf, 1986.

Koch, Beverly Stephen. "The History and Evolution of Women's Pages in American Newspapers." Master's thesis, University of California, Berkeley, 1974.

Kreck, Dick. "Helen Dollaghan More Than Sum of Exploding-Chicken Parts." *Denver Post*, July 7, 1993.

Laughton, Catherine C. *Mary Cullen's Northwest Cook Book*. Portland, OR: Journal Publishing Company, 1946.

Lee, Elinor. "Chicken Has Long and Noble Heritage." *Los Angeles Times*, March 26, 1970.

———. "Chilean Casserole Is a Most Elegant Dish." *Miami News*, October 1, 1953.

———. "Chinese Are Fine Cooks." *Miami News*, September 17, 1953.

Lewine, Frances. "Press Cookbook Simmers Before Done." *Eugene (OR) Register-Guard*, October 17, 1962.

Lichtenstein, Grace. "McSorley's Admits Women under a New City Law." *New York Times*, August 11, 1970.

Longone, Jan. "Feeding America: The Historic American Cookbook Project." Digital and Multimedia Center, Michigan State University. http://digital.lib.msu.edu/projects/ cookbooks/.

Lovegren, Sylvia. *Fashionable Food: Seven Decades of Food Fads*. New York: Simon & Schuster, 1995.

Lovrien, Ruth Ellen. "Good Cook Book Basic Necessity in Every Home." *Chicago Daily Tribune*, January 3, 1941.

———. "Mary Meade's 99 Bread Recipes in Booklet Form." *Chicago Tribune*, November 17, 1939.

Maddox, Gaynor. "Food Fad Flourishing." *Sumter (SC) Daily Items*, September 20, 1971.

———. "Food Pages No More a Woman's Domain." *Rome (GA) News-Tribune*, February 19, 1975.

Manners, Marian. "Food Editors Learn 50 New Recipes at New York Conference." *Los Angeles Times*, October 15, 1954.

"Margot McConnell, Editor, Food Writer." *New York Times*, July 8, 1976.

Marling, Karal Ann. "Betty Crocker's Picture Cook Book: The Aesthetics of American Food in the 1950s." *Prospects* 17 (1992): 79.

"Mary A. Hammond, Food Editor." *Philadelphia Inquirer*, January 21, 1983.

Marzlof, Marion. *Up from the Footnote: A History of Women Journalists*. New York: Hasting House, 1977.

Mathews, Ellie. *The Ungarnished Truth*. New York: Berkley Books, 2008.

"Maude Won't Stay Out of the Kitchen." *Omaha World-Herald*, April 29, 1973.

McBride, Mary Margaret. *Mary Margaret McBride's Harvest of American Cooking*. New York: Putnam's, 1956.

McIntosh, William Alex, and Mary Zey. "Women as Gatekeepers of Food Consumption." *Food and Foodways* 24 (1989): 319–21.

McLendon, Winzola, and Scottie Smith. *Don't Quote Me! Washington Newswomen and the Power Society*. New York: Dutton, 1970.

McNamee, Thomas. *The Man Who Changed the Way We Eat*. New York: Simon & Schuster, 2013.

McNulty, Tim. "Tales from the Test Kitchen." *Chicago Tribune*, December 21, 2007.

McPherson, Heather. "Dorothy Chapman, 1921–2004." *Orlando Sentinel*, December 14, 2004.

Meade, Mary. "Canned Foods Are Easy on Budget." *Chicago Tribune*, November 15, 1963.

———. "Fiesta of Food Ideas." *Chicago Tribune*, September 25, 1956.

———. "Follow Rules When Entering Recipe Contest." *Chicago Tribune*, March 21, 1942.

———. "Mary Meade's Gift to Readers: A Pledge of Continued Service." *Chicago Daily Tribune*, December 25, 1950.

———. "Nation's Food Editors Meet Here Next Week." *Chicago Tribune*, September 2, 1949.

———. "New Canned Foods Give Variety to Menus." *Chicago Tribune*, July 9, 1955.

———. "Newspaper Food Editors Eat, Eat, and Eat." *Chicago Tribune*, October 6, 1960.

"Meatless Days Draws Blank." *Milwaukee Journal*, October 8, 1947.

Mendelson, Anne. *Stand Facing the Stove: The Story of the Women Who Gave America the Joy of Cooking*. New York: Scribner, 2003.

Misch, Robert. "No Pernod in Bouillabaisse?" *New York Times*, June 11, 1961.

Moss, Frank E. "Business, the Consumer and You." Speech presented at the National Food Editors' Conference, Chicago, October 7, 1971. Frank E. Moss Papers, J. Willard Marriott Library, University of Utah, Salt Lake City.

"Myra Waldo's Barbecue Book." *Baltimore Sun*, August 29, 1963.

Nelson, Joyce Kay. "Questionnaire for Betty Crocker Search for the American Homemaker of Tomorrow." April 3, 1970. Ann Valder Collection, MS 90-60, Special Collections, UNLV Libraries, University of Nevada, Las Vegas.

Neuhaus, Jessamyn. *Manly Meals and Mom's Cooking*. Baltimore: Johns Hopkins University Press, 2012.

———. "The Way to a Man's Heart: Gender Roles, Domestic Ideology, and Cookbooks in the 1950s." *Journal of Social History* (Spring 1999): 529–55.

Nickerson, Jane. "Bread from Whole Grains." *New York Times*, February 9, 1947.

———. "Countless Read Her." Obituary of Cecily Brownstone. *Lakeland Ledger*, June 12, 1994.

———. "Creole Tradition Offers Jambalaya to Grace Era of the Buffet Supper." *New York Times*, January 23, 1953.

———. "Delicious and Out of the Can." *New York Times*, October 19, 1952.

———. "Easy-to-Make 'Jambalaya' Produces Festive Party." *New York Times*, January 23, 1953.

———. "Emergency Potatoes." *New York Times*, April 14, 1946.

———. "Famous Classic of French Kitchen at Last Makes Its Debut in English." *New York Times*, May 7, 1949.

———. "The Fine Flavors of Lakeland Flavors Half a Century Ago." *Lakeland Ledger*, August 22, 1973.

———. "Food: Cost of Thanksgiving Dinner." *New York Times*, November 18, 1955.

———. "Food: Vive la France." *New York Times*, February 20, 1957.

———. "'From the Sea around Us.'" *New York Times*, January 4, 1953.

———. *Jane Nickerson's Florida Cookbook*. Gainesville: University of Florida Press, 1973.

———. "The Legendary Cakes of Vienna." *New York Times*, September 16, 1956.

———. "Making the Most of Oranges and Grapefruit." *New York Times*, January 13, 1946.

———. "Meatless Dishes, Italian Style." *New York Times*, March 6, 1949.

————. "News of Food: $50,000 Recipe Award Goes to Housewife." *New York Times*, December 14, 1949.

————. "News of Food: Adding Vitamin D to White Bread Follows Nutritional Trend." *New York Times*, March 12, 1953.

————. "News of Food: Cheeseburgers for Supper." *New York Times*, May 3, 1947.

————. "News of Food: Cutting Home Food Costs 10% Suggested." *New York Times*, May 15, 1946.

————. "News of Food: Graduate of Swiss Hotel School Tells of Study of French Cooking." *New York Times*, May 10, 1954.

————. "News of Food: Food Editors Hear Actor and Chemist." *New York Times*, October 14, 1950.

————. "News of Food: Head of the Baltimore & Ohio Railroad." *New York Times*, June 28, 1951.

————. "News of Food: Nation's Newspaper Food Editors Arrive on Seventh Annual Epicurean Pilgrimage." *New York Times*, October 9, 1950.

————. "News of Food: New Merchandising Feature in Chain Store." *New York Times*, October 31, 1946.

————. "News of Food: New Packages Made Up by CARE Replaces Army Ten-in-One." *New York Times*, February 12, 1947.

————. "News of Food: Oriental Dishes Available to Americans in 'Far Eastern Cookery,'" *New York Times*, September 16, 1947.

————. "News of Food: Stable Retail Prices for '55 Forecast to Cookery Editors." *New York Times*, October 5, 1954.

————. "News of Food: Sturdy New Packages for Frozen Food." *New York Times*, June 13, 1946.

————. "News of Food: Taste-Teasers." *New York Times*, October 7, 1954.

————. "News of Food: Vitamins, Minerals Added to Ice Cream." *New York Times*, January 29, 1946.

————. "Powered by Water from the Kitchen Faucet." *New York Times*, September 28, 1946.

————. "Steak Worthy of the Name." *New York Times*, January 25, 1953.

————. "They Wanted to Cook Like Mother." *New York Times Book Review*, August 12, 1951.

————. "War Brides, Beware!" *New York Times Magazine*, June 17, 1945.

Oettinger, Louise. "Food Editors Are Criticized at Seminar." *Tuscaloosa (AL) News*, March 8, 1972.

————. "News Editors—More Concerned about Consumer Coverage." *Tuscaloosa (AL) News*, March 8, 1972.

O'Neill, Molly. "Food Porn." *Columbia Journalism Review* (September/October 2003): 38–45.

————. "Long Ago Smitten, She Remains True to the Country Captain." *New York Times*, April 17, 1991.

Ostman, Eleanor. *Always on Sunday*. St. Paul, MN: Sexton Printing, 1998.

————. "Tested at 25." *St. Paul Pioneer Press*, August 22, 1993.

Paddleford, Clementine. "Gourmets' Choice." In *New York, New York*, 147–88. New York: Delta Books, 1964.

————. "Grandmother Shopped Here." *Los Angeles Times*, August 18, 1946.

————. *How America Eats*. New York: Scribner, 1960.

————. "To a Man's Heart Frozen Blintzes." *New York Sun*, May 20, 1949.

Paffilas, Polly. "Comments from the Food Section." *Matrix* (Winter 1971–1972): 15.

Parnell, Dorothy. "New York Chit Chat." *Milwaukee Sentinel*, October 22, 1950.

Parsons, Russ. "The Outing of a Restaurant Critic." *Los Angeles Times*, December 30, 2010.

"Peg Bracken Series Will Begin Sunday." *Los Angeles Times*, June 12, 1964.

"Pete Wells, Restaurant Critic, Answers Readers' Questions." *New York Times*, December 3, 2012.

"A Picture Recipe: Mary Meade Makes Creamy Chocolate Fudge." *Chicago Daily Tribune*, October 19, 1956.
Pollan, Michael. "Out of the Kitchen, Onto the Couch." *New York Times*, August 2, 2009.
Pollack, Frances. "Consumer Reporting: Underdeveloped Region." *Columbia Journalism Review* (May/June 1971): 38.
Polson, Dorothee. *Pot au Feu Cookbook*. Phoenix: Arizona Republic, 1971.
Powell, Kay. "Grace Hartley Germon." *Atlanta Journal-Constitution*, September 16, 2000.
Powers, Irene. "Woman of Distinction: Mary Meade." *Chicago Daily Tribune*, November 19, 1959.
"The Press: The Kitchen Department." *Time*, October 19, 1953.
Preston, Andrea. "Former Food Guru and Editor Dies." *Evansville (IN) Courier*, June 17, 2003.
"Price of Milk Boosted Again." *Milwaukee Journal*, January 11, 1954.
Purvis, Kathleen. "She Always Had a New Idea Cooking." *Charlotte Observer*, January 23, 2002.
———. "Words to Eat By." *Charlotte Observer*, February 18, 1998.
Rainey, Joan Osgood. Letter to Robin Morgan, July 16, 1972. Robin Morgan Papers, David M. Rubenstein Rare Book & Manuscript Library, Duke University.
Raskin, Hanna. "Critics Are Just Reporters Who Write about Food." *Association of Food Journalists' Newsletter* (October 2012).
Raven, John. "The History of Chili Cook-Offs." *Texas Cooking*, March 2007. http://www.texascooking.com/features/march2007_chili_cookoffs.htm.
Reardon, Joan, ed. *As Always, Julia: The Letters of Julia Child and Avis DeVoto*. New York: Houghton Mifflin, 2010.
Reichl, Ruth. *Garlic and Sapphires*. New York: Penguin, 2005.
———. "Magazine Editing Then and Now." In *The Art of Making Magazines*, ed. Victor S. Navasky and Evan Cornog, 29–46. New York: Columbia University Press, 2012.
"Restaurant Critic." *Chicago Tribune*, June 4, 2010.
Reynolds, Christopher, and Rene Lynch. "Food Critic Outed and Ousted by Restaurant." *Los Angeles Times*, December 23, 2010.
Reynolds, Doris. "Let's Talk Food: Duncan Hines Much More Than Cake Mixes." *Naples (FL) News*, August 8, 2012.
Richardson, Lou, and Genevieve Callahan. *How to Write for Homemakers*. Ames: Iowa State College Press, 1949.
Richman, Phyllis. "Answering Harvard's Question about My Personal Life, 52 Years Later." *Washington Post*, June 6, 2013.
———. Foreword. In *The* Washington Post *Cookbook: Readers' Favorite Recipes*, ed. Bonnie Benwick, 7. San Leandro, CA: Time Capsule Press, 2013.
Robertson, Nan. *The Girls in the Balcony: Women, Men, and the* New York Times. New York: Random House, 1992.
Robison, Pat. "Humorous Recipes Taste Good, Too." *St. Petersburg Times*, March 6, 1962.
Rocky Mountain News Recipe Book. Denver: Rocky Mountain News, 1964.
Rombauer, Irma S. *Joy of Cooking*. Indianapolis: Bobbs-Merrill, 1953.
Rothman Hasin, Bernice. *Consumers, Commissions, and Congress*. New Brunswick, NJ: Transaction Books, 1987.
Rousseau, Signe. *Food and Social Media: You Are What You Tweet*. Lanham, MD: Rowman & Littlefield, 2012.
Rowlands, Clarice. "Editors' Fare." *Milwaukee Journal*, October 30, 1952.
———. "Food Conference Has International Theme." *Milwaukee Journal*, September 23, 1956.
———. "Food Conference Specialties." *Milwaukee Journal*, November 1, 1951.
———. "Manhattan Merry Go Round." *Milwaukee Journal*, September 25, 1958.
———. "Supermarket Managers Get Customers' Views." *Milwaukee Journal*, January 24, 1957.
Saekel, Karola. "We've Come a Long Way since 1902." *San Francisco Chronicle*, April 4, 2001.

Sarazen, Raeanne S. "Q. We Recently Came across a Booklet." *Chicago Tribune*, October 3, 2001.

Sarkar, Pia. "Scrambling for Customers." *San Francisco Chronicle*, August 4, 2005.

Savage, Kay. *Secrets of Michigan Cooks*. Detroit: Foods Arts, 1962.

"Senator Explodes Bomb as Food Editors Seethe." *Editor & Publisher*, October 16, 1971, 14–15.

"Senator Moss, Posing as Ragged Patient, Sees Medicaid Abuse in New York City." *New York Times*, August 30, 1976.

"Services Set for Daum, Led *Journal* Food Section." *Milwaukee Journal*, October 22, 1990.

Severson, Kim. "Does the World Need Another Joy? Do You?" *New York Times*, November 1, 2001.

Shapiro, Laura. "American Originals: Rethinking the Pillsbury Bake-Off." Speech to the Culinary Historians of Southern California, November 10, 2012, Downtown Los Angeles Public Library.

———. "In the Mix." *Gourmet*, August 2002. http://www.gourmet.com/magazine/2000s/2002/08/in_the_mix.

———. *Perfection Salad*. New York: North Point Press, 1988.

———. *Something from the Oven: Reinventing Dinner in 1950s America*. New York: Viking, 2004.

Sheraton, Mimi. *Eating My Words*. New York: HarperCollins, 2004.

Simms, Jayne E. "Public Relations Information and Practices as Viewed by Women's Newspaper Editors." Master's thesis, University of Wisconsin, 1973.

Sinz, Dorothy. Dallas Times Herald *Recipe Book*, in the *Dallas Times Herald*, October 5, 1964.

"A Six Months' Reprieve." *Lakeland Ledger*, December 20, 1975.

Sloan, Wm. David. *The Media in America: A History*. Northport, AL: Vision Press, 2011.

Smiley, Nixon. *Knights of the Fourth Estate: The Story of the* Miami Herald. Miami: Banyan, 1984.

Smith, Andrew F. *Eating History: 30 Turning Points in the Making of American Cuisine*. New York: Columbia University Press, 2009.

Stage, Sarah, and Virginia B. Vincenti, eds. *Rethinking Home Economics: Women and the History of a Profession*. Ithaca, NY: Cornell University Press, 1997.

Stohs, Nancy J. "Food Team Aims to Help Readers Do Recipes Right." *Milwaukee Journal Sentinel*, January 31, 2012.

———. "Newspaper Institute Raised the Bar for Homemaking." *Milwaukee Journal Sentinel*, April 18, 2001.

———. "A Place at Your Table." *Milwaukee Journal*, March 29, 1995.

Strauss, David. *Setting the Table for Julia Child*. Baltimore: Johns Hopkins University Press, 2011.

Sulzberger, Arthur Hays. Box 169, Food News folder. New York Times Company Records. Arthur Hays Sulzberger Papers, Manuscripts and Archives Division, The New York Public Library.

———. Memo to Mr. Catledge, September 6, 1956. Food News folder. New York Times Company Records. Arthur Hays Sulzberger Papers, Manuscripts and Archives Division, The New York Public Library.

Taylor, Marvin J., and Clark Wolf, eds. *101 Classic Cookbooks: 501 Classic Recipes*. New York: Rizzoli, 2012.

Tenore, Mallary Jean. "Pete Wells Explains His Review of Guy Fieri's Restaurant." Poynter.org, November 15, 2012. http://www.poynter.org/latest-news/mediawire/195580/the-story-behind-pete-wells-review-of-guy-fieris-restaurant/.

Testa, Jessica. "Olive Garden Reviewer Receives Super Serious Award." Buzzfeed, http://www.buzzfeed.com/jtes/olive-garden-reviewer-wins-super-serious-journalis.

Theophano, Janet. *Eat My Words: Reading Women's Lives through the Cookbooks They Wrote*. New York: Palgrave Macmillian, 2003.

"Top Honors for Women's Pages." *Milwaukee Journal*, September 15, 1961.

Tracy, Marian, ed. *Coast to Coast Cookery*. Bloomington: Indiana University Press, 1952.

Tracy, Marian, and Nino Tracy. *Casserole Cookery: One Dish Meals for the Busy Gourmet.* New York: Viking Press, 1948.

Turgeon, Charlotte. "Including Hush Puppies." *New York Times*, October 19, 1952.

Tusa, Rosa. *True Grits.* New York: Bantam Books, 1977.

Valder, Ann. "Cooking with Commodities." *Las Vegas Review-Journal*, June 27, 1971.

Van Gelder, Lawrence. "Poppy Cannon White, 69, Dead; Writer Was Authority on Food." *New York Times*, April 2, 1975.

Vileisis, Ann. *Kitchen Literacy.* New York: Island Press, 2010.

Volpe, Veronica. "Dry Soup Flavoring, Smoked Bear Hams." *Pittsburgh Post-Gazette*, September 28, 1956.

———. "Florida, Pakistan Represented with Citrus and Saucy Recipes." *Pittsburgh Post-Gazette*, October 3, 1955.

———. "Results Warrant Use of Mix Adaptation." *Pittsburgh Post-Gazette*, October 14, 1954.

Voltz, Jeanne. "Almendrado." *Los Angeles Times*, January 24, 1971.

———. *An Apple a Day.* New York: Irena Chalmers Cookbooks, 1983.

———. "Are Americans Programmed to Overconsumption of Sugar?" *Los Angeles Times*, April 19, 1973.

———. *Barbecued Ribs, Smoked Butts and Other Great Feeds.* New York: Knopf, 1990.

———. *The California Cookbook.* New York: Bobbs-Merrill, 1970.

———. "Cheers and Jeers for New Nutrient Labeling Regulations." *Los Angeles Times*, January 25, 1973.

———. "Dining Out." *Los Angeles Times*, February 5, 1961.

———. "Dining Out." *Los Angeles Times*, February 12, 1961.

———. "Dining Out." *Los Angeles Times*, April 30, 1961.

———. "Dining Out." *Los Angeles Times*, July 2, 1961.

———. "Dynamic Influence: Californians Bow to Chinese Cookery, Californians Bow to Chinese Cuisine." *Los Angeles Times*, June 26, 1969.

———. "Enchiladas: They're Easy on the Budget and Hard to Resist." *Los Angeles Times*, March 15, 1973.

———. "Expert Hits Myths on Male Taste." *Los Angeles Times*, February 6, 1963.

———. "Experts Defend Cereals." *Los Angeles Times*, August 5, 1970.

———. "FDA Readying First Guidelines on Nutrition." *Los Angeles Times*, April 8, 1971.

———. "Food Shopping Rapped by Housewives." *Los Angeles Times*, November 4, 1971.

———. "For Gourmets on a Budget." *Los Angeles Times*, January 30, 1972.

———. "Grain Enrichment Law—1970's Gift to Californians." *Los Angeles Times*, December 27, 1971.

———. "Home Made Bread." *Los Angeles Times*, August 9, 1970.

———. "How to Protect Consumer." *Los Angeles Times*, October 16, 1970.

———. "Hungry—A Lot of Talk about It, But What's Being Done?" *Los Angeles Times*, September 28, 1972.

———. "Labeling System Proposed by FDA." *Los Angeles Times*, March 2, 1972.

———. "Lexicon with a Latin Accent for California Cooking." *Los Angeles Times*, August 5, 1971.

———. "Little Water Goes a Long Way." *Los Angeles Times*, February 15, 1973.

———. "Looking into Health Food Movement." *Los Angeles Times*, June 22, 1972.

———. *The* Los Angeles Times *Natural Foods Cookbook.* New York: Putnam's, 1973.

———. "Malnutrition Blamed on Eating Habits." *Los Angeles Times*, February 15, 1973.

———. "Malnutrition Detection Urged." *Los Angeles Times*, September 12, 1969.

———. "Malnutrition in the City." *Los Angeles Times*, September 7, 1972.

———. "Markets Listening to Shoppers." *Los Angeles Times*, October 4, 1971.

———. "A Mexican Party Buffet by the Pool." *Los Angeles Times*, April 27, 1969.

———. "Nutritionists Back School Lunch Bill." *Los Angeles Times*, December 22, 1972.

———. "Overcoming Food Stamp Reservations." *Los Angeles Times*, December 21, 1972.

———. "Panel Rakes Grocers over the Coals." *Los Angeles Times*, June 29, 1972.

———. "Roar of Approval for Curry, as Exotic as Sikhs and Saris." *Los Angeles Times*, January 28, 1973.

———. "Round the World on a Meatball Budget." *Los Angeles Times*, March 4, 1973.

———. Speech at Food Editors Seminar, University of Houston, February 25, 1972. Marjorie B. Paxson Papers, National Women & Media Collection, State Historical Society of Missouri.

———. "Standards on Organic Food Questioned." *Los Angeles Times*, November 11, 1971.

———. "Sushi a Great Snack from Japan." *Los Angeles Times*, February 7, 1971.

———. "Tamales." *Los Angeles Times*, June 1, 1972.

———. "You Can Thank Mad Dogs and Englishmen for Indian Curry." *Los Angeles Times*, June 4, 1972.

Voltz, Jeanne, and Burke Hamner. *The L.A. Gourmet*. New York: Doubleday, 1971.

Voss, Kimberly Wilmot. "Anne Rowe Goldman: Refashioning Women's News in St. Petersburg, Florida." *FCH Annals: Journal of the Florida Conference of Historians* (March 2011): 104–11.

———. "Colleen 'Koky' Dishon: A Journalism Legend." *Timeline* (Summer 2010).

———. "Florence Burge: Representing Reno's Women in a Changing Time." *Nevada Historical Quarterly* (Winter 2006): 294–307.

———. "Food Journalism or Culinary Anthropology? Re-evaluating Soft News and the Influence of Jeanne Voltz's *Los Angeles Times*' Food Section." *American Journalism* 29, no. 2 (2012): 66–91.

———. "Forgotten Feminist: Women's Page Editor Maggie Savoy and the Growth of Women's Liberation Awareness in Los Angeles." *California History* (Spring 2009): 48–64.

Walker, Charlotte. "Food Editors Find Shoppers Sharper Now!" *Charleston News and Courier*, October 5, 1964.

———. "Loved, Lost . . ." *Charleston News & Courier*, February 18, 1968.

———. "Loved, Lost . . ." *Charleston News & Courier*, May 12, 1968.

———. "Pilgrim's Special Is Today's Instant Snack." *Charleston News & Courier*, September 26, 1966.

Ware, Susan. *It's One O'Clock and Here Is Mary Margaret McBride*. New York: New York University Press, 2005.

"Was Home Economics a Profession?" Online supplement to exhibition "From Domesticity to Modernity: What Was Home Economics?" 2001. Division of Rare and Manuscript Collections, Carl A. Kroch Library, Cornell University. http://rmc.library.cornell.edu/homeEc/cases/profession.html.

Wason, Betty. *Cooks, Gluttons and Gourmets*. New York: Doubleday, 1962.

Wells, Pete. "When He Dined, the Stars Came Out." *New York Times*, May 8, 2012.

Wendt, Lloyd. Chicago Tribune*: The Rise of a Great American Newspaper*. Chicago: Rand McNally, 1979.

Will, Joanne. "Lifelong Love Affair with 'Real' Food." *Chicago Tribune*, March 9, 1978.

Willard, Pat. *America Eats!* New York: Macmillan, 2008.

Wilson, Carol. "Wedding Cake: A Slice of History." *Gastronomica* (Spring 2005): 69–72.

Witwer, Stan. "Column Points Readers to Good Restaurants." *St. Petersburg Times*, January 26, 1977.

———. "*Times* Computer Gets an Assist." *St. Petersburg Times*, April 19, 1975.

Women's National Press Club. *Second Helping*. Washington, DC: McIver, 1962.

———. *Who Says We Can't Cook!* Washington, DC: McIver, 1955.

Wood, Morrison. "Amateur Chef Recommends Food Editors Book." *Chicago Tribune*, November 5, 1952.

———. "For Men Only." *Chicago Tribune*, September 20, 1947.

———. "For Men Only." *Chicago Tribune*, August 27, 1954.

———. "How to Cook the Way Mother Used To." *Chicago Tribune*, September 10, 1950.

INDEX